W9-AOL-888

HOW DE BODY?

HOW DE BODY?

ONE MAN'S TERRIFYING JOURNEY
THROUGH AN AFRICAN WAR

Teun Voeten

Translated from the Dutch
by Roz Vatter-Buck

THOMAS DUNNE BOOKS

St. Martin's Press 〰 New York

THOMAS DUNNE BOOKS.
An imprint of St. Martin's Press.

HOW DE BODY? Copyright © 2000 by Teun Voeten and J. M. Meulenhoff BV. Translation copyright © 2002 by Roz Vatter-Buck. All rights reserved. Printed in the United States of America. No part of this book may be used or reproduced in any manner whatsoever without written permission except in the case of brief quotations embodied in critical articles or reviews. For information, address St. Martin's Press, 175 Fifth Avenue, New York, N.Y. 10010.

Published under license from J. M. Meulenhoff BV, Amsterdam, the Netherlands.

Publication has been made possible with financial support from the Foundation for the Production and Translation of Dutch Literature.

All photographs by Teun Voeten/Panos Pictures

www.stmartins.com

Library of Congress Cataloging-in-Publication Data

Voeten, Teun.
    [How de body? English]
    How de body? : One man's terrifying journey through an African war / Teun Voeten ; translated from the Dutch by Roz Vatter-Buck.—1st U.S. ed.
      p. cm.
    Originally published: Amsterdam : Meulenhoff, c2000.
    Includes bibliographical references, p. 305
    ISBN 0-312-28219-2
    1. Sierra Leone—History—Civil War, 1991–   2. Insurgency—Sierra Leone—History—20th century.   3. Sierra Leone—Social conditions—1961–   I. Title.

DT516.826 . V6413 2002
966.404—dc21   2001058496

First published in Amsterdam by J. M. Meulenhoff BV

First U.S. Edition: August 2002

10 9 8 7 6 5 4 3 2 1

FOR EDDIE

Contents

CONTENTS

CONTENTS

PART FIVE: ATTEMPTS AT ANALYSIS

*Brussels, Freetown, Wageningen, Antwerp, Bo,
December 1999–March 2000*

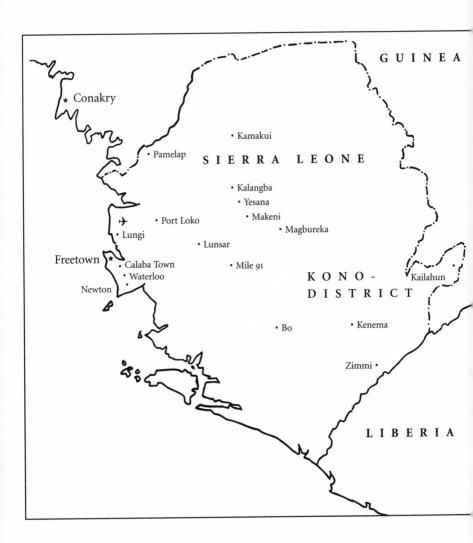

PART ONE

CHRONICLE OF A FAILED REPORTAGE

SIERRA LEONE, FEBRUARY/MARCH 1998

1 | At the Border

The Customs official sits poking his baton up his nose, regarding me with a look of triumph and disdain. The look of a loser experiencing a rare moment of glory.

I know it sounds unbelievable. I mean, consider the size of a baton and the width of the average nostril. But there it is written in black and white in the notebook I have always managed to keep by me. Some people are long forgotten, but there are those I can still see clearly in my mind's eye. Like that obese official in his shabby gray-blue uniform, a badly sewn patch on his shoulder bearing the initials IO—immigration officer—and a cap several sizes too small perched on top of his fat head, extracting a recalcitrant booger from his nose.

Well, he may not have been trying to pick his nose at all. Perhaps it was simply itchy; perhaps it helped him to think better; or perhaps he imagined it would intimidate me. I had no idea and it didn't occur to me at the time to ask him.

"No, my friend, you are not going to enter our country," the

IO has said several times already. The great tub of lard doesn't only say it literally and explicitly; his unwieldy bulk exudes the meaning of the words with relish. His body language is saying without a shadow of a doubt: "You may well think I'm some stupid idiot low down in the pecking order in this backwater Customs post, but even this fool has a modicum of power and influence, and he's going to use it now. My nose tells me, yes, I can smell that you are a filthy spy or worse still, and if I were in charge here, I would kick you straight out of the country. A boot up the ass. Back to your buddies in Guinea."

The setting is the godforsaken border town of Pamelap. A group of immigration officers, Customs officials, policemen, and soldiers of the military junta of Sierra Leone, six men in total, are subjecting me to a cross-examination. I don't know whether I'll come through it, as they are thorough. Deep down inside, a specter looms: not being allowed to enter the country, being sent back, going home with my tail between my legs to be confronted with the scorn of the home front and a financially challenged bank account.

It's a miracle I've managed to get even this far. Before this, I've had to endure all the whims and extortion practices of corrupt police and Customs officials in neighboring Guinea, an impoverished former French colony. At five checkpoints they managed to wrest a total of $150 from me, a sizable chunk out of my travel budget. I'd been warned; I had resolved not to pay a single cent in bribes, but these bastards were clever and cheeky. They came up with all kinds of weird and wonderful taxes and administrative fines. Crooks Sans Frontières.

At the very last checkpoint they had devised a vaccination certificate they said I needed and threatened to send me back to the capital, Conakry, for even more jabs that I'd already had ages ago. The laissez-passer cost me $75. *Vive la francophonie!* The one thing the French left behind in their colonies is a talent for deviousness.

Countries neighboring on war zones. I hate them. They are, without exception, corrupt and tedious and inhabited by pushy, spoiled, badly dressed, grabby, and rowdy natives. They are visited by backpackers with the same characteristics. Every nation gets the kind of tourists it deserves.

Neighboring countries have greasy, rancid food; the souvenirs are tasteless, and their street vendors are con artists and thieves. All topped off with a helping of sickening self-righteousness. Because neighboring countries always think they've got it right. Meanwhile they're doing a nice business, thanks to the misery on the other side of the border. Refugees are a gold mine for neighboring countries such as Slovenia, Costa Rica, Pakistan, and the Dominican Republic, to name but a few of the worst. On the other side of the border there may be a war going on, there may be poverty and misery, but even so values such as hospitality and honesty are still held in high regard.

In Croatia, I've been in villages that were razed to the ground, but the farmers, civilians, and soldiers where I was staying still brought me breakfast in bed with coffee and slivovitz, and roasted pigs in the evenings.

In Nicaragua, I asked a penniless campesino for a glass of water and was immediately served the most delicious meal of rice and beans with thick slices of goat cheese on top.

In Afghanistan, I couldn't walk down the street without being dragged into a house and stuffed full of tea and biscuits, whether by Taliban supporters or Northern Alliance supporters.

In Haiti, a little girl came running after me, waving a ten-gourde bill—worth about twenty cents—that had fallen out of my pants pocket. In a village where there was no hotel, the locals took me to the mayor. He and his wife gave up their bed for me, happy to sleep on the ground.

The less people have, the more willing they are to share. Survival artists. When a village has been flattened or plundered, somehow the destitute inhabitants always manage to rally round. They cultivate the only things they have left, which no one can ever take from them: common courtesy and pride.

Try to find those qualities in countries bordering crisis zones. They don't have much of anything there either, but always just that little bit more than their brothers across the border, whom they scoff at and call barbarians. They hang on like grim death to what they do have, because it is just that little bit that distinguishes them from the barbarians. When the war in Croatia spilled over into Bosnia, Croatia became a neighboring country. In no time at all, the Croatians, too, had become distrustful crooks.

Why not just skip the neighboring countries, then? Simply put, because they are a necessary evil. There you adjust to the climate, pick up the latest scraps of information from relief workers and reporters who hang around the bars of the better hotels; you can map out a safe route overland to the other side, stock up on necessary provisions, leave behind superfluous baggage and papers of any value, post the last few letters, and have one last good meal before venturing into the land of the barbarians.

Back to Pamelap, where the inquisition is still going on. "Can you produce a personal invitation from our head of state?" inquires the police officer in charge of the interrogation. The officer, a captain by rank but dressed informally in jeans and a T-shirt, leans back nonchalantly in the chair behind his desk and gives me a penetrating look. He is in charge of the lot of them and is, luckily, the most reasonable and the brightest among them. He consistently ignores the remarks of his fat subordinate: "Captain, I'm telling you, this man is a spy."

The head of state! Which head of state? Now that's a question. What would be the right answer? Officially, it's the democratically elected president, Tejan Kabbah, but he was deposed last May during a coup by a group of rebellious army officers, calling themselves the AFRC, or Armed Forces Revolutionary Council, headed by the leader of the coup, Major Johnny Paul Koroma.

And then you have the RUF rebels, the Revolutionary United Front. After years of war, the army officers of the AFRC have decided to enter into an alliance with the RUF rebels after all. Partners in crime, you might say. The rebel leader is a shady character named Corporal Foday Sankoh, but I know that he has been in prison in Nigeria somewhere for the past year.

Logically, the guys interrogating me now must be from the AFRC/RUF junta. In which case, I'd better say that Koroma is the head of state. Legally or otherwise, recognized or not, Koroma is the de facto boss now.

Good guess. "I was meaning to write a letter to Major Koroma, but I'm afraid I didn't get the chance." A feeble excuse. "I'm very sorry."

My interrogators nod pityingly. Amateur, they are thinking.

"To be honest, I wasn't aware that you needed a personal invitation from the head of state." I confess my slackness with slightly more self-confidence. Strange, I've never heard of a country demanding anything like that. Usually a valid passport and visa will do. But this is Sierra Leone.

"Aha, a visa," says the fat one, who is now studying my passport. "And how were you able to obtain that?"

"I got it at the embassy in Brussels," I admit lamely.

They can't get around that. I don't have much of a leg to stand on, but whatever leg you do have should be demonstrated firmly but politely. They look at each other pensively. A visa from an embassy. Now that's stumped them.

All very predictable. Time for the thorough inspection of my luggage. Always the worst part. However careful you are, they're bound to find something that can be used against you.

The captain rummages through my belongings and pulls out a pile of boxer shorts. Washed, ironed, and carefully folded. Thank God. There's nothing more embarrassing than Customs grubbing through your dirty linen. Breathlessly, they inspect my underwear. Good quality, Calvin Klein. Each pair of shorts is worth an average month's salary for them. None of the officers or inspectors gathered here will ever be able to afford a wardrobe of this quality. Well, not legitimately, anyhow. They stuff the shorts back.

. . .

The newspaper clippings. Now that's interesting. They turn to the first page. Hastily scribbled names I got from a colleague. "Paddy's Disco" and "Cape Sierra Hotel, Freetown" are some of the more innocent entries.

"Look!" cries the fat immigration officer when he sees where I've written "MIL HQ WILK RD." Fatso is not so dim after all and has managed to decipher my code. "How and why do you know the military headquarters are on Wilkinson Road?" He beams at his boss and waits for an answer.

Here we go again. Just as every American knows that the White House is on Pennsylvania Avenue, every West African knows that the barracks of the Sierra Leone army are on Wilkinson Road in Freetown. "A colleague of mine said that's where I had to go for a press accreditation." It's the truth.

"All lies!" shrieks the fat one. "You are a mercenary."

But the captain believes me. Flipping through the rest of the file at his ease, he now finds a report from *The Economist*. Cut-and-dried facts on soil conditions, gross national product, and literacy levels. The captain considers this secret information. The big one puts the fat in the fire by suggesting the CIA has leaked it to me. It takes me half an hour to explain that we have public libraries and something called the Internet in Western Europe.

Next sheet of paper. I've made a list of the highlights of Sierra Leone's recent history. Presidents, coups, elections, military leaders, takeovers, parties and factions. They go through it all carefully, uttering a cry of recognition every so often.

"I'm very interested in the history of your country." It sounds like bootlicking, but I mean it.

The captain understands. His memory is refreshed, too. But this is where things start to get tense. Will they find the Amnesty International report entitled "Sierra Leone: A Disastrous Setback for Human Rights"? I can't believe I was stupid enough not to leave it in Guinea, with the big pile of junta-unfriendly reading matter I was still struggling through the night before my departure. Fortunately, the captain misses it. I could have talked my way out of it, but that would have taken even more time.

It's the assignment letter from the Catholic humanitarian group Caritas that now catches the captain's eye. The letter confirms that I have to photograph a demobilization project for child soldiers in Makeni. It also gives a brief political sketch, but unlike the Amnesty report, Caritas takes local sensitivities into better consideration. Words like *coup* and *torturing* have been replaced by euphemisms such as *the events* and *certain irregularities*.

Caritas, and Catholics in general, can do no wrong in the eyes of the captain. When he starts to talk about the Dutch soccer stars Gullit and van Basten, I know that everything's cool. This is how every interrogation ends. The fat one is sent out to find his stamp and ink cushion.

It was a tense cross-questioning, five hours long, but surely to them I must look like a bit of an oddball. All the foreigners are busy leaving the country—there's a steady stream in the opposite direction of white jeeps from relief agencies—and then I turn up, all alone, wanting to get in of all things. But you can say what you like, they have behaved correctly all along and haven't extorted one dollar from me, haven't stolen or demanded anything. Remarkable. True gentlemen. Boarding-school discipline. You can see that the English used to run Sierra Leone.

After the liberating stamp and endless shaking of hands, they wave me off enthusiastically and even provide me with an escort of two soldiers. Friendly guys with rusty Kalashnikovs. They smile shyly. It's their job to explain at every checkpoint along the way that I've already been thoroughly interrogated and approved. The two of them are to introduce me personally to each local commander we come across as we go. Now that's what I call service!

The patience of the driver and the passengers of the bush taxi—a beat-up, old Peugeot 504 station wagon—is amazing. They have been taking a nap in the shade or peeling juicy mangoes. They have had to wait half the day for me, and now they are obliged to put up with two extra passengers who have to be squeezed with difficulty into the car. But not a cross word is spoken; they are even glad for me that I have come through the interrogation successfully. Someone hands me a mango and we leave. Welcome to Sierra Leone. Makeni, here I come!

In Search of Child Soldiers

What was I actually looking for in Sierra Leone? And how did I end up in Makeni of all places?

As usual, by coincidence. It was January 1998 and I couldn't wait to start traveling again. My last reporting trip had been three months earlier, and since then I had had nothing but bureaucratic problems, domestic trouble, and money worries.

Conflict areas present their own difficulties, but they do have one advantage: they allow you to leave all your day-to-day worries at home. Let the debt collectors knock on the door, let the bills pile up on the doormat.

So I was in a great mood as I turned out of my street one sunny Monday morning and headed downhill to Brussels Central, to catch the train for the airport. Coming the other way was a convoy of dreary, gray office types, making their weary way up the hill with dark, careworn expressions on their faces. And this was only the beginning of the week, with the sun shining so brightly on this clear winter morning!

They passed me on their way to work in suits and ties, high heels and black brogues. And there I was in a clean pair of jeans, Timberland boots, and a baseball cap, eager to get to my own work. Once again, I had managed to scrape together enough for the trip. Apart from being broke, I was as happy as a king. Poor, but free. I was ready to take on the world again.

Sierra Leone, of all places, was my destination because of the child soldiers. My next big assignment, about Colombia, was not planned until May. Elections were to be held there and violence would be flaring up again, so there would be rich pickings, journalistically speaking. But I just couldn't wait until spring, five more months of sitting at home. I had to get myself an uncomplicated photo job in the meantime. So I was delighted when, at the end of 1997, I came across a brief Reuters report on child soldiers in Sierra Leone:

> The ruling military junta of Sierra Leone has started identifying and registering the estimated five thousand child soldiers in the country. . . . Junta leader Major Johnny Paul Koroma has ordered "the immediate disarmament of all child soldiers" at a ceremony in the capital, Freetown.

Normally so turbulent, Sierra Leone was currently experiencing a kind of peace and cease-fire, which was probably why the ruling junta had decided to demobilize the children who had been fighting in their ranks. Together with UNICEF, no less. The junta was obviously glowing with self-confidence, could do without a few young warriors, and was eager to tell all the world about it. An ideal starting point for a report on child soldiers.

Child soldiers are photogenic. Little black kids parading around with big guns, looking into the lens with wide, serious eyes. Sometimes, for lack of anything better, they practice with a wooden gun, or just an ordinary stick. Cute little rascals playing war games, lost innocence, manhood initiation rites. Metaphors galore.

Armies like to have children in their ranks. Sometimes, the kids flock to them willingly because there is no school or work; sometimes they are recruited by force, kidnapped and conscripted. They are the ideal soldiers. Strength is not an issue. A ten-year-old has no problem handling today's light weapons; a Kalashnikov only weighs about three pounds.

They have not yet developed any fear of death, as they hardly know what life is about. In their innocence they are convinced that they are immortal. Death? That's something that only happens to other people. You can convince them of anything. Promise them heaven or nirvana if they step on a mine and you have excellent little minesweepers. Whole battalions of children cleaned up the front line between Iraq and Iran in a futile war in the mid-1980s.

Tell them they are invulnerable to enemy projectiles and they will run singing and dancing through a rain of bullets. Mai-Mai teenagers in East Zaire functioned as storm troopers for Kabila's rebels when they opened their attack on Mobutu in 1997.

Children are easy to discipline, manipulate, and brainwash. They don't eat much, don't suffer from any infirmities, and don't have that compulsion to visit the whores. What more could a commander want? Tender, young cannon fodder. It's nothing new. The word *infantry* originally meant "child soldiers."

There was a time when warring parties were proud to have children fighting on their side. What's learned in the cradle lasts till the grave. Sacrifice and love for the fatherland. If you have the support of the youth, then you have the approval of the people. But those days are over. Now that slaves and women are more or less liberated, children are at the top of the international agenda. Child labor, street children, child prostitution; it goes from bad to worse. The phenomenon of the child soldier has been a hot topic since the 1990s.

In the 1980s, the Sandinistas in Nicaragua were still proudly exhibiting their youthful recruits for the international press. In 1995, however, UNICEF published a major report heavily criticizing the use of child soldiers. Since then, most warring parties have gradually started to feel embarrassed by the deployment of children. In generally civilized circles, it is no longer considered *bon ton* to press-gang children under eighteen. A movement is afoot to pass a UN resolution to treat this as a war crime.

Of course, full use is still made of children in battle, but nowadays this is concealed from the outside world, far from the TV cameras and photographers. Even the most evil warlords in the most remote regions recognize the importance of a good public image and, since the Gulf War, are aware not only that the media play a role in creating that image, but also that those media can be manipulated. The international community disapproves of rebels with child soldiers. But what the eye does not see, the heart does not grieve over.

I've wanted to report on child soldiers for years now. It's not an obsession, but it's always been at the back of my mind. To no avail. Relief agencies are incredibly enthusiastic when they hear the plans. They swamp me with piles of literature and academic studies. In the field, however, it's another story. "Don't even breathe the words *child soldier*," someone from Doctors Without Borders advised me when I traveled to the Sudan in an attempt to photograph the rebels' child soldiers there. "And please don't mention our name," he added.

How right he was, too. The few times I came across the Sudanese rebels, they posed proudly for pictures, but the moment I pointed my camera at a kid with a Kalashnikov, the atmosphere became forbidding. The message was clear: Of course we have child soldiers in service, we're not stupid. And we couldn't give a damn what you people in the civilized world think about it. But let's keep this between us. Please . . .

I was therefore delighted with the Reuters dispatch. Proud of its progressiveness and humanity, the military junta in Sierra Leone should be keen to show me the demobilization projects and former training camps where there would probably still be a few armed kids left who would like to be photographed. Children are like that. They throng around anything with a lens, yelling, "CNN!" Everything points to its being a simple task. Cooperation guaranteed.

No need to butter up all kinds of rebel spokesmen while sneakily having a secret agenda; no need to travel to the front line to see child soldiers in action at the risk of life and limb. I'm not so keen on that idea, anyway. Children are playful and unpredictable; with a weapon in their hands they are deadly. Just go to the junta and tell them what I want to do. Surely nobody in his right mind could have any objection? No, it will be a piece of cake. No doubt about it.

. . .

I start reading up on Sierra Leone. It's unbelievable. The country appears to be absolutely hopeless. For the past ten years it has been jostling for position at the top of the list of the poorest countries in the world along with Afghanistan, Haiti, and the Sudan. For the past two years, Sierra Leone has even occupied the very bottom place on the list of the UNDP (United Nations Development Program), which attempts to express the level of development in a country as an objective figure, using indicators such as literacy (30 percent in Sierra Leone), life expectancy (thirty-six years), and average annual income per capita ($250).

Since its independence from England in 1961, the country has not only been plagued by a succession of coups, corrupt elections, and greedy despots, but also by long periods of civil war. The war has been flaring up in particular since 1991, when the rebels of the Revolutionary United Front appeared on the scene. With tactics such as amputations, head-hunting, and the kidnapping and brainwashing of children, the RUF has rapidly gained a reputation as the most insane rebel movement in the world.

American writer Robert Kaplan devotes entire chapters to Sierra Leone in his book *The Ends of Earth*. He calls the country the Devil's Poste Restante. The country already had a bad reputation under English rule, when it was known as the White Man's Grave. Not because of the rebels and the civil war, which were not yet on the agenda, but due to the murderous climate (uninterrupted downpours for eight months of the year, temperatures nearing a hundred degrees), the malaria (in all varieties, from serious to fatal), and the diseases (meningitis, polio, hepatitis A to D). In colonial times, half of all white newcomers succumbed within a year.

Sierra Leone is not one of those ex-colonies sucked dry and plundered. It was established with the best intentions in the eighteenth century by English philanthropists and given as a homeland to former slaves who had fought on the side of the English during the American Revolution. In gratitude, their chains were removed so they could start a new, free life on a fertile piece of ground on the west coast of Africa. Hence the name of the capital: Freetown.

In the 1970s, the country's tropical beaches were a top attraction for decadent French tourists, being famed as the most beautiful in all of Africa. Where did it all go wrong? The curse of Sierra Leone is its wealth of natural resources. Not only tropical hardwoods, coffee, cocoa, gold, and silver, but diamonds. In some parts of the country, they literally lie there waiting to be picked up. Diamonds have sown greed into the hearts of the Sierra Leoneans. They have also attracted an international consortium of criminal scum, like bees to honey. Arms dealers, mercenaries, even drug barons.

In the meantime, magic and witchcraft are still alive and kicking. Secret societies carry out lengthy ceremonies in the impenetrable forests. One of them is an association whose members call themselves the Kamajors. Originally, they were traditional hunters who imagined themselves to be invulnerable, due to magical powers. Now they have grown into a sort of national militia.

The more I read about the country, the more fascinated I become. Sierra Leone must be a paradise for journalists and anthropologists. The chief foreign desk of the Belgian newspaper *De Morgen* sends me a newspaper clipping: three war orphans found a giant diamond in 1997 worth half a million dollars. What has become of the orphans, the diamond, and the money is unknown. "Try and find out, if you have the time," says the editor. I promise.

An unexpected problem rears its head. Peace and the cease-fire in Sierra Leone are over. Three days before I'm due to leave, the junta suddenly comes under fire from the West African peacekeeping force called the ECOMOG. The community of West African states had already announced an economic embargo a year ago to force the junta to step down. Naturally, as with most embargoes, this is failing to achieve the desired result. The rulers are shamelessly lining their pockets through smuggling and black-marketing, while the people are becoming increasingly impoverished. The same thing that happened in Haiti is now happening in Sierra Leone. Which is why the peacekeeping forces have no choice but to restore democracy, by any means necessary.

ECOMOG, which is dominated by Nigeria and already has troops in Sierra Leone, is bombing the junta in the heart of Freetown, giving them all they've got. I read the latest news as I'm packing my bags:

FIGHTING RAGES NEAR S. LEONE CAPITAL.
The sound of machine-gun fire and heavy Nigerian artillery rocked the city . . . shelling junta positions . . . another Niger-

ian warplane bombed the area around Freetown's army barracks.

Reuters, February 8, 1998

Fierce fighting has broken out just when I was looking forward
to a peaceful trip. Well, it's too late to cancel everything now: I've
already bought my ticket for neighboring Guinea, organized my
visa, stocked up on malaria pills, and got myself a minor assignment
from Caritas. They have started up projects in the towns of Kenema
and Makeni for converting former child soldiers into poster boys
and want me to do a brief story. I would like to spend a few days
under the protection of Caritas—earn back my ticket and get
acquainted with the local situation—and then go my own way.

But Kenema is a no-go zone, I hear after checking with the
Caritas headquarters. It is situated next to the rich diamond region, where the fighting is the fiercest. Makeni is still quiet and
perfectly accessible overland. Problems in the capital don't yet
mean that areas inland are inaccessible. In all war zones there is
order in the chaos. You have heavy fighting in one place, which
may be the capital or a front line somewhere else. But even there
it's only for a few hours a day. Just fifteen minutes' walk from the
front, daily life goes on as usual and the risks are negligible. At
least, that is what it has been like in all the wars I've ever seen.
Why should Sierra Leone be any different? No, I'll go; I'm not
going to let myself be scared off by a couple of bombs on Freetown. There will probably be trouble for months to come. I'll
complete my assignment in Makeni, then I'll go and check out
the situation in Freetown.

3 | Welcome to Makeni

Buzzing mosquitoes have kept me awake all night. They're trying to get out, but find their way blocked by a dusty mosquito net, full of the shriveled corpses of fellow mosquitoes. It's only seven in the morning, but a sticky heat is already pervading the tiny, stuffy room in Buya's Motel in Makeni.

Buya's Motel is not actually a motel. It may be situated alongside the road, but where is the parking lot and where are the cars? As Buya's is the first and only luxury hotel in Makeni, however, they have the right to call themselves whatever they please.

The hotel is austere, but clean. The floors have been scrubbed and mopped, and up until now, I haven't spotted a single cockroach. There is no running water, but the bellboy discreetly brings a carafe of drinking water and a bucket of water for washing, announcing his arrival with a knock at the door. The water probably all comes from the same tap or well, but it's the idea that counts. The boy will also bring me a thermos of hot water when I want, so the working day can begin with an aromatic cup of Nescafé.

The trip to Makeni was relaxed. Yes, it was a bit of a squeeze with eleven of us in the Peugeot, but the journey went without incident. Night fell quickly, with twinkling stars in the firmament, the waxing moon lighting the scene, the comforting purr of the diesel engine, a companionable mood amongst the passengers, with the odd joke and the spontaneous exchange of bananas, mangoes, and oranges. The third world at its best.

Now and again there was a little tension at the dozen checkpoints we passed, but each time the accompanying soldiers helped me through correctly and quickly. No difficult questioning, no intimidating rattle of weapons, no bribes. The soldiers also introduced me to several local commanders. Once again, all smiles. The commander at Port Loko, who answers to the name of Colonel Croma, even offered to take me to Freetown in the junta helicopter in a few days' time, when I'm finished in Makeni.

On our arrival in Makeni, just past midnight, the soldiers even manage to introduce me briefly at the junta secretariat, where I have my first appointment with the authorities this morning.

Nice guys, those soldiers. They looked shy and helpless when they brought me to Buya's Motel. One said, in a small voice, that they didn't actually have anywhere to sleep and could I possibly treat them to a room? Just for one night? And maybe a cold beer for their trouble?

Again the bashful looks this morning, when they come and ask if I might make a small contribution for the bus ride back to Pamelap. They don't get paid that much. In fact, they haven't had their monthly three-dollar wages for more than six months, they explain.

The soldiers take the bus back at my expense. I go around the corner to the junta secretariat. From a distance, it all looks neat and tidy, the only freshly painted building in the surroundings. From closer up, however, the secretariat has something of the flavor of a banana republic. The walls are covered with crudely designed propaganda pamphlets. Bold capitals scream out "STOP CRIMINAL INVASION!!!" and "KABBAH IS A CANNIBAL!!!" In the courtyard, an elderly soldier is pedaling round and round a mango tree on a children's bike, a silver-colored fireman's helmet at an angle on his head and an old rifle dangling on his back. In the shade of the mango tree, children are trying to sell oranges to other soldiers, who are taking a morning nap.

Inside, however, discipline and order reign. Soldiers with serious expressions are busy typing out big file documents and reports on typewriters. An old woman comes in to report a missing goat—possibly stolen by disloyal rebels? Her story is patiently noted down.

Everyone in the secretariat has a rank, function, and corresponding abbreviation. I am introduced in turn to the OIC (officer in charge), the FPO (first police officer), and the SIC (second in command), until I ultimately arrive at the PRO (public relations officer). It's well organized here. Another legacy of the Brits.

The name of the PRO is Contha Mustafa Sanusi. He is dressed sharply, but not too flashily, in stonewashed jeans, white sneakers, and a canary-yellow polo shirt. Sanusi shakes me heartily by the hand and gives me a penetrating but not unfriendly look. At first sight a decent guy. "Welcome, my friend, welcome," he says. "You are most welcome to see and report the truth." Three times *welcome* in one sentence. That's what I like to hear. Sanusi pulls up a chair and proceeds.

"To be frank with you, we are all sick and tired of this senseless war. But we are the victims of foreign aggression. We have to defend ourselves."

Sanusi expresses the official viewpoint of the AFRC/RUF junta. The West African Peace Force ECOMOG should actually be a balanced reflection of all West African states, but is dominated by Nigeria, the local superpower. The junta therefore never speaks of the ECOMOG but of "the Nigerians."

"Kabbah was a dictator," continues Sanusi. "He put his tribespeople, the Mende, in all the high positions. He also had Abiola's wife murdered. And there were seventy-two thousand political prisoners jailed while Kabbah was in power."

That President Kabbah was no saint doesn't surprise me. I've still to hear of the first untainted African head of state. That Kabbah favored members of his own tribe is not exactly proper, either. But on the other hand, we all want our family, friends, and acquaintances to do well. Nothing wrong with that in itself. If it's to our advantage, we call it solidarity; if we are the victims, then we call it nepotism.

I didn't know about Abiola's wife. In fact, I've never even heard of Abiola. He's not on my list of important figures. Have to look into that. And seventy-two thousand political prisoners out of a population of 3 million, of which maybe only 100,000 can read and write fluently, does sound a bit far-fetched. I note the facts down, but I will make sure to check them before putting them into print.

Sanusi sees me scribbling hastily away, waits until I've finished, then continues his tale. "Now, if Belgium was to come and restore democracy here . . . well, okay, I could understand that. But a Nigerian despot like Sani Abacha, whose hands are stained with the blood of innocent victims . . ."

He almost chokes with anger as he speaks. Sanusi is no hireling slimeball; he sincerely believes what he is saying. And he's right. A regional superpower coming to restore democracy. Now where have we seen that before? Wasn't it los norteamericanos who chased out the communists from Guatemala, El Salvador, Chile, and Nicaragua?

And how sporting of Sanusi to admit that not everything in Sierra Leone is completely kosher. What he is saying between the lines is that the AFRC/RUF junta are no democratic teddy bears, either. But Belgium . . . that's giving it a bit too much credit. If only he knew: Dutroux, the Flemish National Front, the Nijvel Gang, and King Leopold II.

Very astute of Sanusi, by the way, to be able to differentiate between Belgium and the Netherlands. Most Americans don't even know that those countries are in Western Europe. But Sanusi is not stupid. He became friendly with someone who worked at the Wageningen University of Agriculture in Holland when he was on six months' work experience in Makeni. Sanusi is now going to write a letter to his old friend, which I will pick up in a couple of days, as the embargo has also made mail traffic impossible.

We say good-bye and I walk on to the regional headquarters of Caritas. Nice guy, that Sanusi. He knows what journalists want. He will organize an interview with Mr. Gottoa, the governor of Makeni, for this afternoon, and later he will also make a laissez-passer so I can travel back to Freetown without any problems.

Makeni is hot, dusty, and amazingly small for what is supposed to be the third-largest town in the country. Between the peeling storefronts on the only shopping street, a cinema announces that *Malcolm X* will be showing this evening. If there is enough diesel for the generator, that is. Children are playing soccer in the town square where a triumphal arch stands, supported by scaffolding.

On the sidewalk, women are selling oranges, five for fifty leone: roughly ten cents. I only want two oranges, but that's not possible. The vendor has no change and she won't keep the change, either. In Sierra Leone, money not honestly come by is taboo. If it comes into contact with "honest money," the operating capital will become tainted. And that brings bad luck in business. You can compare it to a sensible Western businessman who has a separate black cash box. If you mix black money with white, you end up with tax problems. The woman is not to be persuaded and stuffs all the oranges in the pockets of my photo vest before allowing me to continue on my way. I'm starting to love this country.

"And deliver us from evil. Amen." At Caritas Makeni they start every working day with the Lord's Prayer. I have hardly presented myself at the reception desk when I am propelled toward the conference room, where ebony crucifixes hang above the door lintel. I am expected to join in with the staff, who are all immersed in the morning prayers. No problem.

It's always a bit like coming home again when you are amongst Catholics abroad, whether they are black, yellow, brown, or white. An extraordinary mixture, Catholicism. A healthy dose of moralism, seasoned with scraps of mysticism and a pinch of opportunism. And a commitment not based on sterile concepts, but radiating from a wavering heart. That's something that's hard to find in all those atheistic doctrines.

Once we have all jointly confessed our fallibility and I have opened my eyes again, a young lady stands up and offers me her hand. Decorative silver bracelets adorn her fragile wrist. Her slenderness is emphasized by the giraffes and gazelles on her closely fitting, purple batik skirt. This sparkling presence is Nancy Dankey, the deputy director of Caritas Makeni. The African version of the power girl.

Giggling, she bids me welcome. "I'm glad you made it. To be honest, we weren't expecting you any longer." Her face takes on a worried look. Security is not that good. All the white relief workers left Makeni yesterday. I reassure her that I'm good buddies with the junta clique. "I've got an audience with the governor later," I say. Nancy looks pensive.

Then she clears her throat and comes to the point. Her boss, a certain Ibrahim, is in the Netherlands, promoting the project for child soldiers and raising funds. For the time being, therefore, Nancy is in charge of the project, in which UNICEF and the local Catholic church are also now involved.

The church is strongly represented in Makeni: not only is there the Italian Xaverian order, which runs the Catholic mission, but Makeni is also the residence of Bishop Biguzzi. A generally well-respected figure, he dared criticize the junta in a pastoral letter, but did so in such veiled language that he can still walk around safely. It is Biguzzi who has managed to persuade the rebel leaders in Makeni to collaborate in the child soldier project. The bishop is currently in Guinea for talks with several confreres and imams, Nancy tells me. Although Sierra Leone is predominantly Islamic, there is great religious tolerance. Innumerable Muslims therefore also work at Caritas.

"We want the children to forget the language of the gun," Nancy says, summarizing the objective of the project in a nutshell. The child soldiers have only recently become accessible. Since the AFRC's alliance with the RUF, the Northern Jungle Battalion—as the group of rebels around Makeni calls itself—has gradually been emerging from the bush, with the hundreds of children who have been fighting alongside them in their wake.

The Northern Jungle Battalion has settled in Makeni in the local Teko Barracks. An hour's walk from Makeni, another group of rebels has regrouped in a camp near to a village called—for lack of a better name—Mile 91.

"We are using a subtle game to ease the children away from the rebels," Nancy explains. "Officially, the demobilization hasn't begun yet, but we have had tacit approval from the rebel leader to make a start." That start has consisted of several steps: First of all, one of the Xaverian fathers, Padre Victor, was allowed to visit the children in the barracks from time to time. Later, the children were given permission to have lunch in the mission center. That meant a couple of hundred fewer mouths to feed as far as the rebels were concerned. At an even further stage, the children were allowed to play soccer, watch cartoons, and later even attend classes in the mission center. This is the point at which the children slowly start to open up. The final step, according to Nancy, is to immerse the children in faith, hope, and love, so that they ultimately start to consider these values as normal again and embrace them automatically. "After all, for years these children have known nothing but fear, loneliness, pain, and death."

Nancy is optimistic about saving the child soldiers. "We have to fight the notion that the children are so heavily traumatized that they are irretrievably damaged. And we make no distinction as to whether they have carried weapons or not. The fact of the matter is that they have all seen extreme violence and experienced terrible hardship. But the vast majority can be healed. Give them a normal life—school, family, friends—and see how quickly they become ordinary children again."

Nancy promises to show me everything tomorrow. She is going to put together a program that will let me speak to everyone. If there's any time left, we can also make a day trip to Mile 91.

The residence of Governor Gottoa is on a hill just outside Makeni. Sanusi has been true to his word: a jeep standing outside the junta secretariat whisks me over there. An old army truck is parked just outside the driveway, loaded with an enormous anti-aircraft gun. Cartridges like cucumbers. A few heavily armed, bored young men are dozing in the trailer. They give me a dirty look, even though I'm sitting like a good boy in an army jeep. Do they see me as a white intruder, or have I just disturbed their afternoon nap?

One of the guys is picking the gap between his front teeth

with a dagger and spits out a piece of old food. *Voilà*—the governor's elite troops. The sun is at its highest: the temperature must be somewhere near a hundred. Dogs lie lifeless in the shade, vultures wheel slowly in the sky.

More bodyguards inside. A sweaty soldier is sitting in a stuffy little room full of cupboards stuffed with dusty files: the reception clerk. He takes down my name and asks if I have any weapons on me. I show him my Swiss pocketknife. Instead of chuckling at the little knife, the bodyguard looks at the tiny thing in fascination, pulls out the tweezers, and opens the blade. He passes the knife on to another soldier who is playing with a hand grenade, a grenade launcher lying in his lap.

"Hmm," says the soldier, looking thoughtfully at the little tweezers. The grenade launcher almost falls to the floor. "You could tear your enemy's eyelids off with this." He feels the razor-sharp blade. "And you could rip open his belly with this. Or cut off his balls."

I shudder. The soldier is quite serious; he's not joking. He is a killer who has probably actually done such things at some time, otherwise he couldn't talk about it with such relish.

"Could I keep it?" the soldier asks, looking me right in the eye. His pupils are almost indistinguishable from the whites of his eyes: bloodshot, dark yellow fading to a drab brown. Probably the result of a combination of endemic malaria, syphilis, and all kinds of other nasty diseases and vitamin deficiencies. As with bears, it is impossible to read his mood from his eyes. I'm looking into a dark, unfathomable pool. With some difficulty, I manage to get back my indispensable pocketknife without offending anyone. One thing is clear: these guys have no sense of humor.

I've been waiting for the governor for an hour now. He is in, but is making his guests wait. A bad sign. The small group of people waiting has now grown to almost a dozen.

In the meantime, the soldiers sit belligerently spitting out their vehement remarks. "We will kill the Nigerians," cries Yellow Eyes.

"We will kill 'em all," says his buddy.

"We will cut their balls off," adds Yellow Eyes enthusiastically.

I am forcing an understanding smile when a man in a white baseball cap detaches himself from the group of people waiting. "Eddie Smith, local BBC correspondent, based in Makeni," he introduces himself. A broad smile and a firm handshake. "Are you a reporter, too?" he asks, his lively eyes twinkling.

That's a relief. Finally. A colleague. And not one of those condescending foreign guys who treat you disparagingly because you're a small freelancer, but a local man who knows the ropes. Local journalists in poor countries: they should erect a statue to them. They work in difficult circumstances for subsistence wages in soft currency with the most primitive equipment you've ever seen: it brings tears to your eyes to see the rickety old typewriters, obsolete computers, and dented Soviet cameras the average Balkan and third-world reporter has to work with.

In the meantime, they have to take local sensitivities into account—censorship and dictatorship—when they often have a family to feed as well. To make matters worse, when the shit hits the fan, our correspondent is suddenly no longer the guy from the local rag, but has unwillingly to turn into a war correspondent. Good, simple guys emerge as valiant heroes. Uninsured, naturally. Just like all their fellow countrymen. No golden wheelchair insurance. If anything happens to them, they have only charity, the family, and quite often the Catholic Church to fall back on.

Eddie Smith seems pleased to discover a colleague, too. Most journalists are leaving Makeni left and right because nothing ever happens. No diamonds are to be found here, at best a few peanuts, oranges, and bananas.

Eddie immediately starts to talk about Sierra Leone's troubles, presenting his analysis. None of those exploitation or dependence theories they teach young people nowadays in our social science departments. According to Eddie, everything can be traced back to the leaders' development disorders and personality problems at a young age. "One guy gets better grades than the other, then the other one fucks the first one's girlfriend. They're still fighting out old school quarrels here. But now it's with guns."

War of the Pussy Snatchers. Well, why not? Daniel Ortega and his archenemy, Cardinal Obando y Bravo, were born, grew up, and went to school in the same Nicaraguan settlement. And all the Latin American dictators and colonels who ever deposed, tortured, and murdered each other were once classmates at the Escuela de las Americas, the CIA-run military academy in Panama.

I've never looked at it like that. Eddie has a fresh way of looking at things. I am still considering the implications of his explanation model when we are shown in by a bodyguard. The governor is finally deigning to receive us.

In the half-light of the reception room, a number of people are slouching on chairs around the wall. A corpulent, uniformed man is leaning back in his chair behind an enormous desk. Governor Gottoa himself. A nasty piece of work. The top of the desk is littered with hideous ornaments—shepherdesses and bucking horses in light blue porcelain. The more evil the man, the more sentimental his taste. Gottoa shifts the ornaments about while answering our questions. Well, *avoiding* them would be a better word.

Eddie and I are curious about the latest developments in the military field. Will the ECOMOG succeed in driving the junta out of Freetown? What consequences will that have for the rest of the country? Does the junta have a specific strategy?

Gottoa is no help to us. He looks at us contemptuously and trots out standard slogans, such as "foreign aggression" and "we will never give up."

"Did you come here to fight the Nigerians?" a woman suddenly says with fury in her voice. It is the governor's wife, who has been sitting somewhere in a corner and is now coming to her husband's aid. Why on earth is she sticking her nose in? I explain as amiably as possible that I am a reporter and that it's my job to write, not to fight.

"You see?" she says scornfully. "All journalists are cowards."

"The pen is your weapon," a friendly man adds in a conciliatory tone to the conversation. A terrible cliché, but uttered at just the right moment. The man is sitting in another dark corner and is dressed in shorts and a T-shirt. "You are here to find the truth and record it," he continues. These wise and placating words are from brigadier commander Colonel Momodu. Momodu is the highest commander in Makeni after the governor, the second-in-command. The Sierra Leoneans call him Twicey, a diminutive of *the second*.

"If you have any problems, just come and see me," says Twicey. We take note of that.

At nightfall, Eddie comes to the motel to invite me to go for an evening stroll. He lives in Freetown, where he also has two children, but has been stationed in Makeni for some months now. He works for the capital's newspaper *The Storm* and has recently started making radio reports for the BBC World Service as well. He's staying with two friends in Makeni, T-Boy and Imfahin.

His girlfriend, Zainab, came over to Makeni from Freetown last week. She said she came because she missed him, but according to Eddie, she came to keep a better eye on him as she suspects him of having affairs. Suspicions that are not entirely unfounded, confides Eddie in a conspiratorial tone. All guys together.

Eddie is the life and soul of the party. Everyone knows Eddie, and Eddie knows everyone. He shakes hands and exchanges gossip with every passerby, sharing a joke here, stealing a kiss there, sometimes pinching a woman's bottom, introducing me to everyone as he goes along. A social genius.

"Watch me, Tony," he says gravely. "I'm not just walking around here. I've got my feelers out. I'm working. Checking out the mood. Picking up the latest rumors." We park ourselves next to a group of Eddie's friends. They start rattling on in Krio. Krio is the lingua franca of Sierra Leone, a sort of pidgin English, laced with African, French, and Portuguese expressions. If you see it written down, you can just about make it out, but spoken quickly it's incomprehensible. The lady of the house serves the evening meal. Mashed cassava. Cassava tastes like spinach. Heavily spiced with peppers and served with rice, it's delicious.

Then the palm wine comes out. No bottle, just a two-gallon, plastic jerrican. Undrinkable stuff. Like sour, milky dishwater. I cautiously take tiny sips, but the taste is terrible. I spit out a daddy longlegs that has drowned in my cup. Eddie sees my disgust and slaps me on the back, laughing. "Palm wine is for real men. You have to get used to drinking it." He has already knocked back five pints out of a plastic bowl.

We part later at the motel. Another evening stroll tomorrow. "The sooner you get to know Makeni, the better," he calls after me.

The bellboy at Buya's brings me an envelope. In it is the program Nancy from Caritas has worked out. For the sake of completeness, she has drawn it up retrospectively:

Wednesday, 11th February 98   Arrival from Conakry
Thursday, 12th February 98   Courtesy call to Caritas Makeni

The arrival and the courtesy call are already behind us. For tomorrow, Friday the thirteenth, Nancy has a busy day in mind. Eight-thirty at the Caritas office, after which there are a dozen or so program points to attend to: meetings and interviews with relief workers, padres, and child soldiers; a look at the Teko Barracks; and visits to the food center, a school, and the cathedral. Plus a lunch break in between. Nancy has stuck a yellow Post-it message to the program: "Please tell your 'friends' to give you a security cover note for the visit to Mile 91."

What does she mean by my friends? Sanusi, Twicey, and Eddie? Not that boorish governor and his bitch of a wife, in any case. I listen to the radio. The BBC reports that the ECOMOG has progressed to within half a mile or so of the headquarters of the junta in Freetown. The peacekeeping force is really advancing rapidly. Tomorrow is Friday the thirteenth. Better watch out. Chirping crickets lull me to sleep.

4

Friday the Thirteenth

"AK!" cries Aliu enthusiastically when I ask him what kind of weapon he had. Gabriel, the relief worker, laughs, a little embarrassed. The former child soldiers are supposed to be ashamed of their past now and should softly whisper "AK-47" or "Kalashnikov" with eyes cast to the ground. But Aliu, with his jug ears and buck teeth, swells with pride. He announces it as if he has answered the final question in a children's quiz and is awaiting his prize.

It's also a rather sore point that the children all want to be soldiers again when they're bigger. Those with a little more ambition even want to become a general or colonel. Gabriel explains it away: "That's because the army is the only life they've ever known. But we do have one now who wants to be a truck driver when he grows up."

I'm in the mission center, where Gabriel Mani, the Caritas worker, is introducing me to the children. Gabriel is a mild-mannered, intelligent young man who obviously has his heart in the project. He talks emotionally about the children, who are flocking toward us. I'm soon walking round like the Pied Piper of Hamelin, with three kids hanging on each arm and a couple of dozen skipping cheerfully along behind. The children don't look a bit like little soldiers. If they appear at the mission center in uniform, Gabriel sends them back to the Teko Barracks to change. It's strictly forbidden to carry weapons. Not much good for my photographs, of course, but perhaps the children at the Teko Barracks or in Mile 91 will be parading around in full regalia.

The mission center has simple but strict rules. No weapons or uniforms, no cursing, no fighting. The sanctions are just as clear: no lunch, no washing with real soap and shampoo, and no admission to the Donald Duck videos Padre Victor shows on Friday afternoons. "It works like a charm," says Gabriel. "Once they've tasted the food here, they never want to eat at the barracks again."

Gabriel got involved in the project quite by chance. He was studying economics in Freetown, but couldn't find any work there. In Makeni, he got a temporary job as the chairman of the association for rural youth. After the coup, Gabriel couldn't get back home. Bishop Biguzzi persuaded him to join Caritas and to help in taking care of the children. Now Gabriel wouldn't even consider leaving. "We're the last hope for these kids," he says.

"In the beginning, the people of Makeni had a hard time accepting the fact that we were looking after the child rebels," he tells me, ruffling little Aliu's hair. "The villagers said we were feeding little killers. That's why it was so important to integrate them into the village. So we organized a performance of *The Prodigal Son* with the kids, to show that they wanted to be part of the community." The play had the desired effect, according to Gabriel. Now, the children from the Northern Jungle Battalion can walk round peacefully in the village again without being spat on, sworn at, or threatened.

Aliu is a cheeky little chap who says he's twelve but looks quite a bit older. It's difficult to estimate the children's ages properly. Gabriel has already introduced me to a boy who said he was twenty-one but looked ten years younger. Years of deprivation in the bush obviously do strange things to the body. And the children have probably lost count. I don't suppose they celebrate birthdays in the Northern Jungle Battalion.

Aliu is chattering on in incomprehensible Krio; Gabriel has to translate it into English. How many people has he killed? He doesn't know; he never counted them. "*Dem beaucoup.* Many people." Sometimes, he just closed his eyes and went on shooting until his magazine was empty. He didn't want to see what was happening, he explains.

How did he feel at times like that? I know it's a banal question, but I can hardly ask him what went through his head, can I?

"I felt nothing" is the plain answer. "Most of the time we were high on the *jamba* [marijuana] our commanders gave us."

Aliu is one of the many children who were kidnapped and press-ganged by the rebels. Most of the kids in the Caritas project have similar stories to relate. The rebels raided their village and took the children with them. Sometimes for years on end. Aliu was captured as he walked home from visiting an aunt in the next village. He was assigned to a commander, whose weaponry he had to carry. Later, he learned to shoot with the AK and became a full-fledged combatant.

"It was nothing but running and hiding," Aliu tells me. "The army attacked us every time they discovered our secret camp. Sometimes we had to walk for a week through the bush until we found a new place. But they always found us again, sooner or later."

Mattia is a similar case. He's sixteen now, but says he was kidnapped when he was ten, during a rebel raid on his village. His parents were shot dead and he was taken. "I was too small to fight, so I had to carry the bags and look for food and water. I was sick most of the time. I often had a fever and aches and pains. But you couldn't run away because they were guarding us. And they would kill you if you tried."

Mattia shows me some big scars on his legs: scratches from running day after day through the scrub. "Once, the Kamajors were after us," says Mattia. The Kamajors used to hunt just for wild animals, aided by their mysterious powers, explains Gabriel. When the coming of the rebels made their villages unsafe, the Kamajors started to form civilian militias. The Kabbah government saw them as faithful allies and furnished them with modern weapons. Now the Kamajors are the rebels' archenemies. They are fearless fighters because they imagine themselves to be invulnerable to rebel bullets, thanks to magic amulets and secret rituals.

"We were on the run for six days," Mattia continues. "There was nothing to eat. When we finally reached a safe place, I found a little pool to drink from. I bent over to drink and fell asleep. I nearly drowned."

Mattia has developed an aversion to walking and running. He's the boy who wants to be a truck driver when he grows up. "That way I'll have my own transport and never have to walk again." Gabriel looks at me proudly and smiles a satisfied smile.

The other children recount their stories. Margaret is a cute little girl of eleven, with braids and beads in her hair. Kidnapped at the age of eight, she was in the rebels' SGU, or Small Girls Unit, for three years. She didn't fight, but had to gather wood, cook, carry bags, and set up tents. "We had to work very hard," says Margaret. "They would shoot us down if we tried to escape." Her little brother was kidnapped at the same time, but ended up in another RUF battalion. Gabriel is now trying to talk the rebels into letting Margaret go, so she can be reunited with her family.

Suddenly, we hear yelling and cheering. The children all rush toward an elderly white man with a big beard and a slight stoop, who is making his way across the courtyard. It's Padre Victor, with a soccer ball under one arm, which he throws playfully at Aliu, and the weekly Donald Duck video under the other. Padre Victor kicks the ball around with Aliu and boxes playfully with two other children. The yard rings to his laughter as he disappears into the film auditorium with the little ones.

The sprightly padre is the driving force behind the children's project. It was Padre Victor who first visited the barracks and became good friends with Colonel Isaac, the commanding officer of the Northern Jungle Battalion. Later, the colonel authorized

Padre Victor to take the children to the mission center for the odd afternoon.

"Ah, yes," says Padre Victor proudly, slurping up short strands of spaghetti with cassava sauce. "I remember it well—the first time I visited the kids and threw a soccer ball to Aliu. He kissed the ball, with tears in his eyes. He told me he hadn't touched anything like that in five years. It was only then it really dawned on me how innocent and childlike these kids were."

We're having lunch—the children are watching Donald Duck—and Padre Victor has pulled a chair up to the mission center's long dining table. As the pots of pesto failed to survive the journey from Italy, the padres have to make do with cassava, which, with a little imagination, tastes like pesto. The spaghetti also arrived in pieces. But, after twenty-one years in Sierra Leone, Padre Victor has got used to such things.

"These children have had years of brainwashing," he continues in his heavy Italian accent, sitting with his elbows on the table, wolfing down his food. His table manners are gone for good. "They can take a gun apart and put it back together blindfolded. But they've forgotten their families, so we're trying to bring back their memories of childhood. We ask them what their mother used to cook for them, what kind of presents they had, what kind of games they played with their friends."

Padre Victor licks his empty plate clean. Pieces of green cassava cling to his white beard. Tomorrow he will take me to the Teko Barracks to talk to the children. I work through the rest of the day's busy program with Gabriel. We visit the cathedral, a cool oasis of peace, and take a look at the food program, where well-rounded women are cooking great pots of rice for sniveling orphans. I'm impressed. With very little money, but a great deal of effort, they are working hard to improve the lot of the children here.

The junta secretariat is closed. That's too bad. I wonder what's wrong. Sanusi was supposed to have the letter for his friend in Wageningen ready for me, and he was going to give me the paper that would see me through all the checkpoints without any problems. Maybe they're mostly Muslim at the secretariat and that's why they're closed on Fridays.

Back to Buya's Motel. There, I trip over the grenade launchers lying about on the steps. A couple of soldiers are hanging around in the reception area. The governor is visiting with his bodyguards, the bellboy whispers. And he's not in the best of moods, he warns me.

The lobby of Buya's has a lounge area with a moldy armchair and a saggy three-seater couch on which the governor is sitting, looking equally loose at the seams, a pair of overturned beer cans on the table in front of him. His spotty forehead glistens with beads of perspiration. He's listening to the BBC, which is just announcing that the ECOMOG has now definitely captured the junta headquarters in Freetown. For the governor it is, indeed, Friday the thirteenth.

"That's bad news," I mumble. The governor grunts. For him, it certainly is bad news. Little remains of the self-satisfied, puffed-up frog who was putting me down only yesterday. Now, he's nothing more than a deflated windbag. He'd better start looking for another job. I leave him in peace and disappear discreetly to my room.

So, the junta has fallen. Good news? Well, I'm not convinced of the democratic qualities of the Kabbah government, which will now be returning to power. And is it good or bad news for my story? I don't know. It'll make things more interesting, for sure. Also more complicated. I'd silently hoped—and expected—that the junta would hold out for at least a few weeks. It's all happened too quickly. It's barely a week since the ECOMOG started the attack, and they've already got the junta on the run.

Too bad Sanusi isn't there. I wonder if I can still fly to Freetown from Port Loko with Colonel Croma. Probably not . . . so maybe I should just get the bus to Freetown. But Eddie has asked me to go to the diamond region with him, too. And the Caritas visit to Mile 91? Will that still be on?

Eddie turns up for our evening stroll at the appointed time. It's quieter in the town than last night, but crowds of people are thronging around the bus station. "Just watch," says Eddie, "the people are panicking and starting to leave." From a distance, we can see a soldier dragging the driver out of a minibus and taking off in it himself. "Aye-aye-aye," groans Eddie. "Now, that's not nice," but he isn't letting the situation get him down. "Makeni has always remained quiet," he assures me. "I don't suppose it will be any different this time."

From the palm-wine club, however, we hear disturbing news. One of the workers at the World Food Program, who is half-Nigerian, was picked up by the rebels this afternoon. Luckily, they let her go after a couple of hours. The warehouse of the relief organization CARE has been looted by mutinying soldiers, and rebels have commandeered several Red Cross and World Food Program vehicles.

We decide to make it an early night. Eddie walks back to the motel with me. He is just about to go home when a big, black Mercedes draws up. Twicey jumps out, spots us, and comes over to shake hands. He has no bodyguards with him, just a revolver at his hip and a Kalashnikov in the Mercedes next to the gear-stick. "I can't control my men any longer," he says worriedly. He has spent the entire day returning stolen vehicles, to no avail. "The rebels just don't want to listen anymore," Twicey concludes. "Good luck, guys," he calls, and drives off into the night.

5 | Trouble Has Started

An ordinary Saturday morning in Makeni. The bellboy brings me a thermos of hot water for the coffee and a bucket of luke-warm water for washing. The mosquitoes are still attempting to find a hole in the mosquito net. Outside, the sun is blazing down mercilessly. The street vendors have put their oranges out on display. But the secretariat is still closed. I can't find anyone who can tell me anything. What am I supposed to do now about my paper to get me to Freetown? Oh, well, I'll cross that bridge when I come to it. First I'll go over to the mission center, where Gabriel and Padre Victor are waiting to take me to the Teko Barracks.

Padre Victor is sitting behind the wheel of his dented Toyota pickup, with Gabriel and me next to him in the front seat. We are discussing the fall of the junta. Padre Victor says that the hospital in neighboring Lunsar has been looted. It worries him. We had better put off our trip to Mile 91, thinks Gabriel. The rebels there won't be happy about the ECOMOG victory.

The Teko Barracks are a few miles outside Makeni. The road

is a dusty sand path full of potholes, which Padre Victor deftly manages to avoid. Gabriel points out the bishop's house, a gleaming white villa, the windows staring vacantly in the shade of some big mango trees.

A little farther on is the military base. Two guardhouses in need of paint mark the entrance. They must at some point have been green, white, and light blue, the colors of the national flag, but they are now covered in a layer of black mildew. A soldier leaning against an ancient piece of artillery nods sleepily, indicating that we can drive on.

At first sight, it looks like a holiday resort. Rows of low villas, courtyards with trees, clotheslines hung with wash. Not overly luxurious, but not shabby either. It's quiet, Gabriel remarks. A bare-chested man in shorts with a submachine gun next to him on the ground is sitting up against a house with a transistor radio pressed to his ear. An RUF rebel. We explain to him that we're on our way to see the children. Go on through, he nods, readjusting the knob on his radio.

The deserted yard suddenly fills with children, streaming in from all sides. They flock behind the car. The padre's dilapidated pickup is well-known, and there are not so many cars in Makeni anyway. We stop by one of the villas, where we are greeted by a portly man leading several children by the hand.

It's the Caritas worker Samuel, who has adopted several child soldiers. He has come to live in the barracks, partly to be closer to the children and partly because he is friendly with the rebel leader Colonel Isaac.

I interview a few children, but can't concentrate properly. The grisly stories seem so unreal, somehow. After the fifth interview,

I can't tell one tale from another: kidnapped by the rebels, mistreated, fleeing through the bush, pitching camp, brief moments of terror, then once more periods of endless grind. I take a few photos of the kids, although there doesn't seem much point. Not a single uniform or weapon in sight, but I can hardly ask if they want to play soldier for me.

Okay then, I'll have to settle for some banal snaps of smiling, little black kids. That's what Caritas wants, anyway. "No sorrow photos" were the instructions. The sun is already high in the sky, casting heavy shadows across the children's faces. To make matters worse, they're all wearing brilliant white T-shirts, which makes it impossible to find the right exposure. Eight f-stops contrast difference. Because it will have to be color slides, which I can't correct myself in the darkroom.

"Expose Negroes one f-stop more," it said on the very first Polaroid cameras produced in America in the 1950s. "If in doubt, use a flash." So I do. Hopelessly flat lighting, but all according to the book, nevertheless. The children go crazy when they see the flash go off. This is a new experience for them. Padre Victor looks on, radiant. Caritas should be happy. Mission accomplished. Right, let's get packed and get out of here. Time for some serious journalistic work.

Just before the exit from the barracks, we are stopped. "Come with us, please." History is repeating itself. A brusque officer behind a messy desk launches accusations of espionage and gathering secret information with a real camera. Luckily Padre Victor is there this time. He knows how to deal with these guys. Gesturing expressively with his hands, he explains the matter in fluent Krio, his tone and attitude switching at the drop of a hat. One moment highly indignant, the next a little subservient, then surprised, furious, or disappointed, but always polite. Five minutes later, the man is cordially waving us off. "Phew!" groans Padre Victor. "I've never known them to be so difficult."

I get dropped off at the post office so I can make a quick call home. There is a phone booth, and as the leone has plummeted since the coup, you can buy a phone card for two dollars, which lets you call international for five minutes. No long queues in the post office, just a cheerful, smiling employee who hands me a brand-new phone card. What a country! Everything works, and with the exception of a few smart alecks, everyone is friendly, honest, and helpful. I get through to Brussels almost immediately. I promised to drop a call once in a while. "Everything's cool," I say. "Assignment completed. I'm done with this godforsaken hole. Tomorrow I'm going to try to get to Freetown." There. Short and sweet. Man talk.

At the bus station, they tell me there are still buses running to Freetown. It's all much easier than I'd expected. If I can just get hold of Sanusi, then everything will be sorted out.

I saunter back at my leisure, stopping for a chat with the Lebanese salesmen Eddie introduced me to yesterday. The Lebanese have been living in Sierra Leone for generations. Through hard work—and dubious trading practices—they have acquired a monopoly on import and export. When the first diamonds were mined in the early 1930s, they rushed into the trade in droves. Now, they dominate the lucrative diamond sector and are therefore looked on with some suspicion by many Sierra Leoneans. The Lebanese in Makeni are not worried about the developments in Freetown, they tell me. It's all sure to blow over.

I lunch on a kabob of roasted goat's meat in a small establishment on the main street. A truck full of soldiers approaches. The other guests look up, startled. Behind the truck, a Fiat Panda, with RUF painted on the side and guys in sunglasses with grenade launchers hanging out of the windows, comes screeching up. The governor's elite troops. A few hundred yards farther up they come to a halt. It's not clear what is happening, but the soldiers jump out of the truck and a whole bunch of people run away screaming.

I sneak out of the window at the back of the restaurant and watch from a safe distance. It all quiets down again and I climb back into the restaurant. But then the people start running around again. So much for a quiet lunch. Through the back window, I end up in a maze of muddy alleyways and slums. I find my bearings as best as I can and walk back toward the motel.

Then I hear someone calling my name. It's Samuel, the Caritas worker from the Teko Barracks. "Let me escort you back home," he says. We walk through fields of crops in a wide berth around the center of Makeni, until we come in sight of Buya's. Samuel tells me that some soldiers tried to hijack Padre Victor's car just after he dropped me off at the post office. Padre Victor refused to let them have it and stood his ground. They roughed him up a bit, but he was finally allowed to drive on. I shudder. Things are really starting to heat up around here.

There's still no one about at the junta secretariat, so I go back to the motel for a nap. I'm slowly drifting off to sleep when screaming in the street wakes me with a jolt. I hear the sound of a fighter jet flying low overhead. Outside, everyone is gesticulating madly at a plane circling over the town. "Alfajet, Alfajet!" the children cry excitedly.

I only know the name Alfajet from the BBC bulletins of the past few days. *Alfajets have pounded the junta headquarters in the capital, Freetown,* was the repeated message on the radio. Now I'm seeing one for the first time. Small jet fighters, a bit outdated with their rounded wings and stubby, conical nose.

The people seem to be more curious than alarmed. I, too, watch with interest as the airplane describes big circles over Makeni. Could it be a reconnaissance mission? The precursor of an offensive? Or is the pilot simply lost? Slowly, the jet circles lower and lower. Then it makes a long turn and dives straight at us.

Before I have a chance to jump into a ditch, the aircraft is racing over us at an altitude of about a hundred feet. In a flash, I see the fuel tanks and bombs hanging underneath. Immediately afterward, there are two thunderous explosions. A couple of hundred yards farther on, in the neighborhood of the governor's residence, thick clouds of dust and smoke are rising.

I dash into the hotel to get my camera and walk with the crowd in the direction of the smoke clouds. A mother with a screaming child runs toward us. Only when they have passed do I realize the boy was drenched in blood. The bombs have fallen farther up. Not on the governor's residence, but on the police barracks. One row of houses has been razed to the ground. Nearby, a boy lies with his leg blown off. His jeans are covered in blood; one trouser leg is empty and tattered.

Bystanders watch as the boy's chest heaves painfully up and

down until he finally breathes his last breath. Farther up, a man—he must be dead—is lying half-buried under the dust and rubble of a collapsed building. A woman presses herself, sobbing, against what is left of the wall. A boy with a massive head wound is being supported by two soldiers. Shrapnel is lying everywhere, big, twisted pieces of metal with razor-sharp edges.

Everyone stands looking at the ravages in stunned silence. The police have not been hit; they are on patrol elsewhere. The victims are therefore their families since, in Africa, police and army barracks are intended to house the whole family.

Now Eddie pops up from amongst the bystanders. He has just been visiting the governor at home. Laughing, he starts to tell how Governor Gottoa dived, trembling, under the coffee table at the first sound of the jet. Then the graveness of the situation sinks in. He surveys the damage and questions several bystanders.

"Okay, we've seen enough here," says Eddie. "Let's get over to the hospital." We head toward the center. Halfway there we hear another explosion. Maybe the ECOMOG has dropped bombs with a timing mechanism, or maybe someone has been tampering with an unexploded shell.

Panic reigns in the hospital. Nurses are running around crying, bumping into each other with IV bottles and rolls of bandages. The first victims have already been brought into a darkened room. It stinks like a butcher's where the meat has passed its sell-by date. A sickening stench: a mixture of dead flesh and cheap disinfectant. One nurse is mopping up pools of blood from the floor; others are bandaging bleeding stumps of legs, cleaning the most serious wounds and hanging up IV bottles.

The duty doctor tells us there are two dead and nine wounded—

all civilians. A nurse draws the sheet up over a man with his leg ripped off. "Three dead, now," says the doctor.

We hurry to the post office. Eddie wants to call the BBC with the phone card, but can't get through. On the way back, we see soldiers seizing cars. They are stopping the vehicles under threat and dragging out the drivers. Twicey's Mercedes comes toward us; he recognizes us, waves, and drives on. Great clouds of dust envelop the Mercedes as it speeds away. The street vendors have packed up their wares and disappeared. The Lebanese traders are pulling down their storm shutters. There isn't a living soul to be seen at the secretariat.

"Trouble has started," murmurs Eddie ominously as he drops me off at Buya's Motel. "See you later."

Evening falls. The crickets chirp. From time to time, a rifle shot rings out. Then the crickets fall silent for a moment, only to start up again minutes later. Their chirping would, under other cir-cumstances, be picturesque, but now the creatures are irritating me to death with their infernal racket.

We'd better skip the usual evening stroll tonight, says Eddie. In the distance, we hear the rattle of machine guns, probably Kalashnikovs. The junta soldiers and rebels are getting nervous, he explains. They realize they are fighting a losing battle and have started looting.

Eddie invites me to eat at his house. In the twilight, he leads me through dim alleyways until we reach a small house built of unpainted cement blocks, not far from the junta secretariat. In the courtyard, which is shared with four other families, a couple of women stand, stirring enormous pots. Children run playfully in and out or whine and complain as they are scrubbed clean. It's hard to say who belongs to which house: everyone is walking in and out of each other's home. Eddie wishes them all a good evening and ushers me into his house. By the light of paraffin lamps and candles, his friends T-Boy and Imfahin are sitting on a worn-out lounge suite. T-Boy, a burly fellow with a cheeky face, is smoking a joint. Imfahin, the actual owner of the house, is tall and slim. His eyes are glazed. Malaria, he apologizes, withdrawing to another room. Zainab is Eddie's girlfriend: a good-looking woman with a proud countenance. "*Ebo*," she says in a loud cry as she shakes my hand. It means something like "Well, whom do we have here, then?"

Zainab is in charge of the household and seems to have everything under control. She serves the dinner on orange, plastic plates. Rice with cassava and pieces of dried fish in it as a treat. Zainab likes hot peppers. I have to down cup after cup of water to soothe my scorched throat. Zainab laughs fleetingly, then subsides, a blank, worried look clouding her face. She only came to visit Eddie and is anxious to get back to Freetown and her children as soon as possible. The buses are still running, I try to reassure her.

Zainab sighs. Eddie is at a loss, too. "Don't worry," he says, but the words sound unconvincing. Later, as he walks back with me, he relates more disquieting stories about mutinying soldiers, which weren't meant for Zainab's ears.

The motel staff are standing in the courtyard, gazing at the stars. The quiet of the evening is disturbed by the sporadic rattle of machine gun fire. Star shells and tracer bullets drag red trails across the black sky. The disco across from the hotel is locked up tight, even though Saturday is usually party night. A bus full of well-dressed women and children stops in front of the motel. They get out with heavy suitcases and check in. "We have fled Freetown," they explain curtly when I ask where they have come from. They are reluctant to say any more. Family of the junta leaders, says the bellboy once they are out of earshot.

I go to my room and crawl into bed.

6 | Eddie Will Fix It

I wake up soaked in sweat. A heavy night, hot, humid. I was woken up incessantly by gunfire, and then there were those damned mosquitoes again. At any rate, the shooting has stopped, and it's gradually getting light. The travel alarm says six o'clock. I pull the sheet back over myself. Just another fifteen minutes, then I'll get going. Ask at the bus station if there's still transport.

Ten past six. The first shots. The soldiers are awake again. Now the rattle of Kalashnikovs coming from the direction of the bus station. Maybe I'd better not go over there after all.

I'm standing washing by flashlight in the narrow, dark bathroom when there is a knock at the door. I wrap a towel around my waist and open it, dripping and covered in lather. It's Eddie. He keeps it brief: "Tony, get dressed and get your things together. We're going to my place. It's not safe here any longer." He explains that the junta wants to use the motel as a temporary headquarters.

I try to protest, telling him I actually wanted to go and see if the buses were still running. Eddie shakes his head. "Tony-To, Tony-To," he sighs. He's been calling me that for a day or two now. It makes me sound like a stubborn child. "You're crazy. Just listen to me." Still reluctant, I pack my things, which were half packed anyway with possible irregularities in mind. We drop them at Eddie's and, without stopping, set off to scout around.

Intermittent rifle shots. Not as many as last night, but more than are to my liking, nevertheless. All the stores are locked and barred; no vendors are on the street. Now and again a group of people pass by with mattresses and pans on their heads. "They're leaving for the bush," Eddie explains. The Sierra Leoneans are used to camping in the bush for a week or so in times of trouble until things quiet down again.

Apart from that, there is no traffic on the street, no taxis, no buses, only soldiers and rebels in pickup trucks, which they have more than likely stolen. When we hear them coming in the distance, we dive behind a wall or go and stand around the corner. We watch a truck stopping at the Red Cross offices. Armed men—some of them in army uniforms, others in sports clothes— jump out of the vehicle, walk calmly inside, and come out again carrying big boxes, which they stack neatly in the back of the truck. "There goes the Red Cross," whispers Eddie, lighting a joint to calm his nerves. The men go about their business at their leisure, acting more like moving men than looters.

We walk through narrow alleyways, playing hide-and-seek with the soldiers, who are swarming all over the place. "Hide your camera under your shirt," Eddie orders me. "We don't want any problems."

We speak to a local resident now and again. The picture becomes clear. Last night, soldiers came looting and cleaned out most of the stores and offices. Everything on wheels, down to wheelbarrows and bicycles, has been commandeered, too. The post office has been reduced to rubble; the phone booth is lying smashed to smithereens. Rumor has it that the junta has given the start signal for wholesale pillaging, under the name Operation Pay Yourself. They are also saying that a plane full of weapons and mercenaries is on its way from Ukraine, to support the junta.

"Okay, let's go back," says Eddie. "We've seen enough." We make our way through back alleys. I feel white. Conspicuously white. My heart is in my mouth at every truck of soldiers that passes. Sometimes, Eddie pushes me into a house. The inhabitants barely look up. Some offer me a cup of water, which I down thankfully.

Eddie calls me when the coast is clear again. One time, we walk straight into two soldiers in a passageway. "Don't run," Eddie hisses between his teeth. "Take it easy, just walk normally." My sunglasses hide my anxious eyes as we pass the two as if nothing is wrong. The soldiers ignore us. They're too busy trying to see if there's anything else they can get their hands on.

At Eddie's place I slump into a chair, exhausted, wiping the sweat from my brow. What now? Things are really starting to get out of hand. "Up shit creek without a paddle" is the appropriate expression for a situation like this, I believe. Zainab looks anxiously out of the window. "This is no good," mutters Eddie. "You guys have to get out of here." He steps resolutely outside. "I'll be back in a little while," he calls over his shoulder.

While Zainab is serving breakfast—rice with cassava—the woman next door comes running in, in panic. "They're looting the Catholic Relief Service," she pants. The CRS office is two houses away. Zainab pushes me into the bedroom. "Stay away from the windows," she pleads. I go and stand in the corner, from where I can hear screaming and the tinkle of breaking glass. I look up: corrugated iron. Nowhere to hide. Half an hour later, I hear a car drive off and Zainab comes to let me out.

Eddie comes in with a "Don't worry, trust Eddie" grin on his face. "Everything has been arranged," he says. "Pack your bags, you're off to Freetown in half an hour."

We slip out of the house, wait in the ditch at the foot of the main road until the coast is clear, then quickly dash across the road and walk on to the presbytery. A white Toyota Land Cruiser is parked outside, with "Makeni City Hospital" on the side in large letters. Next to it is a black Mercedes. I recognize the license plates; it's Twicey's. We shake hands. "Don't worry," says Twicey.

"Here we are," Eddie says, and introduces me to the others. "Dr. Baker, the surgeon from our hospital. He has to go to Freetown to pick up some medical supplies. You guys can ride with him. These six soldiers are your escort."

I only count four, but then I notice two small boys shouldering machine guns. They can't be more than twelve. I've seen one of them walking around at the Caritas project, a surly youth with a funny face like a duck's. Finally, child soldiers with guns, but I'm in no mood for taking pictures. "Just to avoid any problems," Eddie goes on, "Twicey will lead the convoy. You'll be in Freetown by tonight."

Eddie is brilliant. Tonight I will be in liberated Freetown, where I can stay with Zainab. Relax for a day, do my laundry, then check out what the ECOMOG is up to.

A white priest appears next to me, Father Daniel. Eddie asks if he might use the mission radio to send a message to the BBC. Father Daniel is reluctant. The rebels are listening in, he explains. The radio could be confiscated. Eddie quickly jots down a rough version of his report for me to ring through to the BBC in Freetown. I'm glad to be able to do something for him in return. An important task, even. Eddie is staying on in Makeni for a few more days, then he'll follow me to Freetown.

Father Daniel has spoken by radio to his colleagues in the town of Lunsar. Mutinying soldiers and rebels have not only looted the hospital, but have subsequently set fire to it as well. The mission post has been attacked; four padres have been kidnapped. I get a funny feeling in my stomach. Lunsar is on our way.

Bandanna and Coconut

Our convoy sets off. Twicey in front, the two children sitting enthroned on the hood of his Mercedes. The smaller of the two, with the duck face, looks about him with a macho expression, his Kalashnikov at the ready. He has the world at his feet, or so he thinks. Little asshole.

Two other soldiers are slouched in the backseat of the Mercedes with their rocket launchers sticking out the window. "Doc" Baker is at the wheel of our Land Cruiser ambulance. Doc is a portly man with a ready laugh, who has every confidence in the trip and is doing all he can to put us at our ease. Next to Doc sits Zainab and beside her a tall soldier, thin as a rake, in a blue tracksuit top. Right Makkah is his name. I'm in the back along with Emmanuel, one of Doc's staff, and a soldier whose eyes flick nervously around, his finger on the trigger of his rusty gun.

We take the main asphalt road to Freetown, but a hundred yards on, Twicey makes a right turn, onto a dirt road. "I guess it's a safer route," suggests Doc. We follow Twicey and crisscross along all kinds of back roads around Makeni. Sometimes we pass a pickup full of looting soldiers and I duck down out of sight for a moment. But they don't bother us; that we have Twicey and the bodyguards with us probably helps. Now Twicey stops at a house. The Mercedes is having engine trouble; a passerby tries to get some diesel fuel from us; someone else wants to join our convoy. Heavy discussions follow, the usual third-world palaver. I just stay in the ambulance. "A lot of bullshit for nothing," Doc curses as we continue on our way an hour later. We're hardly making any progress. Every so often we come across such deep holes in the road that the Mercedes has a hard time handling them. Twicey gets stuck in the mud several times and we have to get out and push him, then do a U-turn.

Twicey stops at almost every village—no matter how tiny. It might be a couple of men he has to speak to, a nephew or a niece to be picked up, a sweetheart he wants to call on or more trouble with the battery, the exhaust, or the diesel pump. Meanwhile, it's getting dark and my hopes of arriving in Freetown by nightfall are gradually evaporating.

We come to a halt again in a tiny settlement, a collection of eight straw huts that nevertheless bears a name: Yesana. Twicey has an important errand to run; he has taken off in the Mercedes on his own for a while. It's starting to get us down. Doc, Zainab, and I sit and wait on a bench, sucking oranges.

"Isn't there a decent restaurant anywhere in this place?" I say, making a feeble attempt at bolstering the general mood. No response. A Toyota Corolla comes round the corner of the forest trail, a monstrous, ugly model from the late seventies, in that dirty brown color. Suddenly, everything starts to happen fast. Out of the corner of my eye I see Doc and Zainab hightailing it. "Run, Tony, run!" I hear Zainab yelling at me.

I jump up off the bench, too, and am starting to make a run for it when I hear an order: "Stop! Stay where you are!" Right behind me, I hear the clicking of weapons being cocked. I turn around and find myself looking down the barrels of five rifles. A bunch of crazily rigged-out, excited teenagers are holding me at gunpoint. The one in front is wearing a bright red bandanna, which he has tied round his head in pirate fashion. His face is covered in scars, and a necklace of cowrie shells hangs at his throat. He has a wild look in his eyes.

His friend's eyes are devoid of expression. He is sporting an orange life vest from which coconuts and hand grenades dangle. Natives with life vests and machine guns are always bad news. They think that the vests are bulletproof. But the coconut doesn't look as if he thinks anything at all. A stupid hanger-on with a face like the back end of a bus, a protruding mouth and thick lips. A white, plastic rosary hangs around his neck. What a photogenically villainous face, I think to myself.

I don't take in what the others look like, just a vague impression of black bandoliers with antiaircraft-caliber cartridges hanging from naked, muscular torsos; knives, daggers, and pistols sticking out from the waistbands of pants and tight football shorts. These are real, hard-core dickheads, straight out of a *Mad Max* film.

"Dirty white man!" screams the hysterical leader with the bandanna. "On your knees!" He tears off my watch. His friend with the coconuts grabs me by the hair and shoves me to the ground.

Something inside me makes me get up and sit on the bench

again. "Back on the ground," the bandanna screams once more. But there's no way I'm going to be picked off like a snake on the ground in the dust. I remain sitting on the bench. "Please, calm down," I try. To my surprise I sound calm, icy cool. I pull a pack of cigarettes from my pocket and offer them one.

"I don't smoke!" screams Bandanna. He snatches the pack furiously out of my hand, rips it up, and throws it away. There goes my first hope. A cigarette usually works wonders. A brief breathing space, a moment of concentration on lighting up, shifting the attention from the potential victim to the cigarette for a second. Soothing nicotine being sucked in by murderers' lungs. A couple of seconds' reprieve in which the original mission—Kill! Maim! Rape! Destroy!—is momentarily forgotten.

I see the crumpled pack of Gauloises roll and bounce across the ground as the others thrust the barrels of their guns up against my head, chest, and belly. All our bodyguards have disappeared. I knew it. This is no good, no good at all. So this is what it's like in practice. The umpteenth death in some foreign rathole. This is it; now they're going to blow me away.

8 | What Went Through My Head

Later, I was to be asked the "What went through your head at that point?" question a thousand times. Very nearly a whole lot of lead, I think now, seated at my writing desk. What does it actually feel like, lead going through your body? In Bosnia I was unlucky enough to experience it one time. I stupidly let myself be taken by a bunch of drunk, high, and reckless soldiers to the front line where a Serbian sniper let me have it from a range of ten yards. The classic beginner's mistake: going with inebriated soldiers to places where you're risking your neck.

A direct hit in the thigh, two holes in my jeans that issued a trickle of red liquid. Blood. No pain, more of a warm, wet feeling, but rather uncomfortable. Like wetting your pants.

That time, no tendons, arteries, or bones were hit. That's when it really hurts. A bullet fired from an AK leaves the barrel at a speed of nine hundred yards a second. If the bullet touches body tissue, it changes course immediately, moving from side to side, crisscrossing through the body, leaving a trail of devastation in its wake. Tissue that hasn't even been in contact with the projectile can be torn apart by shock waves. Sometimes, the bullet shatters into several pieces, each drilling its way in unpredictable spiraling movements through organs and bones. Bone splinters cause even greater damage.

And then we're only talking about a single bullet. A whole salvo is undoubtedly a different matter. Does that hurt more? Or does the nervous system become so overloaded that pain becomes a relative concept? A Vietnam veteran once told me that you don't even notice if you are really seriously wounded. And a character in *Catch-22* whose innards are mangled by a piece of grenade shrapnel dies without uttering a single cry of pain. Does loss of blood make you go rapidly into shock, or do you suffer a massive heart attack so you no longer feel anything and simply slip straight into a black hole?

I don't know. But what I do know is I've got to play for time, make sure the mood changes. I've got to mount a massive charm offensive, get a smile out of these bastards, find a soft spot in their cold killer hearts.

Please, anything to grasp hold of. The cigarette trick didn't work. Now I have to come up with something else. If only I can manage to strike up a spark of humor or understanding, then I can carefully fan it. Not too hastily, mustn't force anything. Slowly, slowly, little by little, pouring fuel onto it. Ultimately, that tiny spark will become a warm fire of camaraderie. Then there will be a few jokes and some mutual backslapping; later we can exchange the names of soccer stars and everyone can finally go his own way feeling a little bit better. At least, that's how it always went in the former Yugoslavia, where they also threatened to put me in front of a firing squad a couple of times. Will it be any different here?

So here they are, sticking the barrels of their guns into me. Bandanna starts ranting and raving again. "You fucking foreigners started this war," he shrieks. "You sell us all the arms. And you're gonna pay for it!" The bandanna and his friend grab hold of me and push me up against their car. Everything goes black. I don't care anymore. Just another senseless death. I'm being shoved up against the shit-brown Corolla; I start passing out, resigned to my fate. "Please, let me sit down for a moment," I hear myself whisper. "I'm not feeling well." My attackers leave me alone for a while. Is there just a trace of humanity in them, after all?

9 |
Right Makkah to the Rescue

I'm sitting on my haunches, on the point of blacking out. The bastards have left me in peace for a moment and I gradually come back to my senses. My knees are not knocking so badly anymore. Cautiously, I stand up. Ready for the next round. Then one of our bodyguards appears on the scene. It's Right Makkah, the skinny guy in the blue tracksuit top. He plants himself right in front of Bandanna, and an exchange of words begins, ending up in an enormous shouting match. Right Makkah holds his AK firmly in both hands and clicks the magazine open, ready. I expect the bullets to start flying at any moment, a chaotic gun battle, like in a Tarantino movie in which it is unclear who is shooting at whom, but when the smoke clears, everyone lies bleeding to death.

But it doesn't get any further than shouting and arguing. Unbelievable the way they can go off at each other. Right Makkah grabs my hand for an instant and squeezes it. That small, tender gesture does me a lot of good. "It's gonna be okay," he whispers to me. I needed that. I'm starting to calm down a bit already. In any event, I'm no longer on my own in this. "Give me your passport," says Right Makkah. He puts it in his pocket for safe-keeping and continues his tirade against Bandanna, undaunted. Plainly to no avail; without any explanation, Bandanna's friends grab hold of me again and throw me into the backseat of the Corolla. In the meantime, Coconut has got my backpack out of the ambulance and chucked it into the car as well. I sit jammed in between the morons, my feet resting on a jerrican of petrol. They are planning to take off with me. "We're gonna torture you," they scream. My muscles go to jelly as I feel myself tossed on the winds of fate. Then just as suddenly, my assailants change their minds again. They kick me out of the car, hurl me against the door, pull off my jacket, and empty all my pockets. The little soldier with the duck face has now crawled out of the bush and is starting to put in his two bits. With a vicious smile, he thrusts the barrel of his gun into my side. He is actually supposed to be my bodyguard, but now he is simply aping his big brothers.

Doc has appeared now, too, and pitches in. He negotiates madly with the rebels, shouting indignantly now and again and raising his hands theatrically to the heavens. Another brief moment of respite for me. Right Makkah takes me aside for a second. "If you hand over all your money, maybe you will come out of this alive." Hope appears on the horizon once more, only to disappear again a second later, as Coconut shoves me up against the ambulance and starts rummaging in my pants pockets. "Where's your gun?" screams Bandanna.

"I don't carry any weapons," I falter. Two of Bandanna's friends undo my belt and pull down my pants. One of them fumbles awkwardly in my boxer shorts and feels my balls. I fear the worst, having heard the tales of castrations. Luckily, they let me pull my pants up again. Evidently they are looking for money.

"How much can you give 'em?" asks Right Makkah, who has now worked himself protectively between me and the rebels with his AK. "A hundred dollars," I whisper. "Get it," he orders.

I pull the notes out of all kinds of hiding places in my back-pack and hand them to Right Makkah. He pays them over to Bandanna. A real bargain, a hundred dollars for a life. But Bandanna is not that stupid. "He wants more," says Right Makkah.

The last of my money is rolled up in a strip of Band-Aids in my medicine bag. I pull it out. I honestly don't have any more, I assure Bandanna, looking him straight in the eye. He nods to show he believes me. We've made human contact for the first time. He counts the money and sticks it in his pocket. His friends are standing around us, looking on with greedy eyes.

I go one step further and ask for permission to smoke. "Okay," he mumbles. I inhale deeply, sucking the calming nicotine into my lungs. Don't make any mistakes now. Don't blow the smoke in his face. Bandanna starts to calm down a bit. "Show me your luggage," he orders.

I obey immediately, gaining a little more time, providing a welcome distraction. I set the backpack and the camera bag down on the hood of the car, and Bandanna searches them systemat-ically. First, he empties the camera bag. There go my Nikons. Two chunky, sturdy bodies with nice lenses, four years of faithful service behind them. Bandanna sets them carefully apart. He can't use the flash or the winder. In the front pocket of the camera bag he finds my talisman: a cowrie shell, artfully bound into a little red box with a leather thong. "Is this juju?" he asks, surprised. African magic, that much I do know from reference books. What should I say? If I say it is, then maybe he will think I possess magical powers. That could go one of two ways. In any event, I would then have to enter into a whole load of explanation, during which I could always say something wrong. I shake my head.

"Just a present from a girlfriend," I say. Bandanna looks at me pensively. He puts the amulet back without a word.

Next round of unpacking: the backpack. Dirty laundry and those damned Amnesty reports again. Why didn't I dump them in Makeni? By the light of the flashlight he already confiscated earlier, Bandanna flicks through them. Well, I am a journalist, after all, I excuse myself. Bandanna nods and stuffs the clippings back.

He leaves the film, too, even the exposed ones of the Caritas children and the bombing. Now he's found my notebooks. I have two: my journalistic notebook and my private diary. Bandanna recognizes the names of junta leaders I wrote down in the beginning. No problems. My diary, he finds more fascinating. Illegible scrawl. It's all about women and love, I explain, "Always problems." A knowing nod. All guys together.

Bandanna continues his search. He can use the radio. I tell him where the on-and-off switch is. World-band receiver, I add. The corkscrew is no use to him, even as a weapon of torture. Filthy drunk, I can see him thinking, degenerate European. Fine with me. The compass and sunglasses go; the cheap plastic alarm clock he leaves.

Now there is only my Leica. The best camera ever made,

extremely expensive, but nothing but a snapshot camera to look at. I'd stuffed it right at the bottom of the backpack, rolled up in a pair of jeans. Bandanna places the Leica on the hood. "Can't I keep that?" I venture. "It's just an old thing, not worth much, but it used to belong to my grandfather." Bandanna is not going to fall for that one. There goes the Leica, along with all the other small accessories that make the life of a reporter abroad bearable. Bandanna puts his spoils on the backseat of the Toyota. But it looks as if I'll live. What more could you want?

I'm overwhelmed with a wave of gratitude and hand Bandanna my business card. "Drop me a postcard when this is all over," I say. He promises to do so. Bandanna also writes his own name and rank on a piece of paper. He is a corporal in the Northern Jungle Battalion. We shake hands.

"Thanks for letting me live," I say to Bandanna. I mean it sincerely.

"It's okay," he mumbles, and gets into the Corolla with his friends. I watch their rear lights disappear into the night. The piece of paper with Bandanna's name is still on the hood.

10 | Between Dream and Deed

"You just went through hell," says Doc when we are on our way once more in the ambulance. Hell? Isn't Doc exaggerating a bit? I think hell must be a thousand times worse. I've only had a glimpse from the portals, taken a cautious peep at purgatory. But his sympathy makes me feel better. I even feel slightly proud of myself. I survived; I got through the initiation ritual. Now I can count myself as a bit of a Sierra Leonean.

Zainab responds differently. "You've caused us a lot of problems," she says reproachfully. "I know," I reply quietly. Of course I know. We all know that, as a white man, I'm an awkward piece of baggage, only causing complications. A monkey on their backs. But let's hope it remains unsaid.

Luckily, Doc quickly changes the subject. He tells us how he contrived to hold on to the ambulance. One way or another, he succeeded in persuading the rebels that he had to go and fetch medicine, and that they had the most to gain by letting him go.

He finally managed to reach a compromise: Doc could continue on his way for the fee of $500.

They could just as easily have stolen both his money and the vehicle. If Doc has paid $500, then he must have more on him. And why did they let him keep the ambulance? Did they really think it was in their interest? In the interest of the wounded warriors of the Revolutionary United Front? Would they think, "Let's be nice to the doctor; you never know when we might need him again"?

They could have gunned me down, too, and gone off with all my stuff just the same. They could have kidnapped and tortured me. A white victim for a change, instead of black ones, which they must literally know inside and out by now.

Everyone is always aghast to hear of people murdering each other. But more amazing is why people don't kill each other all the time. "Between dream and deed, there are laws, and practical objections," the Dutch poet Elsschot once wrote, about a man who wanted to kill his estranged wife. But no such things exist here in the jungle. You can do what you like. No one's going to worry about one more dead man. So why did Bandanna spare my life?

Each wrapped in his own thoughts, we drive on through the night in silence. Muddy, sandy trails with deep potholes, nothing but pitch-blackness and dense jungle all around us. Doc fiddles with the knobs on the radio, but can't locate a station. He curses under his breath, his face illuminated by the dashboard lights. Zainab stares out the window; Emmanuel and Right Makkah have dropped off to sleep. No sign of Twicey. We've left the disloyal bodyguards behind.

A bus comes driving toward us, and I jump out of the ambulance. I want to get away. I can take care of myself, I don't need anybody, maybe the bus is going to Freetown. But it's no use. The bus is packed with refugees, some armed rabble, and another one of those creeps in a life jacket. No one can tell us where the bus is headed. I get back in with Doc. He seems relieved I've decided to stay with them after all. We stop at the next village. Refugees tell us that the ECOMOG have captured Makeni. Maybe we can simply drive back again tomorrow. We knock at a house for water. We can see a light burning inside, but no one answers the door.

"*Ouy, ouy*," cries Doc through a crack in the door. *Ouy* is the local word for water. The people are obviously scared to death and turn out the light. We leave them in peace and eat our provisions, a big bag of oranges. I solemnly thank Right Makkah for saving my life. He shrugs it off.

Right Makkah is tired. He hauls a blanket out of the ambulance and falls asleep under a tree. Doc parks the car in a banana plantation, out of sight of any passing riffraff. We shut the doors and try to get some sleep. Doc and Zainab talk in hushed voices.

Completely exhausted, I fall fast asleep, flat out on a stretcher. I awake now and then, hear Doc and Zainab still talking, and fall asleep again.

11 | Stopover in Kalangba

The next morning. The owners of the house have overcome their fear and bring water for us to brush our teeth. Zainab, Doc, and Emmanuel are looking crumpled. They have hardly slept a wink. Right Makkah rolls out from under his blanket, splashes his face with a few drops of water, and is as fresh as a daisy again.

Doc is undecided. Go back to Makeni, which is supposed to be taken by the ECOMOG? The BBC has yet to announce anything about the fall of Makeni. Drive on to Port Loko or Lunsar? And see there whether Freetown is reachable?

We go for the last option. On the way, we pass groups of refugees trudging down the road with pans and mats on their heads. Now and again, a group turns off onto a side path, in the direction of the bush. They are on their way to villages where it is safe. Which villages those might be, the refugees don't know either. The whole country has turned into a madhouse, they say.

In a couple of settlements, Doc goes to the paramount chief, the head of the village, for news on the situation. The news is troubling. Makeni is a mess. We had better stay away from there. Port Loko is occupied by retreating, pillaging, and looting junta troops. We don't want to run into them, either. Doc sighs. Zainab turns to me. "Tony, Tony, we were so afraid for you yesterday," she says with a harrowed look.

Heavily armed rebels and soldiers are hanging around in all the villages. I get out for a moment and talk to a boy with a rocket launcher on his shoulder. A Liberian, he has been fighting with the rebels for four years. He doesn't have much to say. "Please, stay in the car," says Zainab as we drive on. "And get down if we come across any rebels."

We see more and more of them. They don't bother us, but look at the ambulance with covetous eyes. "It's crazy to go on any farther," says Doc, wiping the sweat from his forehead. "Sooner or later they will kill me for the car. And you, they will get you again. But now you've got nothing left for them to take. Except your life." We no longer have any bodyguards, either. Right Makkah decided to stay behind and rejoin his troops.

In the next village, Doc has friends who run a clinic and the local school. He thinks it would be better to stay there for a few days until the situation has normalized.

Dr. Samai welcomes us with open arms. He runs a small clinic next to the main road, a few hundred yards outside Kalangba. Soldiers are loitering in the village, but Samai assures us they won't hurt a fly. The wave of looting hasn't reached this far yet. Maybe the soldiers don't even know what is happening in Makeni, as all communication has been cut off. And the events in Freetown are evidently too far away to be of any concern to them.

Across from the clinic is the Kalangba Agricultural Secondary School. Doc parks the ambulance there, out of sight from the road. Emmanuel and I move our things into the clinic; Doc and Zainab are going to stay with the principal.

In the afternoon, we are all lying on reed mats in the back garden of the clinic, in the shade of the mango tree. Doc has sent for a pot of palm wine, and one of the workers from the clinic brings a dish of rice and cassava, which we set upon and devour hungrily. We have had nothing to eat but oranges for a day and a half.

Doc has pulled up his T-shirt and is stroking his ample belly, taking a slug of palm wine now and then. "Full of electrolytes," he says didactically. "Good for your eyes."

A naked baby with flies on its face comes crawling through the dust toward Doc. He strokes the baby's head. "African children are the strongest in the whole world," he muses. "At least, as long as they survive the first year of life. Take this little chap, for instance. Someday, he will be one of our political leaders. Or perhaps a rebel leader; that's also possible." The baby burps. Doc laughs, looks tenderly at the child, and takes another swig of wine. I'm starting to get used to the refreshing, sweet-and-sour taste of the stuff and to find it palatable.

"You know," says Doc philosophically, "kids here grow up in the bush. In symbiosis with the wild animals. That's why we're all so crazy." But Doc is an optimist. He dismisses the disastrous situation his country is in as a transient phase. "We are going through dark times. But look at you people in Europe. Where were you in the Middle Ages? And where are you now? Just watch us. The deeper you go, the further you jump . . ."

The jerrican of palm wine goes the rounds. The atmosphere starts to liven up. Doc tells us about his travels. As a promising medical student, he was given a grant to study in what was then the Soviet Union. Later, he traveled round half of Europe on a cheap student discount ticket. Brussels. He was there for two days. The Grande Place he considers to be one of the most beautiful places in the world. He knows Amsterdam, too. The women there sit in the window with a red light on. Zainab splutters with laughter. She thinks Doc is pulling her leg. And now the tall tales start. Doc studied in Volgograd for a while. The Russians there had hardly ever seen a black person. They treated them like escaped monkeys, and he was often set upon by drunken sailors.

"At a certain point I was just sick to death of it," says Doc. "We organized an assault group with a few fellow students from Zaire. One night, about twelve of us went out. We set an ambush. We got the smallest one to walk out in front as bait." Doc laughs off his foolish student pranks. "We soon got a bite. Seven Russians started to have a go at him. Then we jumped out. We beat them to a pulp. With our bare fists. After that, they always treated us with respect."

Then Doc becomes serious. "I've renounced violence now. But I can tell you, if those bastards yesterday had not had guns, I would have killed them myself. I have no problem with killing those kind of boys."

12 | Clash of Civilizations

Behind the clinic is a shower, just a couple of sheets of corrugated iron between which you can soap yourself and rinse off with a bucket of water without too much of an audience. Washed and with clean clothes on, I feel better already. Yesterday evening I went with Doc and Zainab for a nightcap at the principal's house. Nice man. His name is Alfred. He told us that the whole village was plundered by rebels last year, but he thinks things should stay quiet now.

I'm envious that Doc and Zainab are sleeping in Alfred's house, but it's okay staying at the clinic, too. I'm sharing a room with the strong, silent Emmanuel. The nurses are sweet and bring me water for my coffee. Luckily, the rebels didn't take my stock of Nescafé. I still have my packets of tobacco, my clothes, and my toilet bag, too. All in all, the damage could have been much worse. Apart from some cameras, money, and luxury articles, I still have the most important items. Books, for example. A well-considered selection of novels and nonfiction.

First of all, the enormous tome *The Clash of Civilizations* by Samuel Huntington. A controversial book. I've already read a couple of dozen rave reviews. *The Clash* attempts to provide a replacement paradigm for the Cold War philosophy that has determined our way of thinking for the past three decades. A must for global policymakers, blurbs Henry Kissinger. Compulsory reading matter for any journalist wishing to keep abreast of things. After all, isn't every reporter a frustrated policymaker, deep down in his heart? There has to be some good reason why most reporters take such pleasure in hobnobbing with the Greatest Men on Earth. Paralyzed by a lack of commitment, we have opted for the cowardly job of observer on the sidelines. Anyway, a fresh paradigm can't do any harm. And what's more, wasn't it just yesterday that I experienced firsthand a clash of civilizations in the flesh? Maybe *The Clash* will have the answer to all my questions.

I've got Graham Greene's *The Heart of the Matter* with me, too. It's set, quite aptly, in Freetown. A psychological novel about a British Catholic diplomat during the Second World War. Doom and gloom from the first page onward. Colonial villas, thunderstorms, oppressive heat, alcohol abuse, wrecked marriages, consuming guilt feelings, conspiracy and fatal blackmail by a Lebanese diamond merchant. And in the background, those sneaky frogs—Vichy French, no less—cooking up all kinds of dirty plots in Guinea. Great book. Greene's description of Freetown intrigues me no end. Will I ever get see to Freetown? I wonder.

Then some modern English novels. *Enduring Love* by Ian McEwan, Alain de Botton's *Essays in Love*. But first, let's start with Graham Greene. Love can wait.

A cup of coffee, a cigarette, a good book, good weather. I install myself in an easy chair on the veranda. I've earned a couple of days off. On the clinic's radio I hear the BBC reporting that the ECOMOG has now taken all of Freetown. Other towns are on the point of being liberated, too. Not a word about Makeni; Eddie obviously hasn't been able to get through to London. But it can't be long before the ECOMOG seizes Makeni.

I sit, engrossed in Greene's Freetown, enjoying the relaxation. Life in the clinic is peaceful. In the courtyard, several refugees are sitting stirring their cooking pots, and a few women with undernourished children are here only during the day. From time to time, I see a car full of soldiers go by on the road, but they don't bother us.

Lunch. Cassava with rice, followed by mangoes and bananas. One-thirty. Siesta time. I stretch out on a reed mat in the back garden and soon fall fast asleep. Not for long. "Soldiers, soldiers!" screams a woman. Everyone is running off into the bush, which starts just behind the clinic. I take off, too, crouching like a tiger, through the cassava plantation, then into the bush, deeper and deeper until I feel safe. My heart is thumping in my throat; I feel like a fox running from the hounds and curse the soldiers who won't give me a moment's peace. I'd already had it up to here yesterday.

Behind a rock, I await the inevitable. I pray to God. But what is there left to pray for? For Him to set me free? And what should I offer in return? I haven't a clue. Besides, I don't think God is keen on empty promises, especially when made in panic.

The undergrowth rustles; someone is coming my way. Cautiously, I peer out from behind the boulder until I see something red moving through the leaves. One of the women from the clinic. The coast is clear, she says. Some soldiers stopped off at the clinic to ask for a glass of water, nothing more. After they had drunk it, they thanked everyone politely and went on their way.

A moment later, Doc appears. "We saw you running," he announces gaily. "We didn't know white boys could run that fast." I give a bitter laugh. It wasn't that funny. All the same, Doc thinks it would be better for me to come and stay at Alfred's house. That way, we keep together, and besides, the school is little way off the road so we can spot any attackers coming from a distance.

13 | Information and Palm Wine

It seems as if the few days of peace and quiet I so badly need have finally begun. Alfred Kanu, the principal, is friendly and hospitable. He has soft, sad eyes, which twinkle mischievously every so often. He makes me think of Charlie Chaplin.

Alfred talks expansively about his school. It's a sorry situation. Four months ago, he was forced to close the doors, as the teachers hadn't been paid since the coup in May 1997. The classrooms stand empty, the shutters hanging from their hinges; the dust keeps piling up. The junta spends most of its money on weapons or deposits it in foreign bank accounts, says Alfred. Many of the pupils have fled to Freetown over the past year; others have been press-ganged by the rebels.

Alfred's wife, Mrs. Kanu, is a lovely person, with a big, round face that is always smiling. She takes me under her wing like a mother hen, always worried about whether I like the food or not. And I do like it. It may be rice and cassava every meal, but Mrs. Kanu and daughter Annette manage to serve surprising variations three times a day: cassava leaves or cassava roots, raw, boiled, sautéed, poached, mashed, or deep-fried in palm oil.

Annette helps her mother without complaining. With her budding breasts and her giggling, she is one moment a little girl and the next a grown woman on whose shoulders important household tasks rest.

Then there is the couple's son, Peter, and a resident nephew, Andrew. Both are serious young men for whom being unable to get any kind of proper education is a big blow. Andrew would like to study economics; Peter wants to study political science. But with the situation as it is, there is no chance of that.

Peter and Andrew run errands for the Kanu family. Alfred proudly refers to them as his "scouts." They stroll down to the village a couple of times a day to pick up the latest news and fetch palm wine.

Information and palm wine. The day revolves around those two things. Palm wine is no problem, you can get it anywhere and it costs practically nothing. Just climb up a palm tree, explains Alfred, stick your knife in the trunk, and hold the jerrican underneath. The sap comes gushing out in abundance, and there you have your palm wine. "A gift straight from God," says Alfred. The alcohol percentage is unclear: maybe half a percent when you tap it, but rising to at least 10 percent after fermentation. To achieve that, however, you have to leave the palm wine to stand for some time, and we're too thirsty for that. I have finally learned to appreciate the stuff. Eddie was right: it's delicious.

It's information that's the problem. Reliable sources are few and far between. Refugees say there is looting and murdering in

Makeni. Then we hear the hopeful rumor that the ECOMOG is about to uncover the entire junta. Someone comes to tell us that Twicey is in the next village. Twicey, our guardian angel. Should we risk driving over to him and traveling on under his protection? We don't know. Probably it's best to wait.

Waiting for the ECOMOG. Waiting for the BBC. Three times a day, at 15:05, 17:05, and 18:30 we listen to *Focus on Africa* on the World Service. Fanfare. The lively signature tune. The bulletins at 17:05 and 18:30 are usually identical to the one at 15:05.

On Wednesday afternoon we hear Eddie. At least, we hear his message, read out by someone else with an African accent, probably a newsreader in a luxurious studio in London. So Eddie managed to convince Father Daniel in Makeni to let him use his transmitter after all.

Father Daniel himself gets to say a few words, or rather, again, someone speaking for him. There is little news. Eddie talks about the bombing and looting last Saturday in Makeni; Father Daniel tells of his kidnapped colleagues in Lunsar. In the next bulletin we hear the same story again; at 18:30 Eddie is already off the air. Now the broadcast is about Freetown. They are celebrating the junta's finally being driven out.

Our BBC/palm-wine sessions take place under a lean-to of dried banana leaves. From there, we can keep an eye on the road, nearly a mile away. There is a constant coming and going of cars and trucks. One afternoon, I count them: two in the direction of Makeni, four going to Kalangba. The same car, up and down twice. Could that have any significance? I keep asking Alfred and Doc the same questions: "Are they rebels, soldiers, or civilians?" And every time I get the same answer: "What does it matter? Everybody with a car is armed and dangerous." Then I ask what's the best thing for us to do. "Wait until things calm down" is the reply.

Dr. Samai from the clinic comes round to say good-bye to us. He's going to live in the bush for a while, as he is afraid the rebels will kidnap him and conscript him as an army doctor. Two doctors from the next village, halfway to Makeni, have already suffered this fate. Doc looks worried.

Friday brings a ray of hope. At three o'clock, the BBC announces that the ECOMOG has taken the town of Kenema. We nudge each other delightedly; it can't be long before the ECOMOG are on our doorstep, too. We order another pot of palm wine. At five o'clock, the BBC again. The rebels have driven the ECOMOG out of Kambia. Bo is occupied. The RUF is advancing. All our hopes fly out the window. We hear that Twicey is now in another village, even farther away from us. Maybe we can send someone to take him a message. But whom can we send?

"We have to be patient," says Alfred. "We must not give up hope."

I'm not giving up. But I'm getting so tired of waiting. Four days already. Without any prospect of improvement. My cigarettes are nearly all gone; I'll have to start rationing myself. Actually, I should have started three days ago; now I've only got half a pack left. The coffee is running out fast, too. Africans are not really coffee drinkers, but I can't bring myself not to offer Alfred and Doc a cup when I'm making myself a coffee. Then I see them looking thoughtful—do we really want one?—until they decide to drink a cup with me after all, even if it's just out of politeness. Damn! There goes the coffee!

The books. I devoured Graham Greene in a day and a half. I finished de Botton and McEwan in two days. Now I've lent them to a friend of Mrs. Kanu's who is interested in contemporary English literature and have started on *The Clash*. Hard going, dry as dust, heavy and absolutely unenthralling. There is hardly any mention of Africa. Huntington obviously didn't count it amongst the civilizations.

Friday evening. The latest BBC bulletin. An RUF-rebel spokesman is talking. He sounds like a mean bastard, lisping as he trips over his own lies. Some rubbish about revolution, more drivel about "our leader." The RUF scumbag means Corporal Foday Sankoh. He was arrested three years ago and is awaiting trial, somewhere at a secret location, which will probably end up in a death sentence. The rebels are demanding the release of Sankoh. Negotiation is out of the question. "We are freedom fighters," concludes the spokesman. Doc and Alfred shake their heads in disbelief. Freedom fighters. It's just too outrageous for words.

Mrs. Kanu serves up a steaming dish of cassava. We go through the alternatives during dinner. And all the drawbacks. We'll just have to wait. There *is* no alternative. Things have to calm down sooner or later. Mrs. Kanu sums up the situation in a nutshell: "Only the Lord can save us."

Alfred considers for a moment. "The situation is red alert," he concludes in a serious voice. "We have to be prepared for the worst." After the wave of looting last year, Alfred knows how it goes.

We wait until dark and then first hide Doc's ambulance. It was already parked behind the school, but now we push it deep into a field of elephant grass yards high. Andrew and Peter camouflage the roof and the sides of the vehicle until it is invisible; Zainab wipes out all the tire marks with a leafy branch. Then Alfred gets us to pack one piece of hand luggage we can snatch up at a moment's notice in an emergency.

I have little left of any value. The films, notebooks, and *The Clash*. Passport and pens. Apart from that, just a toothbrush and toothpaste, one set of clean underwear, and a thick shirt with long sleeves. Handy as a pillow, as protection against scratches if we have to run through the bush again, warm in the chilly mornings, useful as a towel. Finally, my Swiss Army knife, undiscovered by the rebels. Everything fits neatly into a small backpack. Doc and Zainab as well have quickly reduced their extensive luggage to one holdall.

We stow the rest of the baggage away in the school storehouse. It has a metal door with a padlock, but if they're determined, that won't be of much help either. Zainab and Doc give all their money to Mrs. Kanu for safekeeping. Tomorrow she will dig a hole in the ground and hide it.

We have another glass of palm wine in the moonlight on the veranda. Zainab is weeping quietly. She is worried about Eddie, worried about her children, worried about me. Doc tries to cheer her up with jokes. It doesn't work. We see car headlights on the main road. They stop in the village. Screams, a couple of gunshots. A few moments later, the car screeches off at top speed. Alfred sends Peter and Andrew to see what has happened. It was soldiers looking for fuel, our scouts tell us later. No one in the village had any to give them. The soldiers were furious, fired in the air, looted a house, and left.

"The rebels have to run out of fuel at some point," Doc tries to reassure us.

"And then what?" asks Zainab.

No one knows.

14 | Unexpected Visitors

Mrs. Kanu serves breakfast under the banana leaf shelter. Roast cassava roots with a spicy peanut sauce. How they manage it I don't know, but every meal up until now has been a feast. You have to hand it to African women. Doc digs in, savoring every mouthful.

After last night's dip, morale has again risen slightly. Everything is quiet on the road, and we've seen neither hide nor hair of soldiers or rebels. We discuss possible escape routes, using my map. Escape—our favorite subject of discussion.

It's not much of a map, an ink-jet printout from a Web site on Sierra Leone. No better maps were available in Conakry. And in Makeni the junta had forbidden all maps for reasons of state security. This map, a dog-eared A4 with ink smudges, only shows ten towns and four main roads. Kalangba and the road in front of the school are not on it. Alfred draws them in for me.

It turns out we are only about twelve miles from Makeni. If the ECOMOG takes Makeni, then we should be able to walk there in a day via back roads. Port Loko, where the ECOMOG is now, is a good day's walk, and it's a two-day trek to the border with Guinea. Once we are in ECOMOG territory, we're safe. It can't be all that difficult. But Doc is reluctant to let me go with them. As a white man, I'm a prime target for rebels. Better wait and see how the ECOMOG advance progresses first.

Doc unfolds his ambitious plans for later, when it's all over. Of course he assumes that everything will turn out okay. When I get back to Brussels, I have to buy a Toyota minibus and ship it to Freetown. Secondhand cars are cheap in Brussels, according to Doc. For $2,000 you have a perfectly good bush taxi. There is a flourishing trade in stolen vehicles that reach Africa via Antwerp. No wonder a secondhand car is called a "Belgium" in Sierra Leone. After the war, there will be a great need for public transport. The bus will pay for itself within three months. Then we can buy another one, and a few months later, yet another. Once we have five buses on the road, it will be time for the serious money; investing in a diamond mine. Doc enjoys his job as a doctor, but realized long ago that he will never get rich on the local salaries.

Doc's enthusiasm is infectious. It's not just the prospect of getting rich quickly and easily; it's more his assumption that we will all soon be safe back home. We open another pot of palm wine.

We see a lone traveler approaching on the main road. He is wearing a white baseball cap and heading slowly toward the school. Good Lord, it can't be, can it? Yes, it is! It's Eddie! Zainab comes running out of the house, screaming, and throws herself into his arms. Mrs. Kanu wastes no time in shoving a plate under his nose; Alfred gets his scouts to fetch more palm wine. Once the plate is empty, we bombard him with questions.

How on earth did he manage to find us? Eddie shrugs. It wasn't that hard. In Makeni he heard about our nearly fatal trip through the grapevine. As he gradually made his way toward us, he spoke to more and more people who had seen us. That way he was able to follow our trail. At Kalangba, no one wanted to reveal exactly where we were. They thought he might be a rebel, out to steal the ambulance. Only once Eddie convinced the villagers that he was a BBC correspondent and looking for his wife and a white colleague did a boy show him where the school was. Evidently the entire village is aware that we are here, but they are protecting us.

Makeni is still a mess, Eddie tells us. Soldiers and rebels are systematically looting every house, neighborhood by neighborhood. In a halfhearted attempt at maintaining order, the local junta leaders have set up antilooting brigades, but these are stealing just as fast as the rest of them; even pilfering their ill-gotten gains from each other.

Several thousand junta supporters who fled from Freetown are now hanging out in Makeni. They have smashed the hospital to pieces and thrown all the patients out. The victims of the bombing now lie dying on the street in the hot sun. The hospital has become a rebel hostel, and the governor and his household have moved into Buya's Motel.

Apart from that, Eddie has found out that there is tension within the junta: the AFRC want to give themselves up, the RUF want to fight it out to the bitter end. The ECOMOG is in Port

Loko, ready to advance. It appears that Bishop Biguzzi is holed up there.

Then Eddie tells us how he himself has fared. He was arrested straight after his BBC transmission. The rebels didn't exactly appreciate his reporting. He was held for six hours at the Teko Barracks, where they knocked him about and threatened him. Thanks to the intervention of Twicey, who was around, they let him go again. Eddie is exhausted and Zainab lovingly strokes his hair. They withdraw for an afternoon nap.

In the evening, the BBC announces that the situation in Bo is disastrous. There has been heavy fighting for possession of the town, and bodies are lying everywhere, from which the dogs are benefiting. In Freetown, they are still singing and dancing in the streets. We retire to bed early.

It's a lovely morning, just like every morning. The difference this time is that Eddie's arrival has cheered us considerably. Unfortunately, a reporter's work calls and Eddie is off again to Makeni.

I feel a complete loser. Sitting here like a frightened rabbit, hiding in the bush—without a camera—while all the interesting developments are taking place outside. Eddie has also emphasized a dozen times how grateful I should be to the Kanu family. I realize my dependence on them only too well; Eddie needn't keep rubbing my nose in it.

Finally, we have come up with some new plans. Waiting again, that's what it comes down to. But only for a few days this time, after which Eddie will come back and we'll leave for Makeni, which should be liberated by that time. If not, then we walk to the ECOMOG in Port Loko. Eddie doesn't think it's a good idea to let Caritas know I am sitting safely in Kalangba. "The fewer people who know where you are, the better," he maintains. I don't know, I guess he's probably right.

In the afternoon, we hear good news on the radio. The ECOMOG has finally taken Bo. The liberation of Makeni can't take long now.

Doc starts talking about his business plans again. He figures it out for me: wages for a driver and conductor, the price of a Freetown-Makeni round-trip, the number of people you can get into a minibus. At least thirty, thinks Doc. And another twenty on the roof. I look at his calculations. It's not such a crazy plan.

We're just about to listen to the five-o'clock news when Zainab starts yelling. "Soldiers, soldiers! They're coming!" I stand riveted to the spot. "Go inside the house, Tony. Inside the house!" Zainab screams hysterically. That seems to me about the worst place I could hide. I grab my backpack, ready to flee. I dare not look at the approaching danger; maybe they can see my blond hair, or maybe I will simply be paralyzed with fear.

"There are ten of them, with guns," calls Alfred. "They're heading straight for the house!"

We are behind the house in the courtyard and the soldiers can't see us. If I take off now, they will see me for sure. I'll have to wait for the right moment, until they are closer and the house is blocking their view.

Alfred gets the idea and issues instructions. "Wait for it, wait for it . . . Now! Run!" Doc, Emmanuel, and I hightail it to the back garden; Alfred and the others sprint off in the direction of the elephant grass. We run through the cassava plantations, then through the banana plantations, deeper and deeper into the bush.

I don't dare turn round, thinking of the story of Lot's wife, turned into a pillar of salt.

Doc is panting and wheezing, his body cumbersome. He's wearing shorts and plastic flip-flops. He stops for a moment to dab at a couple of scratches that are bleeding heavily. Behind us we hear shots. We keep running, straight through a piece of swamp, then through dense scrub. We've covered a couple of miles; we must be safe now. We halt by an open space to catch our breath.

Farther on, we spot a man with a dog, walking along a sandy path. Looks like an innocent civilian. Doc shows himself and explains what is going on. The man takes us to his village a little farther on, a group of ten straw huts huddled together. Now it's the villagers' turn to run away. "They think you are a Ukrainian mercenary," the man explains. They are rumored to be twice as brutal as the rebels. The villagers slowly emerge from the bush again. They start heavy discussions. The man fetches two boys who will hide me. Doc and Emmanuel can stay behind.

The rebels are out for my blood, the man says. I'm supposed to have passed on information to the BBC. They threatened a boy from Kalangba to disclose my whereabouts. Alfred has been taken hostage. Every piece of news the man tells us hits home like a sledgehammer. I don't know if it's all true, but I'm starting to feel sick from worry.

The boys take me deep into the bush. When we come to a shallow river, they are nice enough to take me on their backs so my feet don't get wet. They are even bringing along a chair for me. On the other side of the water is an open space under a big mango tree, where they set the chair down. "We will come and fetch you when it is safe," they say, and disappear into the night.

This is ludicrous. Sitting on a chair under a starry sky. Alfred's been taken hostage. I'm surrounded by empty calabashes on poles, looking like headhunters' skulls. In the distance, I hear a car. I have no idea how far I am from Kalangba. Should I turn myself over to the rebels? Then, at least, I would know where I stand; anything would be better than the panic, uncertainty, anxiety, and guilt that are now tormenting my breast. With my hand cupped around the glowing tip—which must be visible for miles—I smoke the last of my cigarettes.

I sit and wait, brooding over the situation. Panic scenarios run through my mind. Should I give myself up to save Alfred, only to be tortured and murdered myself? Maybe they will treat me well. Anything's possible. Carry on fleeing, to the high hills in the distance? I don't know a soul there. And I think it hardly likely I will be so lucky as to come across such Good Samaritans as the Kanu family a second time.

War is no joke. Surely it's a sign of advanced perversion to deliberately go looking for this kind of thing. Someone once accused me of being morally and intellectually bankrupt. Is my soul so dulled and degenerated that I need adventures like this? And aren't things really going too far when other people suffer as well, as a result? My thoughts gradually drift away. Now I see a vision of braised chicory with cheese and ham. Is this the automatic pilot of the subconscious making my thoughts shift to more pleasant things, so the brain doesn't get overloaded and boil over? Or am I simply the ultimate amoral, egocentric narcissist who thinks only of himself? I know exactly what will happen when I get home—if I ever get there—I can see it now. They'll all be patting me on the back and listening, awestruck, to my he-man stories. But the fear, you can't explain that. Stabs of pain shoot through my chest. I never realized you could feel it so physically.

Voices on the other side of the water. Another stab of fear. But they sound calm, not like agitated rebels. Yes, it's the two boys. "The coast is clear," they assure me. They take me back to the village, where I find Doc and Emmanuel have been joined by Peter and Andrew. "The soldiers have gone," they say, "but we've got a new hiding place now, anyway." Everyone is still alive, I hear; Alfred has not been taken hostage. It's an enormous weight off my shoulders.

The moonlight illuminates our new shelter—an open hut, actually a few poles with a straw roof, in the middle of a cassava field about a mile and a half behind the house. Alfred, Mrs. Kanu, Annette, and Zainab have already settled in on some foam-rubber mattresses.

"Don't worry," says Alfred. "They weren't looking for you; they were looking for the ambulance." Annette didn't manage to get away in time and was questioned roughly by the soldiers about the ambulance. The brave girl maintained she didn't know anything, however, so they let her go and stole the entire contents of the house. The radio, the books, the crockery, jewelry, clothes. They were at it for over an hour, Alfred tells me.

"They even made themselves at home and ate a pot of rice and drank all the palm wine," says Mrs. Kanu indignantly. "And they found the money, of course." Mrs. Kanu hadn't had time to bury Doc and Zainab's money and had stuffed it under the mattress for the time being. The family's savings are gone, too.

Everyone is feeling disillusioned. We go to sleep on an empty stomach. All except Doc, who paces restlessly up and down.

15 | Waiting

Doc is leaving. He has found a guide willing to take him and Emmanuel to Port Loko via jungle trails. Risky. But Doc can't stand it anymore. He feels guilty about the raid on Alfred's house. What's more, he thinks the rebels are looking for him. Everyone will know he is here by now. I want to go with Doc but he refuses. "You'll only cause problems for everybody," he says resolutely. I protest, but Alfred agrees with him. No point in moaning about it. Enviously, I watch Doc disappear into the distance with his guide, making a break for freedom. He promises to send help as soon as he reaches the ECOMOG lines.

Alfred comforts his wife, who is surveying with tears in her eyes what the soldiers have left of her house. He curses under his breath. "It's impossible to build anything up in this country," he says. "It's a waste of time planning for the future."

Not only has the Kanu family been robbed of three years'

savings; the money from the village women's saving club is gone, too. Mrs. Kanu was treasurer of the club. Every woman paid in half a dollar a month. Thanks to this African banking system, a lot of women in Kalangba had already been able to set up a little business of their own.

Alfred decides we will have to camp out in the bush. We get the rest of our things out of the school storehouse, which has not been looted, and hide them in the banana plantation. Next to it is an open space under a couple of mango trees: that will be our kitchen and living room. In an emergency, we can immediately disappear into the nearby brush. The hut with the straw roof will be our sleeping quarters.

We get ourselves settled on reed mats in the open space and wait for events to take their course, while Mrs. Kanu and Annette make something to eat on an open fire.

The BBC midday bulletin reports new atrocities. Dressed as Kamajors, rebels have infiltrated Bo, which had been captured by the ECOMOG. When the people came out of their houses cheering, they were mowed down by the fake Kamajors. There is also an interview on the radio with the chairman of the Lebanese Chamber of Commerce in Makeni. He was forced to open his safe at gunpoint. The rebels got away with a million dollars in cash and diamonds. But the chairman was lucky. He tells how the rebels have been slitting open the bellies of diamond merchants to search their guts for any diamonds they might have swallowed.

In the evening, I search the heavens for the Great Bear and the polestar. Nowhere to be seen. I've lost track of north. Huge fires are raging on the horizon, tingeing the sky with orange. Alfred and I are watching the ominous spectacle gradually approaching. Now we can even hear the flames crackling. Apocalypse now. Is it spontaneous forest fire? Or are the rebels aiming to burn down the surrounding bush in search of the ambulance? Alfred opts for the former, a reassuring explanation.

I'm woken every morning at six, by a crowing rooster. The creature is shut up in a basket that sits at my head. Seven of us are sleeping on two mattresses, sharing three sheets. Easy prey for mosquitoes and other creepy crawlies. My malaria tablets have been stolen, and I'm expecting the first signs of fever any day.

The days go by in a monotonous stream. During the day, we move to the open space under the mango trees, where Mrs. Kanu and Annette prepare the cassava on a smoking fire. Breakfast, lunch, and dinner, every meal is the same. For variety, Annette makes cassava fritters. Water comes from a muddy pool nearby. If you let a bucket stand for an hour, the sediment settles and you've got drinking water. Every afternoon, at about five, Annette carries a bucket into the undergrowth, so I can have a wash.

The Kanu family is treating me as an honored guest. They wave away the idea that I am putting them in danger. "God wants us to help each other," says Alfred when I ask why they are all prepared to do so much for me. "God has brought us together and he will make sure that we all come through this alive." Alfred starts every day with a brief prayer: "Please Lord, protect us from the hooligans. And don't let Tony fall sick from the food and water."

Alfred sees me suffering from nicotine withdrawal symptoms and gets Peter to fetch a couple of cigarettes for me every day, an unheard-of luxury that eats away at what is left of our seriously diminished funds for housekeeping. Then Peter discovers some big tobacco leaves at the market in the village. One leaf for the same price as a cigarette. But you can roll at least twenty cigarettes from a leaf like that. Alfred looks on, sympathetically, as I cut the leaves up fine with my pocketknife, roll up huge cigarettes using blank paper from my notebook, and light up the monsters with a blissful smile.

I'm forbidden to go near the road as we have deliberately spread the rumor that I have fled with Doc. I can't move around much; every so often I take a walk alongside the cassava plot, the banana plantation, and the mud pool, where Annette catches gobies, dirty little brown fish, with a sieve to supplement our repetitious diet. I think about making a bow and arrows to shoot a heron or a toucan, but don't get around to it. Someone from the village, having heard about the looting, takes pity on us and donates a tough old boiler, on which the seven of us feast for three days. The hen is given to us alive and Annette deftly wrings its neck.

We listen to the BBC three times a day. At times, it's hopeful news of the advance of the ECOMOG; at others, reports of counterattacks or of atrocities the rebels have committed dash our hopes again. Sometimes there isn't even a mention of Sierra Leone. Then we feel completely deserted. The BBC does, however, announce that Washington is planning to bomb Baghdad again. Frankly, I couldn't give a damn. This waiting is driving me crazy.

Everyone says the ECOMOG could take Makeni at any moment. But they've been saying that for ten days now.

"Just be patient. We have to wait for the ECOMOG," Alfred entreats me whenever he sees me sitting apathetically on a mat, staring into the middle distance.

Waiting for the ECOMOG is like waiting for Godot. Sarajevo waited three years for the UN to intervene. I don't want to spend months in the bush. They must be starting to get worried about me at home by now, too. I'm off on Monday, I announce. On foot to Port Loko. Or maybe I'll just take a raft and drift down the first river I come to. Two weeks is the limit.

The boredom is just about bearable. Little rituals, such as the morning cigarette, the afternoon wash, break up the day. I help Annette shell peanuts and clean the cassava. Once in a while, I take a stroll and look for a suitable landing site for the helicopter that Doc is sure to send. Maybe I should spell out an SOS message in pebbles on the ground. Will Doc have got to Freetown yet? Later, we hear that Doc and Emmanuel are stranded in a village twenty miles on. The area has been infiltrated by rebels and they can't get out of there.

Empty days. *The Clash* was stolen by the soldiers, but I couldn't get into it, anyway. I suppose I could compile an anthropological in-depth report on African village life, but I just haven't got the energy. I'm not only a failed reporter; I'm also a useless anthropologist. Oceans of time, so little motivation. I've even dropped the lessons in Krio that Annette and Zainab were giving me. I didn't get any further than *How de body?*—How are you? *De body feel fine, fine.* I can't even take a nap anymore. I've had enough sleep to last me a lifetime.

. . .

Zainab is starting to get on my nerves. "Tony, don't go there, Tony stay here," she calls in an anxious voice if I venture out for a little walk. "What are you writing, Tony?" she wants to know when I'm making notes. Shut your face, Zainab, I think. I'm just writing that you're bugging me to death.

Meanwhile, the menu has gone downhill. In order to economize, Mrs. Kanu has scrapped lunch. The villagers have given her a goat's stomach, and we are eating peanut sauce with pieces of tripe for breakfast. The evening meal is cassava with gobies. Annette has ground the little fishes raw in a pot, heads, tails, and all, and made them into little balls. I can just about stomach the goat's tripe, but the raw gobies are simply too much for me. I surreptitiously throw them into the bushes when no one is looking.

Despite everything, Alfred manages to keep up morale. "I don't mind a bit of excitement now and again," he says, his eyes twinkling mischievously as we are forced to flee with our mattresses into the undergrowth yet again when we hear gunfire in the village. "It's just like playing hide-and-seek with the rebels." Mrs. Kanu looks at him in outrage. Then Alfred suggests that I might write a book about "our adventure." I don't know what adventure he's talking about. Dying of boredom in the bush?

16 | The Road to Freedom

Hope. Eddie has come back, as promised. They gave him a rough time again in Makeni, but at least he's made it through. He's lost his money and papers; his video camera and cassette recorder have been smashed up. The rebels even tore up pictures of his kids. Eddie wisely decided it was time to get out of there for good. With all his worldly goods: a T-shirt and a pair of socks. He knocks back a cup of palm wine, cursing, while Zainab massages his back.

"When are we leaving, Eddie, what are we going to do?" I ask impatiently.

Eddie grunts and treats me like a small child. And that's precisely what I am. My fate rests in his hands. "Take it easy, Tony-To. Let me think. All in good time. Let me rest a bit first. Then check out the mood. Collect information. Make some plans. And then we make a move."

The peace and calm Eddie radiates are astonishing, but it's driving me mad. He is still lying on his mat. And now he even wants to take a nap. What are we going to do? Walk to Port Loko? Or to the border with Guinea? Or are we going to make for Kamakui, a bit farther on? We've heard that Twicey is supposed to be hanging out there.

Finally, Alfred tells us again that the ECOMOG will be taking Makeni within the next few days. He's got it from a reliable source. I just can't listen to this anymore. The ECOMOG have been just about to take Makeni for the past two weeks now. Everybody has heard it via secret channels, everyone feels it in his water, everyone is deducing it from the passing traffic, seeing it in the stars, the tea leaves, or the chicken entrails. I've had just about enough of it. Fuck the ECOMOG. We're not going to wait for them any longer. No way.

Okay, so we're going, sooner or later; we can worry about the route later, but what are we going to do with Zainab? Do we take her with us? She goes berserk every time she hears a gunshot. And she doesn't have any good walking shoes. A pair of flip-flops you could barely shuffle a mile in. No, Zainab would be an extra millstone around our necks.

Eddie wakes up. Slowly, he comes into action. He questions Peter and Andrew and gleans the latest news from the villagers. He weighs the pros and cons, puts forward a plan, which he discusses in every detail with Alfred. Then he takes another nap. It goes on like that the whole day. We discuss all kinds of possible routes, only to reject them as too risky. Eddie doesn't know what to do. But he doesn't show it.

Sunday morning. We make our decision over breakfast. We'll leave today. Just Eddie and me; we're leaving Zainab behind.

We're going through the bush, toward the highway connecting Makeni with Port Loko. Once we're there, we'll see which way we go after that. I'm seized by a great thrill of excitement. Thirty minutes later I'm standing ready with my backpack. "Tony-To, take it easy, take it easy," Eddie starts again. "Why are you Westerners always in such a hurry? Let's get a good meal inside us first."

We change our plans six times during the day. Stay, leave, wait an hour, talk to the villagers, get going straightaway, listen to the BBC, go to Kamakui after all; no, to Port Loko. Or Lunsar. "You know what?" says Eddie at five o'clock in the afternoon. "Let's leave first thing in the morning. It's getting too late, anyhow. Better to leave once we're properly rested up."

My nerves can't stand it any longer and I crack up. Totally spent. I've been torn this way and that, between extreme ecstasy and deepest disappointment. First thing in the morning? I just don't believe it anymore.

When night falls, I try to get some sleep under a torn sheet on top of a couple of plastic bags filled with straw. But I'm tossing and turning, feeling the sheet tear even further. The plastic is sticking to my body; the straw is sticking in my back. All around me there is a cacophony of terrifying noises. Bats, nightjars, owls, toads, lizards, and mice rustle and squeak past me. The mosquitoes are biting me to death.

The alarm goes at half past five. We dress by candlelight. Alfred begins a solemn morning prayer: in a hushed voice, he thanks God that we have made it through okay this far. We may have been robbed of all our money, but no one is dead, wounded, or sick. "O Lord, please protect Eddie and Tony on their perilous journey," he pleads. We feel invigorated. Time to say good-bye. There is so much to say, but we exchange few words.

We set off at six-thirty. Eddie in front with his last few possessions in a sports bag, me behind with my backpack and my looted camera bag, which is now stuffed full of the peanuts and cassava fritters Mrs. Kanu has given us as provisions. She has even been so sweet as to borrow some money from the church and give us five thousand leone for contingencies. Peter and Andrew will accompany us to the next village.

We are aiming for Port Loko. A sixty-mile walk. We should be able to do it in two days. After extensive discussions with everyone, Eddie has worked out a safe route where we should have the minimum chance of encountering rebels.

We are just passing the last house in Kalangba when we come across the first group of soldiers. My heart sinks into my boots. Luckily, Eddie knows a couple of them. He bluffs his way out by introducing me as a temporary teacher at Alfred's school. They let us proceed on our way. I've just got over the shock when I hear a motor vehicle coming. I immediately throw myself into a ditch and hide in the undergrowth. A tractor drives past. I only crawl out again when the sound has retreated into the distance. "Good reaction," remarks Eddie dryly. "You're starting to learn already. They were soldiers indeed."

No more than ten minutes on the road and we've already had two nasty encounters. A woman coming the other way tells us that there are rebels farther up. If you don't have anything to give them, they chop off your hand, she warns us. I shudder. Eddie looks pensive. He asks Peter to get a letter of recommendation from Alfred in which I am described as a guest teacher in transit. Thirty minutes later, Peter comes back. Even Alfred's helpfulness has its limits. Eddie understands.

"Tony, give me a pen and a piece of paper," he says shortly. Using my back to lean on, he writes a letter of recommendation from none other than brigadier commander Colonel "Twicey" Momodu. "These men have been questioned and approved at my office. They are on a special mission. Please give them free passage."

We have less trouble with the rebels than we expected. When we come across another woman, she tells us it's completely safe. At the first village, we stop for a rest and Peter and Andrew take their leave. "Keep an eye on Eddie," Peter whispers to me. "He is capable of wasting all the money on palm wine." "He is a womanizer," adds Andrew. They leave. As soon as they are out of sight, Eddie and I make a deal: palm wine for him and cigarettes for me.

At the next stop, the head of the village instructs a boy to come with us to act as guide. When it's finally time to leave, Eddie has disappeared into thin air. I finally find him in the arms of a village beauty, with a pot of palm wine at his feet. Eddie protests, but I keep nagging until we set off again. "I'll be back to see you in a week," he calls to the girl as he turns away.

The sun is climbing in the sky; it's getting hot as hell, with a humidity of 95 percent at a guess. We walk hour after hour, stopping once in a while for a drink of water. Apart from that, Eddie doesn't allow me a moment's peace. He's punishing me for spoiling his fun with the girl in the village.

At another village, we run into a soldier with a carbine. We try ignoring him, but he beckons to us. We pretend we haven't seen. Then he shouts at us. Adrenaline courses through my body again. But Eddie keeps his cool. Smiling, he shoves the reference letter under the soldier's nose. He scrutinizes the paper closely. He recognizes the handwriting, even knows that Twicey always writes with a black pen. He lets us pass. Eddie is a marvel. Just outside the village, we both break down in fits of laughter. A black pen. How on earth did he come up with that one? We suspect he couldn't even read. But what would have happened if I had brought a pack of blue ballpoints from Brussels? Would we have been . . . ? A butterfly beating its wings in Japan causes a tidal wave on the other side of the world. Now is not the time for wild speculation.

Two villages farther on, a single soldier with an old-fashioned revolver is sitting in a rocking chair. "Your papers," he demands brusquely. Eddie is becoming increasingly nonchalant and bold. "I am a lieutenant and this is a personal friend of Colonel Momodu's," he bluffs. "We're on a special mission to Port Loko." The soldier looks impressed and wishes us luck.

At another checkpoint we encounter a soldier with a rusty hand grenade. He wants money. "Sorry, my friend," says Eddie, "a couple of your colleagues got there before you." Sullenly, the man watches us go.

Our trek continues, along overgrown jungle paths with here and there a black snake hanging in the branches. In our bare feet, together with groups of refugees, we ford broad rivers that offer my burning soles temporary comfort. We cross open steppes, scanning the horizon for rebels in pickups.

I'm worn out, but Eddie is still bright-eyed and bushy-tailed when, toward evening, we walk into a settlement of six straw huts. African hospitality is astonishing. Not more than ten minutes has passed and we are already sitting in front of a dish of rice and a big pot of palm wine. People dig into the rice with their hands and roll it into little balls, which they pop into their mouths. The villagers are considerate enough to find a spoon for me. After the meal, they take us to a waterhole where we can wash, then show us to a guest hut.

"The ECOMOG has taken Makeni without resistance," we hear on the village radio at half past five the next morning. Eddie curses, "Damn, why did we have to miss that! Tony, get your shoes on, it's Makeni on the double." I struggle to my feet and crawl out of the hut. Everything hurts, but Eddie won't listen to any complaints. He manages to quickly make a date with another pretty girl, then we set off again. The trek is even more arduous than yesterday. My kneecaps feel as if they have seized up, my feet are swollen, I've got cramp in my thigh muscles, and my legs are threatening to refuse to support me.

We pass deserted villages and only one checkpoint with an unarmed soldier, who runs off when Eddie tells him I am a mercenary. As we near Makeni, a crowd of cheering people with white ribbons around their heads walks toward us. No mistake about it. The junta has definitely been driven out of Makeni.

Numb with fatigue, I stumble into Makeni at five o'clock in the afternoon. There they are: our liberators. Forty ECOMOG soldiers are milling around a monstrous howitzer, surrounded by cheering people. Eddie and I embrace the ECOMOG soldiers.

"Thanks for saving us," I utter. "It's okay," mumbles an ECOMOG soldier.

Eddie's house has not been destroyed. T-Boy and Imfahin are still alive, too. Roaring with laughter, they hug us. It doesn't take long for the palm wine to appear and the tall tales to begin. I really ought to get hold of a telephone and call home, but it can wait until morning. I've been away two weeks; one more day won't make any difference. I flop down onto the bed.

17 | The Day of Reckoning

Bishop Biguzzi has returned to Makeni in the wake of the
ECOMOG. Eddie and I have recounted our adventure to him,
and he is more than happy to let us use his satellite telephone.
I call Brussels.

"Sorry I haven't had a chance to call the past two weeks, but
I had some problems. Everything's okay now. I hope you weren't
too worried about me?"

A deep sigh at the other end of the phone. "A team of your
friends was just about to come over to Sierra Leone to look for
you."

A team of friends? They turn out to be my esteemed colleagues
Polman, Dulmers, Van Lohuizen, and Van Langendonck. I nearly
faint with surprise. "What? Why on earth?"

"It's a long story. I'll tell you when you get back."

I don't know what to say. I can't stay on the line; it's the
bishop's phone bill. I hang up. Eddie still has to call the BBC.

What have I done? The crème de la crème of Dutch and Flemish journalists wanted to come down here to look for me? I get a funny feeling in the pit of my stomach. What were they thinking of back home? Were they really that worried? It's not the first time I've been incommunicado for a while. Next thing I'll be in all the papers and there'll be a whole hoo-ha, all over a failed trip. I don't want to know about it. First I need to catch up on all the time I've lost. A friend of Eddie's lends me a camera and I get to work quickly.

Makeni has been ransacked. For two weeks, demoralized rebels and soldiers have been making a complete shambles of the place. After the stores, organizations, and offices, they started on the local residents. "They came banging on the door in the middle of the night, screaming, 'Where's the money, pull the money," says T-Boy. "After the second time, we had nothing left. But they kept coming back all the same and always found something else. The radio, the rice. They wanted to steal the car, but they couldn't get it started. So they just took the wheels."

The rebels evidently lacked rolling stock for their retreat. Padre Victor has a bizarre story. "We were holed up in the mission center. Outside on the street, there were bodies lying everywhere. Soldiers and rebels who had killed each other in gunfights over the spoils of the looting." He relates the tale, bristling with anger. "Together with a couple of children from our project, we started collecting the bodies with a cart, so they could at least be given a proper burial. Then the rebels went and stole the wheels from our hearse! Can you believe it? The next day, a commander came knocking at the door of the mission center asking if we would like to continue. The bodies were beginning to stink. I was furious. I slammed the door in his face."

The mission center was a safe haven during the crisis, explains Padre Victor. "When the rebels were done with looting, then the rumors started that the raping would begin. Girls and young women no longer dared to stay home at night and slept here. On the last few nights, three thousand people were sleeping here. Thank God nothing happened. Apart from the ninety-nine times the rebels burst in looking for the radio."

Here, Padre Victor looks accusingly at Eddie. "That was your fault, young man. You're a dangerous fellow."

Eddie laughs sheepishly. It's not clear whether the padre is cross or not. In any event, Eddie's broadcast had alerted the rebels that the padres must have had a radio. They ransacked the mission center several times, but Padre Victor consistently denied that they had one. "We had already buried it along with our diesel generator," he says with a grin.

In the mission center's dining room sit four stranded Xaverian priests from Rome. They'd arrived in Makeni just before the trouble started in Freetown, for a working visit that was supposed to last a couple of days at the longest. It's turned into three weeks. They silently stir their spaghetti with cassava sauce, unable to swallow a mouthful. One has come down with malaria, explains Padre Victor. Another has a liver complaint, and a third is diabetic. It's a miracle they're still alive. "It was terrible," Padre Victor repeats three times. He has mixed feelings about his child soldiers: the majority stayed at the mission center, but twenty or so kids rejoined the rebels. "Twenty too many," says a doleful Victor.

Farther up, Bishop Biguzzi is standing talking to two elderly gentlemen with bushy, white beards, padres who were in the village of Kamakui. At the first sign of trouble, they fled with their radio into the bush, where they have been hiding, like me, for the past two weeks. A boy from the neighborhood brought them a pan of rice every day. Apart from that, no one knew they were there. Every three days they transmitted a brief message to let people know they were still alive. Yesterday, the bishop radioed a message that brought them out of hiding: "The procession has left the cathedral. The joyful entry can begin." Code for "The junta is out of Makeni. You can safely come home." To prevent people listening in from understanding, the padres often communicate in ecclesiastical adages.

Biguzzi takes Eddie and me to his residence. Everywhere along the way people are waving and cheering the bishop. His return has great symbolic value: everything is normal and safe. The bishop's house, however, has been completely destroyed; he surveys the debris with a hurt look. On the veranda stands a sink the rebels didn't manage to drag off; all the sanitary fittings inside the house are gone. The little carved wooden chapel has been reduced to firewood; the library has been turned upside down. Torn encyclicals lie scattered all over the floor. As a clergyman, Biguzzi is supposed to attach little importance to worldly goods, but I see tears welling in his eyes nevertheless. "Barbarians," he mutters under his breath.

In the Caritas headquarters, the destruction is just as bad. Gabriel Mani and Nancy Dankey embrace me. For two weeks, they have had to seek sanctuary at the mission center, but they have survived. Gabriel is amazed I haven't succumbed to any diseases. "Oh, man, you must be strong." I swell with pride. You can't receive a nicer compliment from an African. But I'm not here to be flattered; I have work to do. Gabriel and Nancy show me the devastated office. Bullet holes in computers, overturned filing cabinets, burned-out wrecks of cars and smashed-up typewriters in the courtyard.

It's just as bad in town. Everywhere I go, people lead me by the hand to show me the destruction. The shopping street where the Lebanese had their establishments has been burned to the ground; the fire is still smoldering. "I've never seen such a mess," says an ECOMOG soldier who is patrolling the streets. He shakes his head. There's not much left of the hospital. The rebels had camped there for two weeks. On a ward stands a bed, the silhouette of a patient outlined on the sheet in coagulated blood, like the Turin shroud. In the mortuary, a corpse lies under a blanket, black with flies. The body has been there for three weeks already and the stench is unbearable. A nurse shows me Doc's little office: the junk is piled two feet high. The operating theater is smashed to pieces.

Another man takes me to the children's hospital, once the pride of Makeni, set up with a lot of money from UNICEF. A large-scale polio vaccination campaign was due to take place shortly. Now, the tens of thousands of vials of vaccine lie ground into the floor. A message has been chalked on a blackboard: "We will return."

. . .

Outside in the street, it is the day of reckoning. Those soldiers who haven't fled are being brought in by the people. The cry of "Thief man, thief man!" goes up from time to time. Then you see a mob of villagers with sticks rounding up alleged looters. The collaborators are first beaten black-and-blue and then taken to the ECOMOG checkpoint. There, the Red Cross nurses stand at the ready with iodine and plasters to tend the worst wounds. Some soldiers come out of the bush of their own accord, with white ribbons around their guns as a sign of surrender.

The ECOMOG checkpoint has become a central meeting place. Retrieved loot is piled on the ground and there is a great coming and going of villagers, checking whether their belongings are there. Padre Victor is also rummaging around and finds to his great joy a stolen wheelchair. My cameras are not there. A group of captured rebels sit in the dirt, some looking around them brazenly, swearing to God they have never had anything to do with the RUF; others are pathetic creatures, emasculated without their guns, like abandoned children, their eyes darting anxiously about.

A white Mercedes comes up the road. Three white guys with cameras and VCRs jump out. International colleagues! Finally. I'm just about to approach them when the sound of jeering and yelling starts up again. A manhandled rebel is being brought in. I focus sharply on his frightened eyes as the people lay into him with their sticks. I can't bring myself to feel sorry for him. Anyway, the ECOMOG are waiting farther up to rescue the man. He only has to walk another ten yards, what's a few more whacks?

The four of us stand in a row, shooting our pictures, until the man is safely in the hands of the nurses. No longer photogenic.

"You're not the missing reporter, are you?" asks one of the three colleagues.

"Well, I wouldn't go so far as to say missing," I reply. "I just had to lie low for a while."

"You're on all the wires," he continues. "We were supposed to look out for you. Everyone had given you up. Have you called home, yet?"

It starts to dawn on me how worried everyone at home has been.

That evening, I'm sitting with the three journalists behind the church hall. They have developed their films with water from the well. Padre Victor has dug up the diesel generator and installed it and is watching in amazement as the three attempt to transmit their pictures via laptops and satellite telephone. The floor is littered with cables and plugs, but they are unable to transmit anything. Probably a piece of dirt in one of the innumerable connections. One of the photographers curses. He uses the satellite telephone to call his office and say he is having technical problems. "I didn't get anything, anyway"—his voice is blasé—"just some mob violence."

The cameraman is Miguel Gil. It turns out we know each other indirectly. During the war in Bosnia he was driving a motorcycle straight through all the front lines. "Do you think I'm a wimp, Miguel?" I ask. "Sitting in the bush like a frightened rabbit for two weeks while everything was happening out there?"

"Absolutely normal," Miguel reassures me. "Very smart." During the unrest in the Congo, Miguel was stuck for ten days in a house in Brazzaville while Cobra militias rampaged through the streets, murdering and looting. "I came back without any footage, but it would have been suicide to go outside."

A helicopter lands on the football field next to the mission center to evacuate the sick padres. They were supposed to arrive three days ago, but I'm used to waiting by now. I follow the three sallow-faced clergymen into the chopper. Eddie is there to wave me off. We say good-bye like cowboys.

"Thanks for everything, Eddie."

"No problem, Tony, don't worry."

"I'll be back, Eddie. I love this country."

"We'll be waiting for you. You're always welcome here."

"Take care!"

"You, too!"

Firm handshakes and a lot of backslapping. The rotor starts to turn. Eddie disappears in clouds of dust.

The helicopter flies painfully slowly, at a low altitude, but we don't get shot out of the sky by rebels. An hour later, I'm in Conakry. If I get a move on and jump into a taxi, I'll have just enough time to collect my stored luggage and Sabena ticket from the Doctors Without Borders office. My return flight was booked for today. Amazing timing.

But things turn out differently. Friend and colleague Dulmers throws himself, cheering, into my arms at the airport. He has been sent by the Dutch Journalists' Association to fetch me and take me home. A nice gesture. But I want to be left alone. Dulmers waves two Air France business-class tickets at me. They shouldn't have.

Champagne in the cabin. I can smoke to my heart's content. Dulmers tells me of the lengths everyone has gone to in trying to find me. All the various correspondence, newspaper reports, and E-mails have been bundled up together, all four hundred pages of them. He slides the package over to me and dozes off. One surprise after another. Journalists' federations in Amsterdam, Brussels, and New York, a string of ministries—from the Ministry of the Interior to Foreign Affairs and Defense—the Vatican, international press agencies, the head offices of Doctors Without Borders and Caritas, virtually every embassy in West Africa, family and distant friends, every one of them has made every effort to find me. It wasn't supposed to be like this. I only went to photograph child soldiers in Sierra Leone. I want to be left alone.

PART TWO

PEACE AND QUIET

BRUSSELS, MARCH/APRIL 1998

18 | Hypertrophy Plasmodium

It's morning when I land in Brussels. They almost had a TV crew waiting for me at the airport, but my friends were able to convince them that I might be too exhausted for that. When I get home, I find my answering machine full. Dozens of people have been unbelievably worried about me. My most heathen friends have been praying and lighting candles for me all over the world. Macho guys admit they shed a few tears when they heard I was missing. How on earth can I thank them all? The telephone doesn't stop ringing. Magazines, radio and TV stations, calling for interviews. They all want an exclusive. I leave the negotiations to the team.

I remember a fantasy I used to have as a child. Being kidnapped by terrorists, cunningly escaping. Then a triumphant welcome at the national airport, complete with a press conference, which I would, naturally, give slumped in my chair, unshaven, with a cigarette hanging out of the corner of my mouth. The unassuming hero.

That dream has now become reality. The reluctant hero. Of course all that attention does me good. But hero is a relative concept. If it had all gone wrong, they would have called me an idiot and an amateur. Then they would all have been shaking their heads and muttering, "There you go, I've said it all along, it was bound to happen sooner or later." Eddie, Alfred, and Padre Victor, they are the heroes. I was just lucky. And all this attention is bad for me. It only serves to aggravate the hypertrophy of my ego, something I've been fighting against for years.

In the evening, a big dinner party is held with friends and family. In the night, I come down with a high temperature. *Plasmodium falciparum,* the examination the following morning reveals. A form of malaria that, as long as it is caught in time, can be treated with excellent results, never to return. If left untreated, within four days it leads to hyperthermia, coma, and—ultimately—death. But I'm in time. Another lucky break. Five days of sweating and shivering till my teeth chatter. Quinine and antibiotics. The research team again takes care of things for me and cancels all interviews for the time being. Finally a bit of peace and quiet.

19

Everything Is PTSD

The malaria is cured; my visa is still valid. I feel that as a journalist I achieved nothing of any relevance last time. Within two weeks, I'm planning to go back. My friends manage to talk me out of it. "It's a typical symptom of PTSD," they say. "Just take it easy for a bit. And you really should go for that therapy." I can get PTSD therapy at the expense of the Journalists' Association. Over my dead body. Real men don't need therapy.

PTSD stands for *post-traumatic stress disorder*. That's what I've got, apparently. Irritability, feelings of alienation, concentration problems, and sleeplessness are just some of the symptoms, according to a brochure from the Dutch Psychiatric Association, which someone has sent me unsolicited. But I'm not suffering from any of those symptoms any more than usual. Aren't they simply part of an anthropologist's standard equipment? I feel great. As if reborn from the flames. No nightmares about rebels. Once, I do wake up in a cold sweat from dreaming that I have triple-booked myself for a dinner engagement. Because my social diary is full to bursting. Eating out with all kinds of prominent people, colleagues, friends, and family who have all made such an effort for me. I can't believe the amount of money the Journalists' Association has spent on me, when I haven't even paid my membership fees. How can I thank everybody? The guilty feelings are starting to pile up. Typical PTSD, according to my friends. Everything is PTSD. Even the fact that I'm surprised I can simply enjoy life again.

20

News of Eddie

The spring sun is shining outside, a blackbird is singing on the balcony. I'm over it now, I think. The publicity has blown over. I have given several interviews, to everyone's satisfaction. Caritas is happy with the photos and the interviews with the child soldiers from Makeni. And the whole affair hasn't done my career any harm, either. An account of my trip under the wonderful title "Run, Tony, Run!" has appeared in illustrious publications in Brussels and Amsterdam. It has also been passed on to a Hollywood agent via an American friend. Who knows? Maybe there will even be a film. I'm back to hatching travel plans.

Then Nina from the Journalists' Association calls. "Bad news," she says. "Eddie Smith, you know, the one who helped you . . ."

She needn't say any more. Eddie is dead. Such a senseless death, at first thought. Shot to pieces while traveling with an ECOMOG convoy to Kono, the diamond region. The convoy drove into a rebel ambush. Nine ECOMOG soldiers were also killed. It was too risky to recover the remains. They have fallen prey to vultures and stray dogs.

I get cold shivers up and down my spine when I think about it. I had deserved those rebels' bullets, not Eddie. I can imagine the scene. Back in Makeni, Eddie and I had taken a ride with the ECOMOG through an area that was still unsafe. You balance on the side in the back of an open pickup, in between soldiers laced into bulletproof vests, while you are sitting in a white T-shirt with your unprotected back exposed to the jungle. Everything's fine, you think. No potholes in the road, there's sunshine and a fresh breeze, an oriole is fluttering around somewhere, and suddenly all hell breaks loose.

I write a letter to Zainab and ask the BBC what they are going to do about his relatives. As a stringer, or local freelancer, Eddie is not entitled to anything is the reply. The BBC does, however, send $100 toward the costs of the memorial service being given by the family in the town of Bo. There's no burial service because there's nothing left to bury. The Journalists' Association is more concerned with the fate of Eddie's family. Money is released from a fund so that his children won't find themselves in dire straits.

I thought I'd got over my trip. I thought I had it all wrapped up and neatly filed under experience, but Eddie's death stirs it all up again. There's no getting around it; I have to admit defeat. Therapy, in other words. The Journalists' Association has given me the telephone number of the Sinai Center in Amersfoort. There, they know how to deal with victims of war.

My hands shake as I dial the number. The receptionist snaps at me. I have to call back tomorrow between twelve-thirty and one-thirty; that's the only time anyone will be available to talk to me. It's twenty-five to two when I call the next day. In her hard northern-Dutch Calvinist accent, the receptionist barks at me again that I'm too late. Call back tomorrow. Six days later, I finally have a therapist's assistant on the line. She is even more blunt than the receptionist. I can make an appointment for an intake interview in eight weeks' time. "But I have the problem now," I plead hesitantly.

"We can't help that, the first appointment I can offer you is in June."

I halfheartedly promise to ring back to set a definite date for an appointment. I foresee a dismal scenario. Taking the train to Holland, being subjected to delays and noisy, jostling school-children; changing three times at those modern designer stations painted in jolly primary colors, waiting in line to buy a bus and tram card and jolting my way past housing projects, shopping malls, and industrial parks to the Sinai Center. Listening at every bus stop to assertive old ladies insisting to the tram driver that they get the senior-citizen reduction, even though they have left their passes at home. Followed by an intake interview in one of those concrete centers with sickeningly cheerful "thoughts for the day" posters on the wall.

Things are always better organized in Belgium. The next day, I am sitting at the desk of a psychologist at Doctors Without Borders in Brussels. Every year, dozens of their personnel get into trouble: kidnapped, wounded, threatened, abused, sometimes even killed. Others end up with a nervous breakdown after years of working under stress in the most appalling conditions.

I'm right on the edge, too, and having difficulty holding back the tears. The psychologist reassures me. First of all, apparently,

I am a YAVIS—young, attractive, verbal, intelligent, sociable. Patients in the YAVIS category have the best chance of recovery. They have no trouble in expressing themselves, are not too ugly, have friends who take care of them, and are not plagued by all kinds of complexes and unhappy childhoods. As a journalist, I also have the enormous advantage of having to talk and write about my adventures and having plenty of colleagues who have had similar experiences.

The psychologist confirms that I am, indeed, suffering from PTSD. But it's something you can deal with, he says, describing the classic assimilation mechanism. The patient swings between two poles: repressing and reliving, switching at a moment's notice from one to the other. These are the mind's defense tactics, he tells me. But, in time, the highest peaks and lowest troughs smooth out. The mood swings tail off, too. Finally, everything starts to ripple peacefully along. Just take it easy for a bit and everything will go back to normal, the psychologist assures me.

And everything does return to normal. But I don't forget Eddie. The last photo I ever took of him stands on my mantelpiece. We have just come out of the bush and Eddie is calling a news report through to the BBC on Bishop Biguzzi's satellite telephone. Eddie is wearing a cheeky, self-confident grin; the bishop looks worried. He's probably thinking about his phone bill.

PART THREE

STRICTLY BUSINESS

SIERRA LEONE, APRIL 1999

By Land, Sea, or Air?

Its engine droning, the MV *Overbeck* moves off and sails slowly out of the port of Conakry. In the distance, the lights of the town disappear in the twilight. The boat will dock early tomorrow morning in Freetown, the town I never managed to reach on my first trip and the one I know only from news reports and Graham Greene's book.

The engine knocks to the rhythm of my heart. Of course I'm nervous. I'm returning, a year later, to the scene of the crime. No, this trip is not meant to be therapeutic; I'm trying to get it into my head that this is strictly business. Besides, it would be just too decadent to use the poorest and most miserable place in the world as a health farm. I've simply become interested in the country, nothing unusual. I'm going back to report on the latest developments. And those are disastrous.

Sierra Leone has sunk even deeper into the abyss, if that is possible. In March 1998, the exiled president Kabbah returned to Freetown. He was received by celebrating crowds. For a while, it looked as if the situation might stabilize. Within a few months, the ECOMOG succeeded in getting almost the entire country under control. The rebels retreated to the east to lick their wounds.

Shortly afterward, it all started up again. Using the jungle paths, the rebel army infiltrated everywhere, gradually recapturing one village after another, one town after another. The ECOMOG had made the classic strategic mistake: advancing too quickly, spreading their troops too thinly over far too many fronts and towns at one time.

Around Christmas, 1998, the rebels mounted a large-scale offensive with an attack on Makeni, managing to drive out the ECOMOG within a few days. After that, there was no holding them. At the beginning of January 1999, they were at the gates of Freetown.

Then began the bloodiest period of the civil war up until then. The rebels mingled with the civilians in the town and forced them to walk in front of them as human shields. Anyone who refused was shot dead on the spot. A few days later, the rebels succeeded in penetrating the center of Freetown. The ECOMOG hit back with all they had, aided by the Kamajors, who had been armed to the teeth by the government. After three weeks of fierce fighting that took the lives of an estimated five thousand people, the rebels were driven out.

The RUF retreated, using the scorched-earth tactic. Operation No Living Soul was the code name for their maneuver. What could not be looted was destroyed. Entire neighborhoods and suburbs were reduced to rubble. Thousands of civilians were murdered, raped, or mutilated. Special amputation squads hacked off arms, hands, or legs, purely for the purpose of sowing terror and avenging the rebels' defeat. In their wake, the rebels kidnapped two thousand more children, who were conscripted as bearers and cannon fodder.

The ECOMOG also did their share: it was rumored that a commander nicknamed Captain Evil Spirit had personally shot dozens of suspected rebels through the neck and then thrown them over the railings of the Aberdeen Bridge into Freetown Bay.

The January invasion received little attention from the international press; not only was the Kosovo crisis on the point of breaking out, but virtually no news came out of Sierra Leone because it was so dangerous there. International relief workers— often the only source of information in crisis zones—had long since been evacuated. Virtually the entire national press, accused of being government sympathizers, were on the death list of the rebels. Nine local journalists were murdered. There were also casualties amongst the international press: an American cameraman was shot dead and his colleagues seriously wounded when they ventured too far into no-man's-land.

Now things have calmed down. In Freetown anyway; three-quarters of the country is still in the hands of the rebels. There, the looting, murdering, and chopping off of hands is going on uninterrupted. So I'm staying well away from those areas, I promise myself. I can't allow myself to get into trouble again.

I can't deny it, it's an emotionally charged trip, so I hardly told anybody I was going back. Those I did tell thought I was either incredibly brave or completely crazy. I'm neither.

The freighter drones through the night. Greasy diesel smoke mixes with the damp evening air and flows into the passenger cabin. The crew have long since disappeared into their cabins with their girlfriends; my only fellow passenger—a Lebanese businessman who is going to see what the rebels have left of his Toyota dealership—is lying snoring on a bench. Sleep eludes me.

A few days previously I had landed in Conakry. I believe in omens, and the initial signs are promising. Customs officials demand a reasonable bribe and the taxi driver is not too much of a con man. Less than an hour after my arrival in Conakry, I bump into Nancy Dankey from Caritas Makeni.

Giggling, she tells me about the latest developments. She was spared the Christmas and New Year attacks as she has for some months now been working in the gigantic refugee camp for Sierra Leoneans just over the border in Guinea. But Padre Victor and Gabriel Mani from Caritas were right in the midst of it. Miraculously, they managed to flee Makeni, reaching the Guinea safe zone after walking for four days through the bush.

Padre Victor is now on leave in Rome, Nancy tells me. Gabriel left yesterday. He wanted to go back to Freetown. He mapped out a special route to avoid running into rebels: bus to the border, then through the swamps along tiny paths, and finally a stretch down the rivers by canoe. I get the shivers imagining the risky journey. Nancy reads my thoughts. "Don't even think about it," she says, laughing and getting into a big white jeep. Nancy is busy, busy, busy. "We'll catch up in Freetown," she calls over her shoulder.

Development workers hang out in the bar of the chic Camayenne Hotel. I go and find out about the options for getting to Freetown. By land, sea, or air? is the question.

The land option has already been rejected. Gabriel's secret

route is only for coolheaded locals who know the jungle like the back of their hand. The main road to Freetown is full of RUF checkpoints. As the rebels are currently losing ground, they are in a bad mood and give short shrift to anyone straying into their territory.

Air is a possibility. A commercial helicopter service has recently been flying between Conakry and Freetown. A Lebanese businessman has spotted a gap in the market, bought an old Russian army helicopter, and put a couple of pilots from Ukraine in them. But the tickets are scandalously expensive and the whole enterprise reeks of Mafia.

Free flights are available with the World Food Program helicopter, but that's booked up for weeks to come. All the relief workers have been evacuated to Conakry, but are slowly beginning to return. Most of them, however, commute daily as they are unwilling to spend one day or night too many in Freetown. Journalists are low-priority passengers and dangle somewhere on the bottom of the waiting list, sometimes for weeks.

By sea would be difficult. A hydrofoil used to make a daily trip to Freetown, but that's now lying somewhere at the bottom of the ocean. Poor maintenance, bombed or torpedoed by the rebels—no one can tell me.

At the UNICEF office, I meet Arnie Hanssen, a sturdily built Norwegian with a big beard. His specialty is organizing convoys and transport to inaccessible crisis zones. Arnie thinks he might have managed to charter a freighter on which I can probably sail. "Just come to the security briefing this evening," says Arnie. "It's a complete waste of time, 'cause you won't hear anything new, but it's fun, anyway."

. . .

The security briefing takes place three times a week in a back hall of the Camayenne Hotel. Some forty relief workers turn up to exchange the latest news on Sierra Leone. The problem is that there isn't any reliable news, only rumors.

The chairman of the meeting is a man with a closely trimmed beard and a spotless photo vest with loads of pockets. He is the head of the World Food Program. The primarily white audience is slightly more casually dressed: pretty girls in wide-legged batik pants in jungle prints, easygoing guys in bleached jeans and sandals, with hip little chains at their wrists. All of them suntanned, with pearl-white teeth, young, beautiful, successful, and self-assured. This could almost be Club Med.

The briefing opens with the chairman reading out a report compiled by the UN military observers. The observations are mostly thirdhand and primarily concern acts of war that took place sometimes weeks ago. Increased rebel action round Makeni, exchange of a few rounds of small-arms fire in Bo, sporadic shelling in Kambia, the chairman reads. I prick up my ears, fervently taking notes, but this is no news to most of the audience, that much is clear. They sit, bored, flicking through papers or making jokes with their neighbors. It's been like this for months; they're not even listening anymore. Only when the chairman throws the floor open and asks what the others know do they perk up. Someone from Doctors Without Borders puts up his hand. He's heard that the RUF have brought in four truckloads of weapons via Liberia. "Can anyone confirm this?" asks the chairman.

A rumble goes around the room. An Oxfam driver claims the rebels plan to attack Freetown on Easter Sunday. Another has information that a plane full of mercenaries is on its way from Burkina Faso. No, from Ukraine, someone else interjects. "Okay," decides the chairman. "That's enough for today. Any additional rumors?"

The meeting breaks up with chuckles, and everyone retreats to the bar. The chartered freighter, however, is no idle rumor, says Arnie. What's more, it's no problem if I want to sail with her. I don't need to report anywhere or fill in any papers; Arnie can't stand bureaucracy and will put me on the boat personally. The captain is a good friend of his. And Freetown is absolutely safe, Arnie assures me. "It's boring as hell."

A brilliantly sunny morning breaks. Together with the Lebanese Toyota dealer, I am standing on deck, watching hills on the horizon loom closer. It must be Freetown. According to the Portuguese explorer Pedro da Sinta, the mountains looked like a lion, which is why, in 1462, he gave the new country the name Serra Leo, or "lion rock." All the way here, I have been looking forward to spectacular mountain ranges, but the lion rocks look more like enormous molehills. The Toyota dealer explains that Pedro da Sinta actually meant lions during the siesta.

I follow the contours of the town on a map to get my bearings as quickly as possible. Freetown is at the most northerly point of a peninsula and surrounded by sea on three sides. In the far west is the Cape Sierra Hotel, the only hotel of any standing that even continued to operate during the invasion. Cape Sierra is the meeting place for all evacuations and the operating base for foreign journalists. The rooms are unaffordable—$200 a night—but I might go there for a coffee sometime.

We sail farther to the east, where the electricity generation plant is situated on a minipeninsula, called Kingtom. King Tom was a powerful chief who sold a piece of ground to the English in the nineteenth century, where they released their freed slaves. The Catholic guesthouse where Nancy recommended I stay is also on Kingtom. It seems a safe idea to me, with water on three sides so if trouble starts to brew again I can simply dive into the sea and swim the half hour to the Cape Sierra Hotel. Behind Kingtom tower the floodlights of the soccer stadium. This is where the rebel advance was halted.

A little farther to the east lies the center of Freetown, marked by several modest skyscrapers. Slowly, the boat steams into the harbor of Destruction Bay. An apt name. At least seven shipwrecks rear up, half out of the water. Just a couple more minutes until the boat lands.

My adrenaline levels slowly start to rise. No going back now. I try to shift my thoughts, thinking about the amount of work I have to do. The agenda is chock-full. Photos, interviews. Make a good story and then try to get in touch with Alfred Kanu. That will be the hardest task. Alfred had asked me in the bush if I could do anything for his school. I've kept my promise and started fund-raising, together with Belgian students, for his school in Kalangba.

We've already managed to collect a tidy sum, but I've had no contact with Alfred for the past five months. The first letters arrived without any problem; the later ones were returned with a big stamp from the post office: "Mail traffic with the country in question has been suspended." It would be suicidal to go to Kalangba and Makeni to look up Alfred, so I'll have to find out in Freetown how things are in the interior. Maybe I can send a messenger who can travel freely in the rebel zones; maybe a member of his family or a fellow villager who has fled to Freetown can help me. No, this trip is not strictly business. I'm here to repay my debts; I stopped being a neutral observer long ago. But where should I start looking for Alfred?

Luckily, Sierra Leone is a small country. I already realized that during an interview with the ambassador to Sierra Leone in Brussels. He was familiar with the surname Kanu. A certain Sapristi Kanu works at the embassy in Bonn. The ambassador immediately called Bonn. Sapristi turned out indeed to be family, a first cousin of Alfred's. Sapristi gave me the name of an aunt who lives in Freetown, at least as long as her house hasn't been destroyed.

That was not the only coincidence. In the middle of the ambassador's desk, lying in a prominent position next to the Bible, *The Clash of Civilizations* was displayed. Wasn't that my copy that had been stolen by the rebels in Kalangba? Could the ambassador be in cahoots with the RUF? Wild conspiracy theories flashed through my head until I was able to convince myself that his brand-new *Clash* could never have been my dog-eared copy.

22 | Welcome to the Nuthouse

The MV *Overbeck* docks. An imposing welcoming committee is standing on the quay: not only heavily armed ECOMOG soldiers and harbor police with pistols in the belt of their pants, but also a bunch of people not in uniform with old rifles dangling from their shoulders. One with a woolly hat and a bead necklace looks sheepishly at me; another in a weird pair of sunglasses is doing a sort of froggy dance on the quay, dragging his carbine over the ground. Welcome to the nuthouse.

The soldiers start shouting and shooing us back up the gangplank. The Toyota dealer and I look out of the porthole to see what's happening. Have the RUF invaded again? A lot of panic about nothing, he reassures me. The soldiers' nerves are on edge and they react hysterically to every minor incident.

When they are rummaging through our luggage, a crew member who protests has almost all his teeth knocked out with the butt of a rifle. I, as usual, am accused of being a spy. Why else would I have that map of Freetown in my pocket? Even worse,

I'm a spy pretending to be a missionary, because I want to stay in the Catholic guesthouse. The same old routine. After an hour's interrogation, ending up in profuse apologies, I am once again a free man. I get into a taxi and head for Kingtom. Yet again, not completely free; I have been given an escort, an ECOMOG soldier, "for my own protection."

At first sight, Freetown looks normal enough. Your average third-world city: dented cars honking their way through a cloud of exhaust fumes through crowds of street vendors crying out the virtues of their multicolored wares. "This used to be called Kissy Road," the taxi driver informs me chattily, "but now they have changed the name to Sani Abacha Road."

"You should tell him why," the Nigerian ECOMOG soldier urges him.

"For all the good work the late president did for the people of Sierra Leone," the driver trots out like a good boy. The ECOMOG soldier nods, satisfied. General Sani Abacha should be pleased, too. The Nigerian dictator lives on in Sierra Leone as the savior of democracy. His successor, civilian president Obasanjo, is slightly less enthusiastic about continuing to pump Nigerian troops into Sierra Leone. The peace operation is costing Nigeria a fortune.

The taxi weaves its way through the crowded streets. Only when we reach the center does the devastation become obvious. We drive through roads where every single house has been burned to the ground or shot to pieces. Churches have not been spared either: only the outer walls remain standing. Children are playing tag on burned-out cars, refugees sit apathetically next to crumbling walls, their eyes dull, trying to sell cigarettes or bags of peanuts to passersby who are surely equally destitute.

The fighting was worst in this part, the soldier tells me. The rebels retreated, looting and pillaging as they went. "It takes a lot of bombs and grenades to actually flatten a house," says the taxi driver. The rebels took their job seriously, he explains. Sometimes they dragged all the inflammable materials from the street into a house, made a pyre on every floor with furniture and mattresses, poured petrol over the lot, then shot a couple of grenades in downstairs.

We drive on past the police station, of which only the blackened facade is still standing, and alongside the old covered market, of which nothing remains but steel constructions contorted by the heat. Throughout the main street the facades of every building are pockmarked with innumerable bullet holes and grenade impacts.

Every hundred yards or so is a checkpoint with heavily armed military, where people are being frisked and car trunks searched. The fear of a new rebel invasion is still very much alive, and the ECOMOG has learned its lesson now that it has turned out that, for months, the RUF had been freely smuggling weapons and men into the city.

As we have a soldier sitting in the front, we are waved on at every checkpoint, a tactic the rebels also make grateful use of. Even if your trunk is full of grenade launchers, all you have to do is pick up a hitchhiking ECOMOG soldier.

The Catholic guesthouse is overbooked with priests and nuns who have fled the interior. The taxi driver knows what to do and takes me to the nearby Kingtom guesthouse, a three-story building in a dead-end street behind the graveyard. "Very safe," he says. "Yes," echoes the soldier. He waits until I have actually checked into the hotel and writes my name and the address of the guesthouse in his notebook. "Security," he mumbles, gratefully accepting a tip for his services.

Melvin, a broad-built lad of about eighteen, helps in the guesthouse and lugs my bags upstairs. The room is simple but clean: a big bed on a scrubbed linoleum floor, a small desk, and a little bathroom. Curtains cover the barred windows; a mountain landscape in oils decorates the wall. Great, I say, and get ready to unpack my things. Melvin lingers shyly in the doorway and, in a timid voice, asks if he can bum a cigarette. Then he shows me a big scar on his thigh. A bullet graze, as a warning from the rebels. Warning for what? He shrugs his shoulders, he doesn't know. "Them rebels are just crazy," he mumbles. His father was executed at point-blank range in front of his eyes because, with his sturdy posture, he looked suspiciously like a Nigerian. Nigerians are built quite a bit bigger than the average Sierra Leonean. Now Melvin is the breadwinner and has to support his two little brothers. Not easy on his wages—the Kingtom pays him about $15 a month. I resolve to give Melvin a fat tip now and again and go down to the restaurant.

"Damn, Tony, fuck, what are you doing here, for God's sake?" someone shouts enthusiastically as I walk into the restaurant. I recognize the accent straightaway and see T-Boy's cheeky face. He and Imfahin are sitting there with a couple of cans of beer in front of them. Eddie's two best buddies from Makeni. They come here quite often for a drink. Laughing, T-Boy slaps me on the back and asks Melvin to bring extra beers. "Unbelievable, unbelievable," he declares, and drains his can to get over the surprise. Then, in a more subdued, tone: "Have you heard about Eddie?" He stares at the ground between his feet. I explain that his death didn't go unnoticed in Europe. "Tragic, terrible," T-Boy murmurs. "We were devastated. Imfahin had his last drink with him in Makeni. Eddie wanted to slow down. We were planning to set up a cinema, the three of us, in Freetown. But first he wanted to do a couple of stories in Kono. We warned him he was risking his neck there. But he wouldn't listen: he just had to be there for the recapture of Kono. Eddie couldn't have stuck an office job. He always wanted to be where the action was."

T-Boy sighs. Eddie was not only against the RUF; he was also critical of the government. He was respected by everyone for his courage. After his death, even the infamous rebel commander Maskita paid tribute to Eddie on the rebel radio, announcing that the death of such a dauntless reporter as Eddie was a tragic loss for the whole country.

T-Boy and Imfahin had known Eddie since school. "We were like brothers," says T-Boy. "We used to own a piece of land together in Kono, where we were prospecting for diamonds. Imfahin is the godfather of his children." T-Boy stares reflectively into his beer can. "Damn, his little daughter and son, Lois and Mambu. Poor little kids." Imfahin nods in silent sympathy.

I now hear from T-Boy that the mother of Eddie's children is not actually Zainab, but another woman from whom he was long since divorced. "His first wife didn't want anything more to do with him or the children," says T-Boy. "Zainab took care of the children as if she had given birth to them herself. She sent them to school, took them on holiday to Makeni once in a while, or on a boat trip to Conakry."

T-Boy comes up with more dirty linen. "Eddie and Zainab were engaged, but his family objected to a marriage because Zainab was from another tribe. Once Eddie was dead, they just took the kids from her and placed them under the custody of an uncle.

"Zainab was brokenhearted," T-Boy continues. "She didn't get anything from Eddie's estate. She was simply shoved out of the way. Now she's staying with family somewhere in Conakry. Damn." T-Boy sighs and contemplates the plastic tablecloth. He doesn't know whether the children received the financial support from Europe. If the uncle has it, T-Boy thinks that Lois and Mambu won't get to see much of it: the uncle has enough children of his own. We'll look into it over the next few days. Eddie's children mustn't be allowed to suffer, that's for sure. But how have things been with T-Boy himself this past year?

He perks up. He was lucky during the invasion; he was safe in Aberdeen, where he had been staying with his parents. Everything was okay. But then . . . "Oh, man, Tony, damn." He laughs. "It was hell." T-Boy orders another round of beers and settles into a narrative mood. Story time. The staff of the Kingtom joins us at the table.

T-Boy was able to get a lift from a relief convoy leaving for Makeni. It was a month after the invasion and everyone thought the route would be safe. A rebel leader had even given safety guarantees. "Thirty vehicles," says T-Boy. "A procession a mile long. Passenger buses, four-wheel-drives, and trucks with a total of at least a thousand sacks of rice."

Just outside Port Loko all hell broke loose. "One-mile ambush! They threw everything at us." T-Boy gestures wildly with his arms. "Mortars, bazookas, RPG launchers, Kalashnikovs . . . Bang, bang, bang, they just kept coming. Those who weren't wounded or killed outright fled into the bush, in all directions. Our group walked a couple of hours in the direction of Lunsar, until we fell into the next ambush. A group of fifty rebels, some of them no more than thirteen, fourteen years old. Some people who tried to resist were shot on the spot; a couple of girls were dragged into the bush. We could hear yelling and screaming . . . And then it was our turn. We were stripped clean, and I mean literally the shirts off our backs. First they took our money, documents, passports, deposit books . . . then they took all our clothes. They set us free in our boxer shorts." T-Boy can't help laughing.

"We finally arrived in Lunsar. The villagers there gave us something to put on. A truck driver was willing to take us to Makeni for ten dollars. There was hardly any fuel; the truck was running on a mixture of palm oil and diesel. Clouds of black smoke out of the exhaust. Fifteen miles outside of Makeni the driver threw us out when he discovered we didn't have any money. We continued on foot to Makeni. We stumbled into town in the middle of the night."

T-Boy stayed on in Makeni for a few days, after which he managed to get back to Freetown by hiking over bush tracks for four days, blisters on his feet, knees swollen. "Damn, my mother had given me up, she almost had a heart attack when I got back home." He laughs. "She told me to keep my ass in Freetown." T-Boy tells his story with a heavy black-ghetto accent. He has never been to America, but he has undoubtedly picked it up from films and from gangsta rappers like Tupac Shakur and The Notorious B.I.G., who are incredibly popular in Sierra Leone.

Newton, May 2000. A Kamajor/Civil Defense Force fighter.

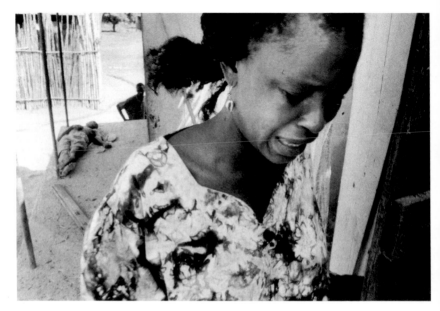

Makeni, February 1998. A jet from the West African Peace Force, ECOMOG, has bombed Makeni. A woman cries when she sees the destruction.

Makeni, February 1998. After the bombing, bystanders watch a boy die.

Makeni, March 1998. Makeni is freed from the rebels and military junta. The people take revenge by berating a suspected junta collaborator.

Magbureka, March 1998. A ECOMOG commander discusses the military situation with Kamajors.

Freetown, April 1999. A woman sells cigarettes and sweets in the shade of a burned-out vehicle.

Calaba Town, April 1999. A man walks with his child through the destroyed village center.

Freetown, May 2000. Women walk by a mural of the late rapper Tupac Shakur.

Freetown, April 1999. A woman on her way to the market.

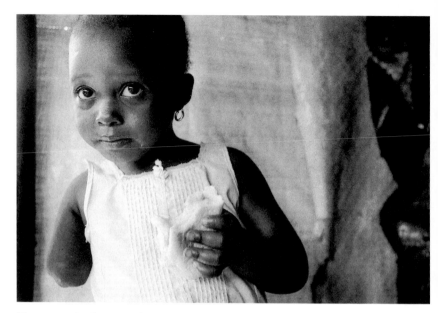

Freetown, April 1999. Three-year-old Memuna Mansarah, whose arm was amputated at the elbow by rebels.

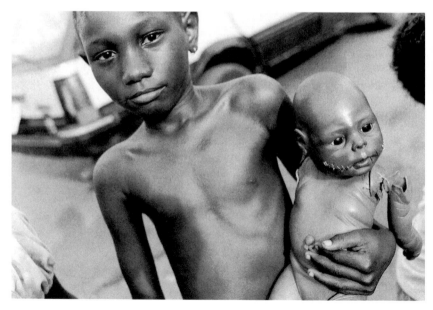

Freetown, May 2000. A girl with her favorite doll.

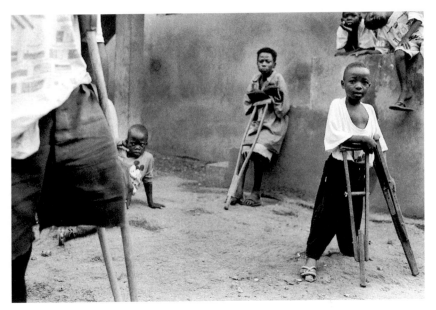

Freetown, December 1999. Kids at a shelter run by the aid group ADRA. Some had their limbs amputated by rebels; others were wounded in the war.

Freetown, December 1999. Displaced children at an old factory (the National Workshop), now a big refugee camp.

Port Loko, December 1999. RUF leader Foday Sankoh is escorted by soldiers of the ECOMOG to a rebel camp near Freetown to talk his men into disarmament.

Freetown, December 1999. At a ceremony celebrating the registering of the RUF as a political party, a woman holds a banner depicting former AFRC/RUF junta leader Johnny Paul Koroma.

Freetown, May 2000. Playing soccer at the beach.

Freetown, May 2000. A boy walks in front of a hairdressing salon.

Zimmi, May 2000. Girls dressed up in traditional costume sing and dance to raise money.

Freetown, December 1999. Women supporters of Foday Sankoh perform a traditional dance to celebrate the transition of the RUF into a political party.

Along the Bo-Kenema Highway, May 2000. Workers dig away the topsoil to get to a layer of gravel that contains diamonds.

Zimmi, May 2000. At a diamond pit, men start the final wash of gravel that contains diamonds.

Kenema, May 2000. The main street of Kenema, lined with diamond shops.

Kenema, May 2000. A diamond dealer showing some "stones."

Newton, May 2000. Civil Defense Forces, also known as Kamajors, on their way to the front line to repel a rebel attack.

Newton, May 2000. Army and Civil Defense Forces (CDF) have captured a rebel and are bringing him back to Freetown.

Newton, May 2000. CDF fighters get out of their truck.

Newton, May 2000. CDF fighters smoke cigarettes on the hood of their pickup.

Freetown, April 1999. A girl proudly shows a sculpture made out of clay. Her right hand was amputated by RUF rebels.

Imfahin has been listening patiently and looks a little abashed. His story is not as impressive as T-Boy's. Imfahin had the bad luck to be in the center of Freetown when the rebels stormed the city. There was no escape and he had to hide out with ten other people on the top floor of an office building, like rats in a trap. Four days without food or water. From where they were, they could see the rebels rampaging through the streets like wild animals.

"We could even hear them discussing when they should loot our building and set fire to it," says Imfahin. His voice still sounds scared, but at the same time relieved and proud that he has lived to tell the tale to yet another receptive audience. "If it hadn't been for the ECOMOG striking back at the rebels the next day, we would have been roasted like chickens."

T-Boy slaps him on the shoulder. "Like chickens!" T-Boy cries, laughing and gesturing to Melvin to get another round of beers. It seems that telling thrilling tales is the national sport in this country. Therapy for a population suffering collectively from PTSD. After all, in one way or another, everyone in Sierra Leone has been affected by the war. I haven't set foot outside the King-tom yet, and I've already heard the worst tales. I feel completely at home. Particularly when T-Boy briefly recounts my story for the Kingtom personnel.

The beer is starting to take effect on T-Boy. "Eddie, Eddie," he mumbles thickly. "They never recovered his body. Damn, at first we couldn't believe he was dead. We thought he had been kidnapped and maybe he'd manage to escape. Eddie always managed to pull something out of his sleeve. And poor Zainab, she still thinks he can turn up alive at any moment. They never recovered his body." He repeats himself a couple of times, now mumbling to himself, now shouting in anger. "They never, ever recovered his body."

Then he decides it's time to call it a night. He gets Melvin to flag down a taxi for him outside the hotel and shambles off unsteadily.

The Kingtom guesthouse may well display a neon sign advertising, "Air-Conditioning, Cold Drinks & Hot Meals, Private Rooms with Hot Showers and TV," but in reality things are rather different: the beer is warm, the shower emits a thin trickle of cold water, the menu on the wall offers nothing but rice and cassava, the TV is a hopeless old black-and-white set that only receives the national channel, and the air-conditioning in the rooms makes such a row you can't sleep without earplugs.

The staff, however, do their best to make things as nice as possible. The tables in the restaurant are decked out with plastic flowers in empty rum bottles wrapped in foil. The walls are hung with colorful advertising posters featuring tulip fields and windmills, courtesy of the brewery that provides the local beverage: Royal Dutch, undrinkable Premium Export Lager. Melvin is constantly on the go with a bucket and mop and has already informed me that if I need anything, he will see to it. Electricity is no problem, he boasts. I'm lucky; Kingtom houses the municipal power plant and is therefore the only place in Freetown never without electricity.

"Be back before six," he calls anxiously when I leave for an afternoon stroll. For security reasons, the government has imposed a six-o'clock curfew. Everyone out on the street after six is picked up by the ECOMOG and rewarded with a sound thrash-ing or a night in a cell.

Cautiously, I set foot outside for the first time alone. Here I am, just walking peacefully around in Freetown. I can hardly believe it; I expect a pickup full of gun-toting rebels to come screaming round the corner at any minute, bullets flying. The only people with weapons driving around are the odd ECOMOG patrol or a group of Kamajors. These days, they are known as Civil Defense Forces and are just as scary in appearance as the rebels, with their beads and amulets. But the Kamajors don't give me a second look, either.

Even the inhabitants of Freetown seem hardly to notice me, a welcome change from other exotic lands where everyone con-tinually stares at you, speaks to you, or calls after you because you are white. All meant in a friendly way, but tiresome. Being completely ignored, however, is going to the opposite extreme, so I don't feel entirely comfortable. Is it a form of politeness? Is it the anonymity of the big city, or do the people here have enough to think about without being bothered with foreigners?

As I get out my camera to take a picture of the devastation, five or six young men cross the street and group around me, looking hostile. "What's the nature of your mission?" the biggest one asks threateningly. *Mission* is a bit of a heavy word, I counter, I'm just a foreign reporter. My knees are beginning to shake; the boys are making me nervous. Just act confidently, I think, you've got nothing to hide. And who might they be?

"Concerned citizens" is the gruff reply. They want to know why I'm walking around in this particular area, why I chose to take pictures of that row of devastated houses in particular, and other such questions. They take a good look at my papers and letter of recommendation, which they find to be in order. "We have to be vigilant," the biggest one apologizes, and they walk on.

Still shaking, I realize their suspicion is understandable. White skin is no guarantee of innocence. The war has been attracting a dubious collection of foreign scumbags. In the mid-1990s, South African mercenaries were used against the rebels. Now the rebels have Ukrainians fighting on their side. During the invasion, too, Italian identity papers were found on a number of white men killed. The arrest of an Israeli army officer who had previously trained death squads in Colombia has given fuel to the rumor that drug cartels are trading cocaine for diamonds. What's more, the Russian Mafia has discovered the diamond trade for laundering its money.

And then there are the few opportunists who operate on the outer fringes of legality. The Lebanese, who control virtually all the trade in the country, appear to have concluded mutual agreements to keep prices artificially high. In Conakry, I heard that a Belgian soccer trainer has been buying up the top players in Sierre Leone's national team for next to nothing and selling them to foreign clubs at an immense profit.

Even the numerous aid organizations that have set themselves up in the country are being looked upon with suspicion. The average Sierra Leonean only sees them driving around in shiny white jeeps, while it is entirely unclear to them what good deeds they actually perform. During the invasion, even the International Red Cross was kicked out of the country. Neutrality being their watchword, the Red Cross was also at work in rebel zones, reason enough for the ECOMOG and the government to accuse the organization not only of espionage, but even of supplying arms.

"The Sierra Leoneans are the most racist people in the world," the Lebanese captain of the boat had already warned me. "It is written into the constitution that, as a foreigner, you will never have the right to vote, although we Lebanese have sometimes been living in the country for more than four generations. At the same time, foreigners get blamed for every problem the country is plagued with."

I walk on and come to the soccer stadium, built in the 1970s by the Chinese government and once the pride of West Africa. Now it serves as a refugee camp. Women are cooking pots of rice on the field over smoking fires; their husbands lie listlessly on mattresses in the catacombs. They object to the term *refugee*.

"We are not refugees, we are temporarily displaced people," says an old man indignantly in UN-speak. He comes from the western suburb of Calaba Town, where, according to him, no stone has been left standing after the destructive retreat of the rebels. "Refugees are people running away from problems," explains the man. "We have no problems. We have simply lost our houses." There follows a brief but fierce tirade against the international community, which has never raised a finger to help Sierra Leone. Other refugees mill around us. Indirectly, the accusing finger is being pointed at me; after all, I am a representative of The International Community. The old man pronounces it with capital letters. If I have any further questions, I can come back tomorrow, he says. Then I can speak to the camp spokesman. I'll do that, I say. I buy a bag of peanuts from a woman and leave.

According to the map, Whiteman's Bay should be in between the stadium and Kingtom. It's now half-filled by garbage. What's left of the bay is just a stinking pool in which a couple of kids are swimming. A layer of oil glistens on the surface because, a little farther toward Kingtom, the rubbish belt evolves gradually into a scrapyard. A group of people have set up homes next to a burned-out wreck of a car. The washing has been spread out to dry on the rusty hood. A screen has been knocked together from a couple of sheets of plastic and a car door, to keep out any onlookers. I don't dare ask whether they are refugees or displaced people and leave them in peace.

Here and there you still see a car wreck, but now the gravestones are gradually starting to take over and the scrapyard flows into the Kingtom graveyard. The dates and names on the few monumental gravestones are no longer legible, but those on the graves from January 1999 are still clearly visible. If you can call them gravestones. They are nothing more than hastily daubed planks of wood that will never survive the coming rainy season. Now and again you see a big hole in the ground. The rebels had considerable arms caches here, which they unearthed during the invasion.

I arrive at the guesthouse just before six. Melvin is at the gate, anxiously looking out for me. A steaming dish of cassava is waiting in the restaurant.

23

Dem Bats Beaucoup

I am not in the mood for a halfhearted conversation with surly displaced persons in the soccer stadium, so I go and take a look around the town center. One of the attractions worth seeing in Freetown is the Cotton Tree, which stands in the middle of the main thoroughfare, Siaka Stevens Street. The tree is depicted, without fail, on the few picture postcards in circulation. The Cotton Tree is impressive—its trunk has a circumference of twenty-five feet and the crown reaches higher than most of the surrounding office buildings.

Around the tree is a busy traffic circle, where a policeman is attempting with little success to get the congested traffic moving. Crippled polio and rickets victims hold out their hands to the packed taxis and overflowing minibuses. The lucky ones among the beggars are in rusty wheelchairs; the less fortunate are leaning on rickety crutches. The very poorest shuffle along on their knees, where monstrous calluses have formed.

In between the beggars are street children, all hawking the

same type of diapers to passersby. The diapers are probably part of a looted consignment from the port, or maybe a Lebanese businessman managed to get his hands on a batch of seconds, which kids are now selling on the street for a small percentage commission. That's the way to get rich in this country.

Up in the tree, there is an incessant squeaking, chirruping, and twittering, as if from an enormous flock of sparrows. But, no matter how hard I look, I can't pick out a single bird. High up the huge trunk, withered leaves are hanging, swaying gently in the wind. Suddenly, there's a loud explosion in the street. I stiffen. No, it's not a grenade, just an exhaust backfiring. The air is suddenly black with flying creatures. The dry leaves fall away from the tree, fluttering up and then landing again. From the shape of their silhouettes and the nervous way in which they flutter, I judge them to be bats with a wingspan of at least eighteen inches.

Passersby see me looking up, fascinated. *"Dem bats beaucoup, beaucoup,"* I mutter in what I hope is fluent Krio. *"Dem big, big,"* says a man walking by, smiling.

I walk to the end of Siaka Stevens Street. The facade of the UN office is riddled with bullet holes after the battle, but since the building is constructed of reinforced concrete, the rebels have been unable to reduce it to rubble. ECOMOG soldiers are guarding the empty building and gesture to me with their rifles to move along quickly.

Farther up are a couple of banks and the post office. Barclay's Bank has been open again for about a week; the post office is still closed, but through the railings I can see that everything inside looks dusty, though undamaged. Newspaper salesmen are jostling each other for a place in the shade under the eaves. I count eight different daily papers. I buy them all and go and sit on the corner to read them. Next to me, a woman is selling cold Coke in the shade of a wrecked car and is nice enough to shove over an empty crate for me to sit on. There's nothing nicer than going through all the local newspapers on a lovely sunny morning.

"Rebels Hunt for Medical Doctors" . . . "50 Tons RPGs for RUF" . . . "Mischievous RUF Attacks" . . . "ECOMOG on the Move" . . . "Massacre in Makeni" . . . "RUF Plans for New Invasion," the headlines scream. I don't know what to believe. Generally, an anonymous source is credited, or a "spokesman who can produce documentary proof." The same photo of dead civilians is featured again and again, sometimes printed as a mirror image, but each time with different captions. Here they are victims of the invasion of Freetown; there, butchered villagers in Makeni; here again, innocent market traders killed in an ambush at Port Loko.

No international news, not a word about the NATO bombings in Yugoslavia or the refugees from Kosovo. The back page is reserved for sports and miscellaneous news. The Africa Cup is in full swing. Unfortunately, Sierra Leone has been disqualified because the national soccer team didn't turn up for the qualifying rounds in Conakry. These took place just after the invasion of Freetown, but the Africa Cup Committee can't take those kind of extenuating circumstances into account. Every African country has its own problems.

Amongst the miscellaneous news is a piece on Michael Jackson's latest nose operation. Then I read a remarkable article in the *Concord Times* about a "witch crab" that fishermen from the harbor area of Kissy have caught. The monster, a spider crab three feet wide, is suspected of being responsible for the sudden increase in infant mortality in the area. Now that the creature has been ritually burned by a medicine man, the locals are hoping to have been released from the curse.

In the sports section, the Rex Mining Company has placed a big condolence announcement: ". . . heartfelt condolences to the people of Sierra Leone for the great loss they suffered as a result of the January 6 invasion." A bit sick, frankly, as Antwerp-based Rex Diamonds is one of the shady background players in the conflict in Sierra Leone. Rex is suspected, amongst other things, of having supplied major quantities of arms to the successive regimes in Freetown, and the diamond merchants were not exactly bothered by which party was in power, whether it was the army, the rebels, or the civilians.

Having finished the papers, I am strolling through the center, wondering how and where I should begin to try to contact Alfred, when I literally run into the answer. It's Samuel, a fellow journalist whom I met briefly last time I was in Makeni. He's not the only one who's here, he tells me; virtually everybody from Makeni and the surrounding area has fled to Freetown: the Caritas workers, the hospital staff, even Dr. Baker. . . . I stare at Samuel in surprise. Is Doc here in Freetown? Oh, sure, he doesn't have his address on him now, but he can give it to me tomorrow.

I can't wait until tomorrow. I jump into a taxi and go over to the Kingtom to look through my old notebook. Doc's address is in there, written down neatly next to his telephone number.

Fifteen minutes later, I'm knocking on the door of his house, not far from the Kingtom. I'm met with a roar of welcome. Doc has gained some weight, which has done nothing to quell his good humor. He reminisces merrily over the good old times in the bush. The palm wine sessions, the cassava, and that time we broke all speed records together after the raid on the Kanu family's house. Doc can't remember any more pleasant experiences. Actually, there weren't that many, either. How was his trip back? I'm more curious about that.

"Emmanuel and I did the right thing in leaving straightaway," relates Doc, "because in the village, the son of the paramount chief told me that the soldiers were looking for me. The soldiers had threatened to raze Kalangba to the ground if they didn't hand over the doctor. Luckily, the son managed to trick them into thinking I'd left long ago." Neither Doc nor Emmanuel had a map, just a list of the names of the settlements on the route to safety in Port Loko. Helpful villagers showed them the way to the next village at each stop.

"We went as fast as our feet could carry us that morning. Everybody for miles around knew that a doctor and a white journalist were somewhere there, but we spread the rumor that they had both already fled to Guinea the week before. We must have covered forty miles the first day. I was shattered. My feet were all swollen up; I couldn't put one foot in front of another. We stayed a couple of days in a village until I could move again. I was stiff from the painkillers the villagers had given me. Three days later, we arrived in Port Loko. Then we got a lift to Lungi with a truck full of Kamajors. And from there, we took the boat to Freetown."

Later, Doc went back to Makeni. "We spruced up the hospital again and went straight back to work. The busiest time in my entire career: amputations, bullet wounds, knife wounds—everything from the northern provinces came our way."

Christmas, 1998, the trouble started again. Luckily, Doc was able to get away safely. "The hospital is all smashed up now," he sighs. "What we saw the first time was nothing. They'd only made a mess and turned over a few cupboards. This time, everything has been smashed to pieces and destroyed. Everything."

Doc is working in a private clinic here in Freetown at the moment. He's due on duty any minute now. "Have you visited the Kanus yet?" he inquires casually as he gets his things together. The Kanus? What does he mean? Are they here, then?

"Sure. They arrived a couple of months ago." Doc explains that the Kanus are now living in the house that belonged to Alfred's deceased mother-in-law. It's near the clinic. He can drop me off there.

I'm stunned. I had imagined going through the most convoluted process to find Alfred, and now he turns out simply to be living around the corner. What an anticlimax. It didn't have to be that easy. As Doc maneuvers his car though a maze of narrow streets, I prepare for what will, undoubtedly, be emotional for all concerned. But I hardly get the chance because a few minutes later we are already there.

The neighborhood has gone slightly downhill: open sewers and wooden huts with rusty corrugated-iron roofs. Next to an open space already being used as a garbage dump stands a row of brick houses. And there, on the veranda, sits Alfred, daydreaming. A big smile spreads across his face when he sees Doc and me getting out of the car. "Tony-To," he cries enthusiastically, running to meet me. Mrs. Kanu and Annette appear, too, and throw their arms around me, laughing.

A joyful reunion! Luckily no tears of joy, as Africans don't tend to go in for that kind of thing. Alfred sends his giggling daughter to fetch some Cokes, and we install ourselves in the Kanus' cramped living room. Mrs. Kanu is all smiles; Annette just can't stop giggling. "Tony-To, Tony-To," she laughs.

As head of the household, Alfred takes the floor and gives an account of the past twelve months. After I left last year, the situation in Kalangba stabilized. An ECOMOG battalion was stationed in the neighborhood, and after the summer—the rainy season—Alfred was again able to open the doors of the school. Until the rebels drove the ECOMOG out of Makeni and the surrounding area during the Christmas holidays, that is. Shortly afterward, things heated up in Kalangba.

"There was nothing left to steal in Makeni, so the rebels moved up in our direction. It all started when they took over Dr. Samai's clinic to use as a control post again. Right after that, they looted the school. They took the paper, the typewriters, and the duplicator. Can you imagine? They started making travel permits and passes with our school materials," says Alfred indignantly.

"It became more and more dangerous. We went back into the bush. We had to cook at night; otherwise the smoke would have given away our presence. I came out now and again to take a cautious look around. You know how nosy I am," says Alfred with a cheeky grin. Mrs. Kanu shakes her head. "But my students warned me, 'Please, don't go back, Mr. Kanu, they want to kill you.' The rebels had concluded that, as principal of the school, I must be a rich and powerful man, and they were looking for me. They even beat the children: 'Where's the teacher? Where's the teacher?' but they tricked the rebels and said I had fled long ago. We finally left there in February. We were worried about Annette. We dressed her up as an old woman with a head scarf and cushions under her dress. It took us a week to get here."

It must have been an incredible haul, fraught with danger, but Alfred reduces the whole trip to a few sentences, as if trekking through the bush for a week is the most natural thing in the world. In fact, that's just what it is in Sierra Leone. Fleeing is the least of all evils. The Kanus therefore don't blink an eyelid at my journey with Eddie. Alfred can't help laughing when I relate how we pulled the wool over the soldiers' eyes with the false letter of recommendation. "Only Eddie could come up with something like that," says Alfred. Then he grows serious again: "It was a big shock for us when we heard he was dead."

The last time they had seen Eddie was when he came to pick up Zainab to take her with him to Freetown. A couple of weeks later they heard on the radio the news of his death. They haven't seen Zainab since. Alfred has heard that she is in Conakry now. We all fall silent for a few moments.

Then Alfred finishes his story. After walking for four days, the Kanu family came to Kamajor territory. Only then were they sure they were safe. The Kamajors escorted them to Port Loko, from where they got a lift to Freetown with the ECOMOG. "It was a blessing in disguise that this house had become free," concludes Alfred. "Otherwise, the whole family would have been in the soccer stadium right now."

I look around and try to imagine how they all—five including Peter and Andrew—must have to live here. In Kalangba, the family had a house with four rooms and a big courtyard; there was even a school outbuilding where Peter and Andrew slept. There, they had space; they were in the middle of the country-side. Here, a muddy alleyway a yard and a half wide runs in front of the veranda; right opposite is the next block of houses. "It's a bit of a squeeze," says Alfred. "When we want to go to bed, we have to spread the mattresses out over the floor." All the same, Mrs. Kanu has managed to make the cramped living quarters cozy: a couple of cheerful posters on the wall, couches and coffee table and reed mats covering the concrete floor.

Alfred wants to reopen the school as soon as possible. The fund-raising campaign therefore couldn't have come at a better time, and I tell them about all the activities we have organized. Alfred is touched when he sees the campaign newsletter I made with Belgian students to sell at school. In the middle of the newsletter stands the letter he had sent me from Kalangba in which he explained what the school needed. We've still got a long way to go; we'll get down to the details over the next few weeks. Alfred has rejected an offer to teach at a refugee school in Freetown: "I'm afraid I would never get away again otherwise. And I owe it to my students. They would be only too pleased to be able to return to Kalangba." The Kanu family now lives on the meager salary Alfred receives as principal. His teachers, how-ever, are less fortunate; they haven't seen a penny for more than six months. "The cost of living is high in Freetown. You have to buy everything here," says Alfred, "even the palm wine. In Ka-langba, everything grew in the fields and on the trees."

As usual, Alfred is optimistic about the peace negotiations between the RUF and the government, but foresees a dark scenario nevertheless: "If they manage to achieve peace, there will be the problem of crime afterward. The rebels have never had to work before. They are used to getting everything for free or stealing it. They are so selfish. Only interested in power and money. They scream, 'We are against!' but if you ask them what they are against, they don't know. 'We are against!' they shout again, and then smash everything to pieces." Alfred sighs. "A bunch of spoiled brats, that's what they are."

Spoiled is putting it mildly. But then Alfred is a mild-mannered person and can't bring himself to use more colorful expletives. He stares unseeingly ahead, with sadness in his eyes. We've still got so much catching up to do, but I've got to go. We will see enough of each other in the weeks to come.

Alfred helps me find my way back through the labyrinth of little streets. The neighborhood is bursting at the seams from the influx of refugees and displaced persons. In Freetown alone fifty thousand people have lost their homes. Children are playing in open sewers; dozens of women swarm around a water pump. Other women are selling little bags of hot peppers, as Mrs. Kanu did in Kalangba. A group of amputees is sitting under a mural of the rapper Tupac Shakur. "They're always there," says Alfred. "They have nowhere else to go, so they sit there begging all day."

24

CO Cuthands

The dead have taken their grisly tales with them to their graves. The amputees still live to tell theirs. Systematic amputation as a war weapon: it's the first time it has appeared in the modern theater of war. Murder and manslaughter, rape, looting, destruction, arson—those have been the most common methods for sowing terror. The history of hacking off hands and feet is therefore short.

In the Afghanistan of the Taliban they have taken up the practice again; in Saudi Arabia it has always gone on, with the cross-amputation variant: left hand and right foot. In those countries, people invoke the *shariah*, and the removal of limbs is a punishment imposed on criminals by the government. Doctors ensure that it is carried out in a responsible manner, sometimes even under local anesthetic.

The first records of mass amputations were in the former Congo. Natives from the interior who resisted the rubber exploitation had their right hand cut off by Belgian colonizers—

the difference being that those refusing to work were first killed before having their hands removed. The hands served not only as proof that the punishment had successfully been carried out, but that each bullet used was accounted for with a hand. Only as an exception to the rule—in order to save bullets? out of charity?—were people subjected to amputations while still alive.

The Mozambican rebel movement RENAMO also punished their opponents with mutilation, but went no further than cutting off ears and pieces of noses. The only three other opposition movements that could vie with the RUF in insanity and cruelty— the Sendero Luminoso in Peru, the Lord's Resistance Army in Uganda, and the Khmer Rouge in Cambodia—may have been guilty of the most ghastly torturing and maiming, but always had the death of the victim as the ultimate goal.

In Rwanda, the Interahamwe death squads sometimes severed the Achilles tendon of their Tutsi victims, not to cause lifelong disability, but to prevent them from running away so that the final slaughter could take place with ease.

Land mines are a dubious case. In former Yugoslavia, all parties made use of *pashtetas*—small land mines that were so named because they are similar in shape and size to tins of liver pâté. *Pashtetas* were specially designed to blow off only the victim's foot. That's all that is needed. Lifelong mutilation is more demoralizing and disrupting than death.

The RUF has realized that, too. But where did they learn it? That's the big question. We do know that the phenomenon of amputations only raised its head relatively late—in 1995. According to the English anthropologist Paul Richards, who has carried out extensive research on the rebels in Sierra Leone, it reflected not diabolic cruelty, but a "set of simple strategical calculations." After four years of battle, the RUF was confronted with heavy losses and lack of food. Their ranks were threatening to shrink as recruits deserted, fleeing to their villages because the rice harvest would soon be brought in. To prevent desertion, the harvesting had to be stopped, says Richards. In Sierra Leone, women traditionally work the land, therefore they became the target. It took only a few amputations. Word of mouth did the rest. No one ventured outside any longer. No harvest, no desertion. Where the rebels were supposed to get their food from, the anthropologist doesn't mention.

A year later—in 1996—the second round of amputations started. The government had held overhasty elections. The RUF felt excluded, as it had not had the opportunity to organize a political wing and was therefore unable to participate in the elections. So they opted for active sabotage. Voting is done with the thumb in Sierra Leone, by dipping it into an inkpot and pressing it onto the voting slip. People can't vote without hands. A simple solution.

The rebels drew extra inspiration from the canvassing slogan of the hated presidential candidate Tejan Kabbah—"The future is in your hands." Two birds with one stone. The well-known rebel remark dates from that time: "Go to your president. He will give you new hands."

As time went on, the rebels seemed to enjoy amputating and devised all kinds of cruel variations. Sometimes, the victims were allowed to choose which part of their body they wished to relinquish; other times the rebels made the victims draw straws representing nose, ear, hand, arm, or foot. And what has now become a classic is the tailor's joke "How would sir like it? With long or short sleeves?"

During the January invasion, staff from Doctors Without Borders came across a new sort of mutilation: deliberate paralysis. Eight children were brought in, each with three shallow ax wounds: one on the cheek, one in the back of the neck, and one in the lower spine. The first blow ensured an enormous scar; the last two caused total paralysis.

Like the bats in the Cotton Tree, the amputees have become part of the Freetown scenery. They lean against the wall outside the gates of the hospital and sit in the town's squares, begging in groups. They waddle on the street like penguins, feebly waving short stumps bound in big, white, bulky bandages—all that is left of their arms. In Aberdeen, there is even a special camp for refugee amputees. Organizations such as Handicap International are trying to fit the victims with prostheses such as a double hook in the form of pliers, which can be closed tightly by means of a leather belt pulled with the teeth.

"We learn the same lesson from every war," UNICEF man Arnie Hanssen had said to me in Conakry. "Bury the dead and forget them as quickly as possible, so we can concentrate on the survivors. The amputees in particular . . ." The big Norwegian sighed deeply when he spoke of it. "It is they who are the ultimate losers in this war. They can no longer work the land; they can't even feed themselves. They have to be fed by their families like little children. Nothing is more humiliating for an adult." Hanssen told me he was setting up a program to find work for the victims. "If needs be, we teach them to use a keyboard by pressing the keys with a stick between their teeth. Then, at least, they can do simple administrative work."

I've already seen dozens of amputees, but I still can't get used to the sight. I hardly look at them the first few days, don't dare to speak to them. It is also ironic that *How de body?* should be the phrase with which people greet each other. Then I overcome my timidity and go to the Connaught Hospital in the center of town. An older man with a blank expression is leaning against the gate. Lansana Sesay is his name. About fifty at a guess. No arms, no elbows, the *double short-sleeve* amputation in rebel terminology. Sesay is anxious to tell his story. "So the world knows what has been going on here."

I'm not sure if I should offer him a cigarette, but I do so anyway. Thankfully, he takes a Marlboro between his lips and bends forward for a light. Sesay can smoke, talk, and breathe all at the same time.

It was February 1999, just after the invasion of Freetown. The defeated rebels were retreating. Sesay lived in Kissy, an eastern suburb of Freetown. It was right in the middle of the rebels' path of destruction.

"Suddenly, there were hundreds of rebels in my street," Sesay begins. "They went from house to house, banging on the doors, stealing anything of any value and demanding money. Those who had nothing to give were taken away. They saw my fourteen-year-old daughter. They wanted to take her with them and gave her five minutes to pack her bags. I went with her into the back room, but got her to climb out the window, so she could escape. The rebel leader was livid. 'If you fail to produce your daughter, we will get rid of you!' he screamed. I went for him and managed to knock him to the ground."

Sesay would like to gesture expansively with his arms, but he can only shake his stumps impotently. "Some other rebels overpowered me," he continues. "They smashed my teeth in. The rebel leader screamed that the ECOMOG had murdered his wife and he had no sympathy for anyone. They lined me up with some fifty other neighbors under the mango tree outside. 'You people are against us, you are for the president,' the rebels yelled. A few people were shot dead on the spot. One guy was waving a big ax with stickers from the World Food Program on it. They had just finished looting their warehouse. He had CO Cuthands written on his vest. 'Commanding Officer Cuthands,' " Sesay explains the abbreviation for me, spitting out the butt of his cigarette.

"One by one we had to lay our arms on a table for them to be cut off. My eyes filled with tears; I couldn't stop crying. The other rebels were standing around drinking beer and laughing. 'Go to your president. He will take care of you,' they said. They stuffed the cut-off hands in a plastic bag and took them with them." Sesay has no idea why they took them. Maybe as proof of the work they had carried out, or perhaps for certain cannibalistic rituals. It was three days before Sesay managed to flee through the front lines. He collapsed, unconscious, at the first ECOMOG checkpoint he came to. When he came round, he was in the hospital. "My daughter made it," Sesay breathes gratefully. "Thank God."

. . .

Dr. Baker has taken care of a good many amputees who've come stumbling out of the bush into Makeni. "It's a simple procedure," Doc explains coolly. "First you have to see how clean the cutting face is. Generally, the flesh is rotten and eaten by maggots. So we have to carry out a second amputation, a little higher up. The normal procedure is anesthetic, disinfection, and a surgical saw. Then we file the bone off smooth, sew the muscles and tendons together, pull the skin over, and then close it up."

Why don't the amputees bleed to death? "What we get to see is most likely only the tip of the iceberg," says Doc. "The vast majority have probably not been able to find medical help in time and bled to death in the bush. But then those who do survive . . ." On reflection, he is unable to come up with a medical explanation that quickly. "It has something to do with the coagulation processes, which are accelerated by a state of shock, circular muscles around the arteries that immediately close. But it remains a great mystery. Just call it Divine Providence."

An operation called the Krukenberg maneuver is performed on some patients. This procedure, named after the German surgeon Hermann Krukenberg, originated in the First World War and was performed on soldiers with hands torn off by grenades and mortars. Forgotten for decades, the Krukenberg maneuver has been resurrected in Sierra Leone. A deep incision is made between the radius and the ulna in the forearm. The skin is wrapped around the two bones and sewn up again. The result is an arm that appears to end in two monstrously fat fingers like a crab claw. After the operation, with a bit of practice, the patient can hold a spoon or a fork. Nothing more.

I can't stop thinking about Lansana Sesay and Dr. Baker's stories as I walk back to the Kingtom. Evening is coming on; the bats are fluttering wildly around the Cotton Tree. The white jeeps of relief organizations are speeding to Cape Sierra to arrive before the last helicopter leaves for Conakry. The atmosphere in the guesthouse is tense. It is Good Friday and rumors persist that the rebels will attack during Easter. After all, they have a preference for Christian holidays. The first RUF invasion was just before Easter, 1991, and coincided with the twentieth anniversary of Sankoh's first conviction for involvement in a coup. Christmas, 1994, the RUF began a massive offensive at Mile 91; around Easter, 1995, there was an unsuccessful attack on Freetown; Christmas, 1998, the capture of Makeni took place, which ultimately culminated in the invasion of Freetown around New Year's, 1999. Where that preference for religious holidays comes from, nobody knows. Is it pure sadism, is it superstition, or do strategic considerations play a role? For the Sierra Leoneans, it is a foregone conclusion that Easter, 1999, would fit perfectly into the pattern.

On the black-and-white TV in the restaurant, the national station is transmitting an Easter mass. There has been a power cut and the guesthouse's emergency generator is humming away. We see and hear a snowstorm and a lot of white noise, with psalms in the background. Images of the choir now fade into a close-up of a stained-glass window where Jesus hangs on his cross. The cross wobbles and shudders, disappears off the bottom of the screen, only to reappear again at the top. Melvin is just lighting the candles in the silver-foil vases when a shot rings out in the distance. Jesus is now quivering on the screen, like the image from a jammed film projector. Round the corner from the King-tom, two dogs start a fight. I feel as if I'm in a trendy New York gallery where an installation by a Japanese video artist is being shown.

25

The Spin Doctor

Easter has passed without an RUF offensive. Up in the hills of Freetown a cool breeze is blowing, a breath of fresh air after the oppressive, filthy clouds of smoke that pervade the packed streets in the center. The English colonials used to have their villas up here, to escape the germs and the malaria mosquitoes below. Now, relief organizations and embassies have their offices here. All the way at the top is the official residence of President Ahmad Tejan Kabbah, where I have an appointment with his spokesman, who answers to the wonderful name of Professor Septimus Kaikai. Kaikai has a reputation for unimpeachable integrity, a white raven in government circles. Everyone in Sierra Leone knows him because it is always he who interprets the official standpoint of the government in impeccable English on the BBC.

Welcome back to civilization. The signs are unmistakable as you approach the official residence. Brand-new Mercedes in the parking lot, a tennis court and a swimming pool behind the presidential lodge. The guard at the entrance gate looks like a macho bouncer from a swanky nightclub, dressed in a spotless black, tailor-made suit, complete with GSM and metal detector, stylish Italian sunglasses, and shoes that glint in the sun.

After being thoroughly searched, I'm shown by the guard to the reception room, lavishly furnished with Louis XIV chairs and curtains of a gold-colored fabric. Otherwise it is just like a refrigerator, as the air-conditioning is turned up too high. In the corner stands a color TV, connected to one of the few satellite dishes in Freetown. For the first time, I see pictures of the refugee drama in Kosovo on CNN. For most Sierra Leoneans that war is still too far from home to attract much attention. I've only seen it mentioned once in the papers, and on the sports page at that: no soccer matches in group eight due to the NATO bombardment in Yugoslavia. Melvin sometimes asks about Kosovo when he sees me listening in the evening to the latest reports on the BBC over the eternal rice and cassava. Then he asks, "Why doesn't NATO bomb the rebels?" True, a couple of cruise missiles on the rebel bases in the jungle and the RUF would soon be history. But I have no answer for Melvin. When he repeats his question, I suggest tentatively that maybe the world doesn't care about Sierra Leone.

There's a knock at the door. The guard comes in and escorts me to the professor's study. Kaikai is sitting behind an overflowing desk on which personnel are continually placing fresh paperwork and newspaper articles. Kaikai is in his fifties, but still looks youthful and vivacious. A white streak in his short-cropped, frizzy hair lends him an extra air of mischievousness. He lived in America for thirty-five years, where he managed to climb to an excellent position as a university lecturer in economics. After his election, President Kabbah flew personally over to the States to ask Kaikai to become his presidential spokesman. Kaikai took the challenge seriously. He carefully studied the style of various White House spokesmen. His flawless presentation and rather smooth ways have earned him the nickname the Spin Doctor in Sierra Leone.

Why has Kaikai swapped his affluent life in America for a job in bankrupt Sierra Leone? "I wanted to do something for my country," he remarks modestly on his astonishing remigration. "A lot of people here were cynical about my return. They thought I would leave again at the first sign of trouble." The January invasion was almost fatal for him, too. The rebels were threatening to lock Kaikai up in his own house, but he managed to escape just in time by clambering over a six-foot-high fence. He fled to the radio station, which was also attacked shortly afterward. But he made it. "Oh, everyone has his own story," Kaikai says, making light of his alarming experiences. "The president of the Supreme Court wandered for ten days in the bush; another minister managed to escape the rebels in a rowboat. We've got some quite good Hollywood scripts here."

A smile briefly illuminates the Spin Doctor's face—maybe he sees himself acting in a film—then he continues with his task: explaining the official government policy. "We are implementing a two-track approach," Kaikai summarizes. "On one hand we are engaged in defeating the rebels at a military level, on the other we are discussing peace." Heavy negotiations for a peace treaty are currently under way in the West African country of Togo. If it's signed, then it will be the third or fourth treaty so far. I've lost count.

"We will never give in to the rebels' demand for power-sharing," says Kaikai confidently. "The RUF can transform itself into a political party and present their case to the people. We'll see how far they get in the next elections."

According to Kaikai, the RUF is definitely on the losing side. They still possess three-quarters of the country, but can only maintain their hold on the people through terror. And those people are gradually filtering through to the liberated areas via bush paths, through the front lines, so the rebels will ultimately be left without food, shelter, or human shields.

"Their morale is low," explains Kaikai. Rebel deserters have been providing information. "The RUF is suffering from food shortages, logistics problems, and a lack of medical care. The rainy season is coming on. They'll get tired pretty soon."

Kaikai might have every confidence in a rapid conclusion to the war, but he sometimes gets disheartened by the enormous task of rebuilding the country. "After eight years of civil war and twenty years of corrupt regimes, we have inherited a totally collapsed system. And as one of the few African countries in the throes of an honest democratization process, we get precious little international support." Kaikai is not one to blame the international community, but it still smarts that Sierra Leone is being forgotten. "They are quite right to intervene in the Balkans. But it seems the Western world is unaware that we have already had five thousand casualties here, too."

Five thousand is a magic number. Much later, I see a BBC documentary on Kosovo. A representative of the Kosovo Liberation Army says that a Western diplomat once informed him they could only count on intervention after five thousand deaths.

26

Press Trips

The working days are short and wearying in Freetown. Everyone heads for home at about five, to be sure to be in before the curfew. As it is virtually impossible to get hold of a taxi or a seat in a bus at that time, however, most people call it a day at around three. In the whole of Freetown, only three phone booths are in working order, so the only way to make an appointment with anyone is to turn up in person. Traveling in town is also enormously time-consuming due to the control posts where cars and passengers are subjected to a thorough search.

For days now, Alfred and I have been trying to organize the simplest of matters for the campaign for his school: open an account at one of the banks, which are just cautiously reopening their doors to the public; start an E-mail account in a recently opened cyber café; request an appointment with the Ministry of Education. There, we speak to the deputy minister of education, Dr. Bobson Sesay. We want him to guarantee that the Belgian students' support campaign will not jeopardize the regular government subsidy.

What should have been a brief discussion turns into a major event. Sesay receives us in full regalia and has called the national TV station in for the occasion. Before the cameras he praises the unselfishness of Alfred, who thought first of his students and only later of himself. Let this be an example for all Sierra Leoneans! Alfred fidgets uncomfortably in his chair and smiles shyly. But Sesay doesn't stop there. "You are in company with such great men as President Kabbah and the English ambassador Penfold," he continues. Kabbah and Penfold came up with the idea that every school in Sierra Leone should be adopted by an English school.

Alfred and I appear on TV in the evening. The entire staff of the Kingtom guesthouse witnesses the broadcast, which is repeated three times. From special guest I have now been promoted to guest of honor. Policemen and soldiers at checkpoints recognize me and want to shake my hand. People wave at me. Freetown at its best.

But I'm not getting anywhere as a journalist. Too busy with humanitarian and social affairs—Alfred and T-Boy. With the latter, I try to find out what is happening with Eddie's children. We finally hear that they staying with an aunt in Bo. There's no way of getting to Bo, but we manage to get an envelope to them with something in it via a roundabout route. The whole operation takes almost a week because T-Boy is a social animal who does everything at his own speed.

My original mission, more in-depth interviews with child soldiers, is complicated. UNICEF has taken the children to Lakkah Beach, a former holiday resort that now functions as a shelter. The staff are shielding the children from the press. "They've already spoken to too many journalists over the past month," says the UNICEF press officer firmly. "The children are starting to get the idea they are something special; they're even beginning to be proud of everything they've done."

A British reporter helps me out, giving me a lift to Lakkah Beach. He is allowed there because he is on an assignment for the English division of UNICEF. And London needs some positive images. Once we arrive in the crisis center, the Englishman opens the trunk of his car and starts doling out buttons, stickers, and T-shirts left, right, and center. Ten smiling children in UNICEF T-shirts—UNICEF buttons pinned to their chests, UNICEF stickers stuck to their foreheads—pose willingly in front of the UNICEF car. This is all I get to see of the child soldiers. I get my camera out anyway, so as not to disappoint the kids.

If I'm not going to get anywhere with the child soldiers, then I'll try to follow the ECOMOG. And they've just organized a press outing. Everyone from the local press has been drummed up and instructed to report to the headquarters of the peacekeeping force at 7 A.M. sharp. One by one, the bleary-eyed correspondents turn up, grumbling about the ungodly hour. After a three-hour wait, boredom and irritation set in. Then we are all loaded into the belly of a worn-out cargo helicopter and flown over to Lungi Airport, six or seven miles farther, on the other side of the water. A large group of Sierra Leonean army recruits are traveling to Nigeria for military training.

The recruits are standing in line, waiting in the hot sun in front of the reception lounge of the shot-up airport. We are not allowed to talk to them; we can only walk around them and take pictures from a distance. Neither are we allowed to approach the top brass of the army or the supreme commander of the ECOMOG, the Nigerian general Khobe. They have retired to the VIP lounge, where journalists are not permitted. They emerge after an hour and a half; a soldier installs a microphone and an amplifier and starts up a diesel generator so the speeches can begin.

General Khobe, a lofty man dripping with medals, addresses the recruits like little children, giving them a lesson in democracy: "There is nothing wrong with having the ambition to become head of state, but wait until you have finished your national service. If you don't have the patience for that, then quit the army early and take part in the elections. The time for military coups is over." A colleague photographer considers it scandalous that I have yet to point my camera at the general. True, I forgot. To avoid insulting anybody I take a portrait shot of the general behind his microphone. After a wait of another two hours, with most of the reporters taking a nap in the shade, the helicopter flies back. The working day is over again. Net result: one portrait of a man with medals talking into a microphone. Taking pictures at the front appears not to be in the cards, either. The front lies a little way on from the small town of Waterloo, twenty miles outside Freetown. The numerous control posts on the way turn the trip there into a half day's haul. It's a depressing journey, through the suburbs of Wellington and Calaba Town. The displaced persons from the stadium were not kidding when they used the expression *razed to the ground*. It's shocking to see that is exactly what has happened to these villages.

The ECOMOG's Waterloo base is situated behind an enormous refugee camp. Anytime I want to speak to the commander, I have to walk through a sea of plastic tents. Here, too, the word *refugee* is taboo, the camp elder, who has appeared from nowhere, informs me in an accusing tone. All the relief organizations have left the displaced in the lurch, he complains. Oxfam built five latrines. They took a photograph of them, went away, and never came back again. But the latrines are already overflowing. And where's the food? Couldn't I send a food convoy? I promise the camp elder to bring the affair to the attention of several relief organizations in Freetown. They, in turn, promise to send an exploratory mission at some point.

The ECOMOG commander at Waterloo keeps stringing me along. Every day he asks me to come back again the following day. He thinks it is too dangerous to go to the front. Is he hostile toward the press because they have reported extensively on the misconduct of the ECOMOG, or is he really concerned for my safety? Not that I have any desire to see any real action. The Alfajets are screaming over my head, and in the distance I can hear the rumble of heavy artillery.

On the fourth day he concedes. Together with a journalist from *The Democrat,* a local paper, I crawl into the back of an armored car brimming with grenades and cartridge belts. They take me to the recently recaptured village of Newton. Not much to be seen there. Burned-out huts, blackened corrugated iron. ECOMOG soldiers lying asleep under the palm trees. They answer all my questions derisively, "Military top secret. None of your business."

My colleague is also having difficulty in writing an exciting story. "Corpses from rebel fighters were all over the village," I read the next day in his paper, which has "Truth Sets Us Free" as its motto. I can't remember even seeing a dead dog or cat. "Well, we have to make it a bit more lively for our readers," the *Democrat* reporter defends his white lie. His article is about the unrelenting, successful advance of the ECOMOG, who are recapturing village after village from the rebels.

The ECOMOG is, indeed, slowly but surely winning ground. A week after Newton is taken, the little town of Songo is captured. There, the ECOMOG come across the half-burned bodies of thirty civilians, slaughtered by the rebels. While the RUF leaders negotiate peace in Togo, the terror in the field goes on unimpeded. A month after Newton, the strategic town of Masiaka falls. A couple dozen hacked-off hands dangle from ropes in a mango tree in the village square. The rebels are deploying the two-track approach as well.

PART FOUR

PEACE IN SIERRA LEONE

SIERRA LEONE, DECEMBER 1999

27

Testimony of Hope

It is December 1999. Officially, there is peace in Sierra Leone. The government's two-track approach and the bloodier version implemented by the rebels have brought the two parties to an agreement. In July, the Kabbah government signed the treaty with the RUF in the neutral country of Togo. The rebels have come out of it well. Not only have they been granted total amnesty for all their crimes, but several RUF heavyweights have also been incorporated into the government. Once sentenced to death, the rebel leader Foday Sankoh has now been released and is residing in Freetown, where he holds the office of vice-president. Disarmament and reconciliation are the new catchwords. On paper, at any rate.

Naturally, I go back to Sierra Leone. My interest in the country has only grown. Rebels in the government: now I'd like to see that. Freetown should also be full of demobilized child soldiers, who will hopefully be approachable. And I want to know how several people I met on my first trip are doing. The undaunted Xaverian padres continue to fascinate me. They have been kidnapped and almost murdered time after time. How do they cope with that?

Apart from which, there is still the campaign for Alfred's school. In Belgium, the money is still pouring in, enough by now to reopen the school. But that has not happened, as Alfred has written me in the E-mails I regularly receive from him. Kalangba is still unsafe. Then there are Eddie's children. I want to meet them, too. Now I know for sure that they are in Bo, but I didn't manage to get that far last time. In short, I've got a lot of catching up to do. Luckily, everything is gradually starting to function again in Sierra Leone. Well, at least in the capital. Because, despite the peace treaty, the rebels still control three-quarters of the country and plan to keep it that way.

In Conakry, I have no problem getting a scheduled flight to Freetown. An hour later I'm checking into the Kingtom guesthouse again, where the entire staff, headed by Melvin, greet me enthusiastically. They had expected me before now. The telephone in the guesthouse is working again and I manage to track down Padre Victor in three phone calls. It's a good eighteen months since I met him in Makeni, but he remembers me well. I can drop by right away, he is in Freetown.

For the time being, Padre Victor is staying in the Xaverian mission center, a walled villa in the devastated harbor district of Kissy Dockyards. A guard unbars the heavy gate and takes me to the padre, who receives me in the dining room of the mission center. His hair has thinned a little more, his beard is shorter, and he seems weary. He rattles around in the kitchen with a coffeepot and asks me about my trip. Skip the pleasantries, I think. Tell me, Padre, what's going on?

Padre Victor pours out Italian espresso, sits down, and starts in. "I don't know what on earth has happened," he sighs despairingly, "but things will never be the same again. People have lost their pride and their trust. They were even stealing from each other when they took refuge in the mission center. The Sierra Leoneans are very peace-loving by nature. Now, arguing children scream 'I will kill you!' at each other. An eight-year-old girl told me she was raped several times." Padre Victor shakes his head. "Unbelievable. In all the years I've been here, I've never seen anything like that."

All the same, he can't wait to get back to Makeni. "I feel like a refugee here," he grumbles. Still, Makeni has almost been the death of him three times already. The first time was during the fall of the junta in February 1998. I was with Alfred in the bush at the time. Padre Victor spent seventeen anxious days in the mission center with stray rebels on the rampage outside.

The second time was Christmas, 1998, when the rebels mounted their surprise offensive on Makeni. Padre Victor tells me the whole story. "It was ten o'clock in the evening," he begins in an ominous tone. He has regained his energy and nothing can stop his flow now. "The attack had already been in progress for an hour or two. The ECOMOG had retreated to the Teko Barracks, and the RUF started to surround the mission center. They had posted heavily armed rebels at all the entrances. They hammered on the door, screaming, 'Where's the father, bring us the father!'"

He was the only white man in Makeni and the surrounding

area at the time—maybe that was why the rebels had it in for him in particular. One group of rebels succeeded in getting inside. The former child soldiers from the Caritas project saved the padre's life: "I hid in a ditch with about ten of them sitting on top of me and all around me. They managed to divert the rebels. It was fantastic," says Padre Victor enthusiastically. "Later, I crawled under the wall through an open sewer with a few of my staff and the children. The kids got me to put on an African robe. We came across a few more rebels, who shone their flashlights onto us, but the children kept on getting in the way of the beam, so they were unable to get a good look at me. Saved by the children for a second time." What was utterly amazing was that one of them stole into the mission center later to fetch the passport Padre Victor had had no chance to take with him as he fled.

For the home front in Rome, Padre Victor has compiled his experiences into a slim pamphlet: *Testimoni di speranza*, "testimony of hope." With mild reluctance, he hands me one of his last few copies. It is an emotional report of his work with the child soldiers—*"Bambini Soldati"*—that turns into a chilling account of his first adventure—*"Ostaggio dei Ribelli per 17 Giorni"*—and his second escape at Christmas—*"La Fuga da Makeni."* Padre Victor has spared no efforts in putting together his brochure, including background information on the diamond trade, the origins of the RUF, statements from former child soldiers, even photographs downloaded from the Internet. Style, on the other hand, is another matter. To inject excitement and tempo into the story, he ends every other sentence with three dots . . .

The text is lightened now and again with typical Padre Victor anecdotes, such as the time a rebel put a gun to his head and demanded all his money. Padre Victor gave him everything he had left in the world—a few sheets of toilet paper. "Do you really have nothing else yourself?" asked the rebel. Padre Victor was, indeed, stone broke. Totally speechless, the rebel pulled out a two-thousand-leone note—a dollar—from his own pocket and handed it over to the padre.

"If you show them you are scared, they kill you immediately," says Padre Victor, explaining his sometimes reckless attitude. "Do you remember the first time, when they kidnapped that half-Nigerian woman from the World Food Program? I got so angry then. 'I curse you animals!' I yelled in their faces. They let the woman go. Later, the rebels used to even come to me for advice: 'We want your opinion before we take any action, Father.' "

Testimony of Hope had hardly been stapled together when Padre Victor escaped by the skin of his teeth for the third time. It was six or seven weeks ago, in October 1999. Fighting had broken out between ex-junta soldiers and mutinous RUF rebels.

"This time was worse than ever," says Padre Victor. "A new conscription of rebels arrived, some from Liberia and Burkina Faso. Totally doped-up animals. It was no use talking to them. Luckily, we had built up excellent relations with the local rebel leaders over the years. The bishop even slept in Superman's bed." Padre Victor sees my look of surprise. "It's true!" He laughs and gives me a complex summary of the most important warlords in the vicinity of Makeni.

There are two commanders, who answer to the nicknames of Rambo and Superman. Then there is Colonel Isaac—the man who had given Bishop Biguzzi permission to demobilize the children of the Northern Jungle Battalion. To make it even more complicated, there is also a certain Colonel Ishah, who is the archenemy of Colonel Isaac. And then you have commander Maskita, the rebel leader from the region bordering Liberia, popping up now and again to create even more havoc.

Isaac and Superman are conspiring against Ishah and Maskita, Padre Victor explains. Rambo wanted peace, but Superman didn't, so Superman shot Rambo dead. He is buried in the village square at Makeni. Rambo's wife has fled to Freetown. Padre Victor knows her well because she lives around the corner. "As poor as a church mouse and deserted by everyone," he sighs.

Then he goes back to last October. "We had fled to the bishop's residence. But we weren't safe there, either. Rebels burst in and stole everything they could lay their hands on. Mercenaries from Liberia. No respect whatsoever. Bishop Biguzzi almost lost a finger when they tore off his signet ring. Colonel Isaac took us to safety. He came with a truck to pick us up and escort us to Superman's house. We stayed there for a day until Isaac and Superman were able to guarantee us safe passage."

The news of the disappearance of the bishop and his padres made headlines all over the world. Everyone feared for their safety until the company reappeared later in Bumbuna, twenty-five miles northeast of Makeni. They made radio contact from a mission post, and a helicopter went to fetch them the next day.

Why does Padre Victor keep returning? "We represent the only scrap of hope the people have left," he says resolutely. He pooh-poohs any dangers. "We are the first to arrive and the last to leave. I know we are used by Freetown to build schools and hospitals, things the government should be doing itself, but our presence is a sign of normality. As soon as we are gone, the rice prices double, then triple the next day. Apart from that, I've been here for twenty-two years now and I've enjoyed every minute. But sometimes . . ."

A note of doubt enters his voice. "I don't know what's going on. Is it the drugs? Sometimes I wonder if our child soldiers can ever be normal again. If they're no more than ten or eleven years old, yes, maybe. But the older kids, once they've murdered with sticks and clubs . . ." All the same, Padre Victor sees signs of hope. Signs of pride, forgiveness, remorse. He recounts the story of a local woman who recognized in the street the boy who had amputated her hands. She started to scream; bystanders wanted to lynch the boy. "Don't kill him!" the woman cried. Then he took out all his money, $20, wanting to give it to her as compensation. The woman refused it. "All the money in the world can't give me back my hands," she said proudly. "I leave your case to the care of God." The boy was allowed to go his way; the bystanders, touched, held a collection for the woman on the spot.

In a similar case, a boy without hands ran into his youthful assailant. The rebel, eye to eye with the result of the double amputation he had carried out, burst into tears and begged forgiveness. "I have forgiven you," replied his victim. "Go home. But don't ever forget what you have done." It was too much for the rebel boy; he went to a soldier he was friendly with, borrowed his pistol, and shot himself through the head.

"The longer I am in Sierra Leone, the less I understand the country," concludes Padre Victor, "but the more I love it."

. . .

Rambo's wife is called Theresa. Padre Victor arranges a meeting with her at the mission center. "Whatever you do, don't forget to give her some money," he urges. "The poor woman hasn't got a penny, and two children to support."

I had imagined Rambo's widow as a self-assured, proud woman, but what I see sitting opposite me is a shy girl with sad eyes and two crying babies on her lap. One has its head covered in eczema, the other is peeing on the couch where Theresa has sat them for a moment. These are Rambo's sons.

Theresa tells about her new life. "I go and beg at the mosque every Friday. Sometimes I come home with five thousand leone." This sum, worth a couple of dollars, has to last her and the children a week. "I went to Sankoh's house for assistance, too. But they told me that The Pa wasn't there." A powerful chief, Sankoh enjoys bestowing favors and goods on his followers, which is why they call him The Pa. Providing for the surviving relatives of his commanders is evidently not high on the rebel leader's list of priorities.

Theresa was with the RUF for five years altogether. In 1993, she was kidnapped at the age of fourteen from her village in the Kono district, in the east of the country. Theresa was forced to fight. Escape was impossible; she would have been killed. She was given a gun and some military training. Not much, because the preparation for an attack consisted primarily of the compulsory taking of drugs. Refusal to comply meant death. Now and again, one of the rebels went into Freetown to buy drugs.

Jamba—marijuana—but also cocaine, heroin, and other—unidentified—powders.

"There was a big pot of light-brown stuff in the middle of the camp," Theresa tells. "Some people sniffed it up, others injected it or mixed it with gunpowder. Then they made a cut in their skin, rubbed the powder in, and stuck a plaster over it."

How did it feel? "Brown-brown makes your mind go bad." Her eyes fill with fire. "It makes you feel like killing. Afterward, you don't know what you have done. You forget everything, you fall asleep." According to Theresa, most civilian casualties fell in cross fire, when the rebels were fighting with government soldiers or Kamajors. "The RUF didn't want to kill civilians; the *sojas* cause that" *Soja* is the Krio word for "soldier." Theresa says that her rebel group did not carry out any amputations. "Rambo was against it. A real RUF fighter will not cut hands." Prisoners of war, however, were granted no mercy. "We tie the hands, we kill the Kamajor. Bam, bam, one or two gunshots."

After Theresa had been with the rebels for a while, Rambo asked her to become his wife. A request she could not refuse. "I was afraid. If I not love him, he will kill me." Once she was at Rambo's side, she no longer had to fight. "Rambo was a good man. He gave me food and money; he played tapes for me." When he returned from one of his raids, he even brought jewelry and presents for her. The other rebels were friendly toward her, too. Nevertheless, she missed her home terribly.

"I often cried all day. I thought about my brother and sister, my father and mother. I just wanted to go back to school. Then Rambo would ask what the matter was. I said, 'Nothing.' 'You don't want to run away, do you?' he asked. 'Because if you do that, you're dead.' Then I stopped crying. But when I was alone, doing the laundry by the river, then the tears would come again. If Rambo was away for a couple of days, then the others kept an eye on me. They begged me not to run away. 'If you run away, then we will have to shoot you. But we don't want to and Rambo will kill us. So, Mummy, please don't run.' "

In September 1998, a dispute arose between Rambo and the rival commander Superman. Theresa doesn't know why; she was not that interested in politics. "They used to be the best of friends. Superman always gave Rambo advice and called him 'my brother.' " The murder happened in a village near Makeni where the rebels had set up camp temporarily. "I was in the kitchen cooking the dinner," Theresa explains. "Rambo and Superman were in the lounge. Suddenly, I heard a gunshot. Pow! And Rambo was lying there. Dead."

Theresa escaped, already six months pregnant. She gave birth in the village of Medina, not far from Lunsar. Later, she returned to the area where she was born. "My parents' house was burned to the ground," she says. "No one could tell me where they were. I went to Freetown, but I didn't know a soul there. I was sitting in the street crying when an old woman came up to me. She took me home with her and gave me shelter." Theresa calls her "Grandmother." "We pretend that we are family. We don't want anyone in the neighborhood to know I was with the rebels."

Padre Victor and I take Theresa home. She lives right opposite the mission center in a couple of poorly constructed huts built of sticks and corrugated iron, in the shade of an enormous cotton tree. This is Grandmother's shack. She comes out, smiling, and shakes hands with us, surrounded by a large group of giggling children. "It's astonishing," says Padre Victor as we walk back. "That old woman has nothing herself, but she has already taken in twenty refugees from the street. Now that's also Sierra Leone."

I have listened to the stories of the courageous bishops and their brave padres with mounting amazement. Bishop Biguzzi, however, makes light of it. "Of course, we do take risks sometimes," he says modestly, "but we try to weigh them up carefully. Some things, however, are unpredictable."

During the January 1999 invasion, Biguzzi even organized a rescue mission: the archbishop of Freetown, Monsignor Ganda, was kidnapped by the rebels. Ganda had escaped, but was stuck in no-man's-land. He succeeded in sending Biguzzi an SOS with his exact location by means of a street child. Biguzzi didn't hesitate for a moment and went personally to the ECOMOG base to request an armed escort to go to fetch Ganda. Everything went according to plan.

In the expectation of more peaceful times, the displaced bishop is now staying with Archbishop Ganda, who has his residence high up in the hills of Freetown. As Biguzzi and I talk on the cool veranda, a fresh breeze carries a breath of sea air; a servant brings us big glasses of cool water. A couple of Catholic magazines are lying on the reading table—*Amici dei Lebbrosi* and *Messaggero di sant'Antonio*—which are clearly targeted for your average elderly missionary group: the "friends of leprosy patients" magazine is full of advertisements for electric wheelchairs and stair lifts. *Mondo e Missione* carries similar ads, but also a big article on Sierra Leone with photos of amputees and a reference to the good works of the Xaverians in Makeni.

Biguzzi doesn't recognize me immediately and I have to refresh his memory by reminding him how Eddie and I came back out of the bush and used his satellite phone. "Eddie Smith," Biguzzi recalls. "Ah, yes, the BBC reporter." Biguzzi had some problems with him at the time. "Eddie was making rather too free with my phone without every paying anything, even though I am sure he received quite good expenses from the BBC. I had told him it had to stop. He grumbled about it for a couple of days, but Eddie wasn't a difficult person. By the time we celebrated Easter he wasn't mentioning it anymore. We danced and sang together at the festivities. We parted as friends. A few days later he was dead." Biguzzi sighs. "What a tragic accident." We both fall silent. Those are the risks of the job. Biguzzi is aware of them, too, and goes on to talk about last October.

"Everything pointed to the situation being normal. We were in the process of gradually moving and had brought mattresses and furniture from Freetown." As Biguzzi says, the residence in Makeni had been made uninhabitable after two rounds of plundering—no windows, doors, or plumbing fixtures, even the roof had disappeared. The Xaverians were to lodge temporarily in the former home of the Sisters of Mother Teresa. The troubles came as a complete surprise.

"We were looted three times. We had nothing left but the clothes we had on. Finally, we went to Superman, who offered us protection. There I complained about the signet ring that had been torn from my finger. Even Superman thought that was going too far. He personally ensured that I had it back the next day.

It's like the medieval style of waging war," adds Biguzzi, arguing the extenuating circumstances. "In those days, the warlords had no money to pay their men either, so, instead, the soldiers were granted the right to take anything they could over a period of three or four days. Once the time was up, the commander stopped the plundering."

Superman organized free passage for them and even brought the stolen mission car back, albeit in a vastly deteriorated state. Biguzzi can't help laughing. "Smart guys, those rebels. It was a brand-new Toyota; they had taken out the engine block and replaced it with a completely dilapidated one. The same with the tires. But it drove. And Superman kept his word. At the first checkpoint, the barrier was raised, no questions asked. 'We were expecting you,' the rebels said, and waved cheerily after us."

The highlight of the diocese adventure so far. Now Biguzzi explains what it's like to be mugged by teenagers. "The most shocking thing is the complete violation of your physical integrity," he says. Biguzzi puts it politely—words like *animals*, *monsters*, and *idiots* do not pass his lips—but his voice quavers with rage. "You are entirely at the mercy of a group of people who cannot control themselves; you're overwhelmed by a boundless sense of insecurity and vulnerability, because they can do anything, literally anything they like to you. . . . No laws or values . . . just an explosion of pure, senseless violence." I listen breathlessly. He needn't tell me; it's etched into my memory. "We were lucky," concludes Biguzzi. "Padre Victor was almost shot in the foot and one of my staff received a heavy blow from a machete.

"Human beings are capable of almost anything," Biguzzi continues. "From the most beautiful things to the most heinous assaults on human dignity. And not only in Africa. Our generation has been through two world wars, the School of the Americas still exists, with torture still on its curriculum. Here in Sierra Leone you see that the child soldiers were the very first victims. Victims turned into killers. Grown up in an environment of fear, hate, and mistrust, where the only way to survive is to continually prove how tough you are. And then there are the drugs, which destroy any moral conscience. When they're not on the drugs, then they're just like Boy Scouts.

"One of the worst things is the systematic undermining of the traditional culture. Respect for pregnant women and elders has totally disappeared. In the past, you wouldn't even speak to a senior. Now, child soldiers are cutting off the noses of village elders, forcing chiefs to undress in public. The worst form of humiliation for a Sierra Leonean." Biguzzi is unable to suppress the disgust in his voice. What happens to pregnant women, the bishop doesn't mention. He probably can't bring himself to dwell on the details.

Like Padre Victor, he has his doubts that some of the child soldiers will ever be able to lead a normal life. "It depends whether the family is prepared to accept the lost child again. Acceptance is essential for the healing process. But the family may be wary of the criminal element; the neighbors might object."

Biguzzi pinpoints the central role of the family in the social life of Sierra Leone. "In this culture, people never break the ties with their families or the spirits of their forefathers. It is a survival mechanism; the family is there to fall back on in times of need. Without any family, you're socially dead." Biguzzi feels the rejected ex–child soldiers could constitute a big problem in the future: a new class of pariahs with nothing to lose.

In his *Testimony of Hope*, Padre Victor also emphasizes the importance of the family and cites the devilish practices of the RUF, which forces new child recruits to make a radical break with all their family so they ultimately come to see the rebel movement as their family. Some children are even forced to kill their own parents.

The fear of rejection, in Biguzzi's opinion, is also the explanation for the incredible level of tolerance in the nature of the Sierra Leonean. "Here, people are more inclined to accept those with other beliefs, because people cannot do without each other. Five percent of the population is Roman Catholic, the vast majority is Islamic, but in schools and at work everyone mixes. Muslim prayers are said in the same breath as the Lord's Prayer. President Kabbah once said that religious tolerance could be one of Sierra Leone's major export products." Biguzzi feels that tolerance is the key to solving the conflict and refers to the great influence the Sierra Leonean interreligious Council—a sort of national ecumenical council of leaders of all the religions in the country—has had on the peace negotiations.

Some are less condoning of that tolerance. Biguzzi tells me that an Islamic delegation from Nigeria has accused the Sierra Leoneans of superficiality and levity in religious matters. Padre Victor had told me of a Pakistani imam on a working trip to Makeni who was amazed by what he saw: women with bared breasts, mixed schools, Muslims as staff at the Catholic mission. The man went back to Pakistan in total shock.

"We Catholics have made mistakes in the past, too," Biguzzi

admits. "There was a time when we put heretics on a stick and burned them alive. These days, however, it has become part of our belief to accept the religious convictions of others. We don't try to convert the people, but try to appreciate the positive aspects of their culture."

Biguzzi is therefore hoping that everyone—civilians, child soldiers, rebel commanders, Christians and Muslims alike—will turn up for the services he will be holding at Christmas, 1999, in Makeni cathedral. Padre Victor is just about to go on ahead to prepare things, while Biguzzi stays behind to work on his Christmas sermon. Reconciliation and forgiveness will be the themes. The bishop is sparing no one and will speak in plain English. He gets out the rough copy and reads parts of it for me: "a wounded country that yearns for healing . . . we cannot remain prisoners of the past, but that does not mean that we must forget the past . . . forgiveness might be contrary to human logic . . . truth and justice are conditions for forgiving . . . evil done must be acknowledged . . . forgiving must come from the side of the victims . . ." "And that can only happen when the perpetrators admit their crimes and demonstrate remorse," says Biguzzi. "It will be a lengthy process, which will need to be carried out in phases. The first phase is disarmament. Without disarmament, hate and revenge will triumph. But admission of guilt remains the most important point. We can live with the amnesty. That has been signed by all parties at the negotiation table. But we spiritual leaders can touch upon matters that transcend the pure legal aspect. In worldly terms, the rebels have been granted amnesty by the state. Now they must get it from God. But you can't negotiate with God. He will not tolerate any compromise."

28

Let We Forgive

Up in the cool hills of Freetown, not far from Professor Kaikai and behind Bishop Biguzzi's temporary abode, is Sankoh's residence. Former public enemy number one, Corporal Foday Sesana Sankoh was held at various secret locations for eighteen months, awaiting the hangman's noose or a bullet from a firing squad. Now, since the signing of the treaty, he has moved into a luxurious villa. There, Chairman Sankoh, as he is now known, poses as the angel of peace, while his former archenemies, Nigerian ECOMOG soldiers, stand guard twenty-four hours a day to ensure his safety.

At the entrance to Villa Sankoh is a big army tent, surrounded by sandbags from which heavy machine guns protrude. I give my name at the gate and am asked to take a seat outside, on a sandbag. Let the waiting begin. There is a general coming and going of visitors. International delegations and organizations, national politicians, but mostly Sierra Leoneans who believe Chairman Sankoh owes them a favor. Destitute women from the countryside, but also former rebels, fresh from the jungle, with an absent look in their bloodshot eyes. I keep my distance, as I have no wish to get too cozy with RUF followers. In a minute, I'll say something wrong and then the shit will hit the fan. Maybe I'll run into Bandanna again. Who knows, perhaps he has presented Sankoh with my Leica. The rebel leader is, after all, quite a creditable photographer. Maybe I can ask him when I finally get to speak to him.

Meanwhile, the ranks of those waiting begin to swell. A few weeks before, Theresa had turned up, too, in the hopes of getting some sort of widow's pension. But the gate is seldom opened to anyone, and most people trail away empty-handed after waiting all day.

The chairman likes to keep people waiting. Last week, he kept the American ambassador and the ECOMOG supreme commander waiting for six hours for a helicopter trip to a disarmament center. A month before, the American secretary of state, Madeleine Albright, also had to sit twiddling her thumbs all morning before the chairman finally decided to appear.

Sankoh is well aware that he is being cosseted. It's a miracle that he has asked his warriors to lay down their arms. It is also a miracle that, with the exception of one or two stubborn commanders, most of them have done so. Sankoh knows he can shatter the fragile peace with one nod of his head. No one trusts him. Every week, fresh rumors go the rounds that the RUF are going to pick up their cached arms once more and recapture Freetown. The unpredictability of the rebel leader is notorious. He negates every conciliatory remark with a threat as soon as it is made. Some suspect that all those years of confinement and jungle war have seriously affected his mental capacities.

I'm keen to speak to Sankoh because I want to know what the RUF actually stands for now. Of course the answers will be predictable, but maybe I can note down a few juicy remarks. I've spent weeks organizing an interview. According to the RUF press officer, Mr. Collins, it was no problem: "The chairman is eager to exchange ideas with the international press." But Sankoh has failed to show for three appointments in a row. This time I have been waiting for several hours when Collins finally comes to fetch me. He takes me to the inner courtyard, together with thirty other people. This is a delegation of petty traders from down in town who have traipsed over to Villa Sankoh to declare their support and loyalty. First it's their turn, Collins explains, then I can have my private interview with the chairman.

A figure with a white beard in a robe woven in gold emerges from a doorway. He leans on a walking stick with a silver knob and seats himself on a chair Mr. Collins has hastily pulled up for him. I hold my breath; this is the war criminal Foday "The Pa" Sankoh in the flesh. The audience applauds quietly. Sankoh spreads his hands in a gesture requesting silence. Then the oracle begins to speak.

"Let we forgive."

Everyone has gathered round him in a circle. "Yeah," shouts someone. Sankoh makes a joke. I don't understand it, but everyone else laughs. Sankoh offers a couple of cases of Fanta to his thirty guests. They have, after all, waited for hours in the sun. Mr. Collins informed us earlier that the chairman is a little weak, due to his rather overbooked agenda. That's why he had to take a nap. The audience completely understands.

Collins hands out the bottles and the grateful public puts the lukewarm soda to its lips. Sankoh promises his guests five bales of rice. They don't have to go back home empty-handed. Applause. The Pa smiles benevolently. He is an old man with fleshy, pouting lips. Heavy bags are under his eyes, which look tired, closing now and then as he is subjected to yet another expansive eulogy from some tradesman.

It has been a long, hard road for Sankoh. He failed to rise further than the rank of corporal in the army. His military career ended abruptly when he was involved in an unsuccessful coup in 1971. Sankoh was jailed for eight years and swore to have his revenge one day.

Free once more, the flunked corporal earned his living as a photographer. He trailed over bush paths, year after year, from village to village, taking wedding photos and portraits of local dignitaries. At that time, God whispered to him in a dream that it was his duty to bring down the corrupt regime of profiteers in Freetown. Sankoh obeyed God's command. He formulated a liberation ideology, a vague mixture of scraps of Pan-Africanism padded out with slogans from Qaddafi's *Green Book*. In Libya, Sankoh was instructed in a number of guerrilla tactics; after all, Qaddafi likes to support young revolutionaries with fresh ideas.

Another source of inspiration was the film hero Rambo: a loner rejected by society who ultimately succeeds in vanquishing the corrupt establishment. Rambo videos were an essential part of the schooling for Sankoh's top men.

Sankoh received further moral and financial support from the Liberian warlord Charles Taylor. He still had a bone to pick with the regime in Freetown, which had allowed the ECOMOG to use the town as an operating base from which to bring him to his knees in Liberia. What's more, Taylor had his eye on Sierra Leone's diamonds.

In 1991, Sankoh set up an army of some hundred men, including a few dozen mercenaries from Liberia and Burkina Faso. With them, he invaded the east of the country, the diamond region, so further financing of the war would not pose any problems. Kids without any future were susceptible to Sankoh's rhetoric and Rambo's romanticism and flocked en masse to join the RUF.

Soon, however, the revolutionaries revealed themselves to be ruthless bullies, out only for money and power. Nothing came of the originally planned land reforms and distribution of the country's mineral wealth. Instead, the rebels plundered and murdered at random. Their ranks were strengthened with hundreds of kidnapped children, who, after the necessary drugs and brainwashing, were transformed into unscrupulous killing machines.

Military defeats forced Sankoh to the negotiating table at the end of 1996, where he signed yet another peace treaty. In the field, however, the battle continued as fiercely as ever before. When, at the beginning of March 1997, Sankoh appeared in Nigeria to buy weapons, the authorities arrested him at the request of the newly elected President Kabbah of Sierra Leone.

After that, the release of their leader became one of the RUF's major demands. In October 1998, Sankoh was sentenced to death for high treason. The Kabbah government had no time to carry out the death sentence because, a month later, the rebels had overrun virtually the entire country. Just before the January 1999 invasion, Sankoh was transferred from his heavily guarded death cell in Freetown to a secret location: probably a British navy vessel lying off the coast of Sierra Leone.

The war went on unabated; with their hit-and-run campaigns, the rebels were indomitable. Nigeria also announced that it wanted to withdraw its ECOMOG troops. With its back up against the wall, the Kabbah government was forced to negotiate a treaty with the rebels. Sankoh was released and signed the peace treaty in July 1999, in Togo.

According to Sankoh, the same God who summoned him to start a war has now whispered in his ear that it is time for peace. The RUF has been transformed into a legitimate political party, the RUFP, with Sankoh as its chairman. The suffix—P for "party"—is supposed to suggest the democratic qualities of the former rebel outfit. What's even more shameless is that the man who plunged his country into the abyss has now adopted the national symbol of a lion as his party's emblem.

"Our party lion is standing vigilantly rampant," Sankoh says when defending himself against criticism. "The three lions on the national flag are taking a nap." Efforts to set up party headquarters have so far been fruitless: any attempts to lease premises have foundered under heavy protests from the local residents who would rather not have rebels as neighbors.

"Let we forget." Chairman Sankoh is center stage in the courtyard. More applause. "We are all victims of war. . . . But if you love and forget, peace will prevail!" Resounding applause. Sankoh looks around him, satisfied, at the loyal fans who are jostling one another to catch a glimpse of him. *Forgive* and *forget*. The two words sound so alike they could easily be confused.

Sankoh and his rebel rabble would have preferred their crimes to be forgotten. But forgetting is not that simple. Ask the amputees who have to face each new day wondering who will dress them or feed them their cassava pap for breakfast. Such things are not so easy without arms.

Forgiving is sometimes possible. The two victims Padre Victor mentioned granted their tormentors forgiveness. That is a sign of hope. Forgiving begins with remorse, Biguzzi said. And some rebels do show remorse for the hacked-off hands, the raped girls, the slaughtered babies, and the burned-down villages. Many of the atrocities were carried out under the influence of drugs. Possible extenuating circumstances. Like all the others. Peer pressure. Conformism. Self-preservation. The law of the jungle. And that law was simple and clear: kill or be killed.

But aside from those cases of rebels who have repented, there are also enough who are proud of their crimes. In Freetown, a rebel boy was grabbed by the scruff of the neck by a man whose left arm he had cut off. "Be happy that I left you with an arm," the boy yelled brazenly. A furious mob would have covered the rebel with gasoline and burned him alive had it not been for the intervention of an ECOMOG patrol. And in *The Democrat* I read that a former rebel has moved into Kissy Road and is not only bragging about all the houses he set fire to during the invasion, but is even terrorizing the local residents once more.

Forgetting starts with denial. And the RUF seems to have a monopoly on denial. No, they know nothing about the atrocities.

Hasn't the RUF always fought against corruption, tribalism, and nepotism? The opposing party carried on like animals simply so they could blacken the name of the RUF. The ECOMOG and the Kamajors, they carried out the amputations. It's been repeated so often the rebels have even started to believe it themselves.

I want to hear these words directly from the chairman, but it could take some time before my interview with Sankoh. Another hour and a half and then it's my turn, Collins assures me, bringing me a Fanta to keep me quiet. Next to me, another journalist sits waiting in his Sunday best. It's Foday Fofanah, editor in chief of the daily newspaper *The Star*, which is deploying a steady pro-Sankoh policy. Fofanah stands bolt upright, his hands respectfully clasped behind his back, listening to Sankoh's empty slogans—"It's no time for politics. It's time for peace"—while I am thumbing through the latest edition of *The Star*. Three and a half pages of advertisements; not even a sports page.

"We have to earn money, too," Fofanah explains slightly irritably when I teasingly point out the low information content of his paper. The one-half page of news is taken up with an article on Chairman Sankoh. "All roads lead to Sankoh," the headline acclaims. The article is a hymn of praise about the wisdom, integrity, and modesty of the rebel leader. The chairman will surely be charmed by the piece, which is why Fofanah has come to present it to him personally.

The *Star* editor looks weary when I ask him about the atrocities committed by the RUF. Atrocities? "The chairman has emphasized on several occasions that his men are not responsible for any acts of terror," retorts Fofanah, proving the innocence of the rebels beyond a shadow of a doubt.

"Mr. Collins just informed me that we need to learn to forget," Fofanah continues, winking at Mr. Collins. He comes over to us. Another two hours. "Great," says Fofanah. "Super."

Several hours pass. Fofanah has started interrogating me out of crabbiness. Things are pretty sad when journalists have nothing to do but interview each other. What is my opinion of the RUF? What do I think of Sankoh? I keep my answers vague; I don't want the sycophantic editor in chief portraying me tomorrow in *The Star* as an RUF-hostile reporter.

In the meantime, the curfew approaches. It hasn't been scrapped yet, but due to improved security has been moved to nine o'clock. I can forget my personal interview with Sankoh. "The chairman is a busy man," Mr. Collins apologizes. "Try again tomorrow."

"You have to be patient," whispers Fofanah. "This is Africa."

29

Getting Away with Murder

On Wilkinson Road, right by the ECOMOG headquarters, is the office of the American human rights organization Human Rights Watch. Due to the seriousness of the situation, they have had permanent representation in Freetown since April 1999. It takes me a while to find them; there is neither a flag outside the door nor a nameplate on it. The stairwell is dark; I feel my way to the top floor and knock on several doors before one opens, revealing Corinne Dufka. She greets me enthusiastically and shows me into her office. Stacks of newspapers and documents everywhere, a laptop humming on an occasional table. The big photo bag is propped up somewhere in a corner. Dufka makes instant coffee, which she serves with chocolate brownies. "My mom sent them from New York," she says, a hint of endearment in her voice. "You know how mothers are." She excuses herself; she just has to sort out a labor dispute with her driver, who is demanding a considerable wage increase due to rising gas prices.

Corinne Dufka is an old acquaintance of mine. I first bumped into her years ago—in 1993—in Sarajevo. At the time, she was working as a war photographer for the same alternative photo press agency as I was. After a few years, she had seen it all in Bosnia. Especially when her car drove over a land mine, leaving her with a big scar on her forehead. She left for Africa. I regularly saw her pictures from Mogadishu in *Time* and *Newsweek*. In 1994, our paths crossed again in Rwanda. Reporters abroad only have to meet each other a couple of times for a direct bond to be forged. After Rwanda I lost track of Dufka, but continued to see her work. In 1996, the most shocking pictures of the civil war in Liberia were published: chopped-off heads, executions, faces contorted in the throes of death. They had been taken by Dufka and won her the World Press Photo award. The last time I had dealings with Dufka was when I was missing. From Nairobi, she provided my friends with important information on Sierra Leone, where she had been numerous times.

Now, Dufka has shelved her work as a war photographer for the time being and is working as a human rights activist. "I'd had enough of rushing from one hot spot to another," she says. "You're only concerned with incidents without any opportunity to go into the subject in any depth." The turning point came during the bomb attack on the American embassy in Nairobi. She had been out of the country for a week when it happened. "I was more sorry that I had missed the photo opportunity than I was about all the victims put together. Then I realized it was time for a break." Many journalists build up calluses on their souls that are hard to get rid of after years of war. Those with any sense make the decision to stop for a while.

"Too many close calls, too much stress," Dufka continues. "It's not the shooting that's the worst thing; it's the hate. Being surrounded by a group of armed people looking at you like you are a piece of shit." In Rwanda she was threatened with machetes by a death squad. How does she solve situations like that? "You try to play the helpless woman; attempt to evoke sympathy in one of the leaders. Once you have that, you're halfway there."

Actually, it's kind of taboo in our profession to talk about these issues, but I feel comfortable with Dufka. We swap some more experiences over coffee and brownies.

But then it's time to get to the point. Dufka hands me *Getting Away with Murder, Mutilation, Rape,* the latest Human Rights Watch report on the January invasion, "the most intensive and concentrated period of human rights violations in Sierra Leone's eight-year civil war," according to the report. It reads like a catalog of all the acts of terror people are capable of. Under headings such as "Massacres," "Fire-Related Deaths," "The Use of Games to Maximize Terror," "Human Shields," the various methodologies of the rebels are described, based on grisly statements. The atrocities of the ECOMOG and the Kamajors are also extensively documented. These become more understandable when you read the way the rebels have tortured and mutilated captured Nigerians. Just as sickening are the accounts of civilians accusing each other of being rebels. Settling old scores. Old neighborhood quarrels or stolen sweethearts. Those falsely accused were taken to Captain Evil Spirit, who shot them dead without any kind of trial.

Hasn't she been desensitized by all the horror she has seen? "Ten years of war prepare you for this work," she says decidedly. "It's not so much the corpses and the blood that get me; it's more the way people's lives are shattered. The heartbreaking tales you hear here." Dufka tells of a girl she spoke to yesterday at the camp, amputated and raped. "The sweetest little thing . . . She was totally broken, but went back to the rebel territory to look for her parents regardless. The courage and strength of some people here is absolutely astounding."

Just as astounding is the ferocity of the war. Dufka has no idea where it comes from. No one, in fact, has any explanation. "An enormous amount of hate and frustration has built up amongst a generation that has been excluded for decades," she says, an explanation suggested by anthropologist Paul Richards. One of his books is lying on Dufka's coffee table. A rather unsatisfactory theory. A lot of frustrated people are out there, but they don't go around mowing down their fellow citizens. On the other hand, there was recently that spate of killings in the United States, high school kids and day traders who blew away everyone in sight.

"Maybe the rebels have learned their tactics from Liberian mercenaries," Dufka offers. "They have no affinity with the people of Sierra Leone. On the other hand, even the Liberians, who are used to quite a bit, thought their fellow Sierra Leonean rebels were sometimes going over the edge."

We have misgivings. And the Liberians then? Where did they get it from? The Liberian president Charles Taylor is reputed to have drunk the blood of murdered enemies on various occasions.

Now Dufka starts to pick her words carefully. "My bosses in New York would hate me for saying this, but I think the way of killing is a reflection of society. The Holocaust in Germany was well planned and efficient; here in Sierra Leone traditional rituals are of a quite bloody nature." Dufka means the former secret societies that had cannibalistic customs. Officially, these were forbidden and banned during English colonial rule. "The step between being familiar with violent rituals and practicing them is not that drastic," she suggests.

Dufka pours another cup; I help myself to a few more brownies. Maybe barbarism is characteristic of every war. The Western world uses laser-guided bombs to spread terror; poor countries have to resort to machetes and Kalashnikovs. That a war is fought with cheap weapons—in some parts of Africa an AK only costs $20—doesn't mean that it's primitive. And Africans don't have a monopoly on brutality. The Serbians in Kosovo, the Americans in Vietnam, the Belgians in the Congo, the Dutch in Indonesia—there's a long list. In *An Intimate History of Killing*, English historian Joanna Bourke describes how the most healthy and normal boys turn into ruthless, sadistic murderers. It may be human, but still . . . Dufka was in the thick of it for fifteen years, I've had the odd sniff of war in the past five years, but we never cease to be amazed at the savageness and cruelty. Perhaps you have to have been personally involved to understand it. And even then, there's probably nothing to understand; it's all perfectly normal.

The question marks and doubts are gone as Dufka takes on the role of committed activist. "The lesson of Sierra Leone is that if you ignore a small country for so long, you ultimately end with big problems," she says decidedly. "It doesn't have to be like that. Look at East Timor; it only took two weeks of violence before the United Nations intervened." Sierra Leone just recently appeared on the UN agenda. In October 1999, the Security Council decided to send in six thousand UN peacekeepers. None too early after eight years of war. In practice, it will make little difference, as the ECOMOG soldiers who are already here will make up the majority of the UN force.

"It's pure racism," Dufka remarks scornfully. "Imagine what would have happened if the Kosovars had come staggering across the front lines on bloody stumps. The Western world would have been screaming for air strikes immediately.

"Blank amnesty is and should be out of the question. What we have now is peace by extortion. And peace without justice will never work. Of course these individual acts of reconciliation and forgiveness are very positive. But something has to happen at an institutional level. It's the international community's obligation to prosecute the guilty parties for their crimes."

Dufka thinks that, sooner or later, the same fate awaits Chairman Sankoh as General Pinochet. "The chairman?" she sneers. "The butcher, you mean. Killers are now given ministerial posts and they think it's the most natural thing in the world. That's the wrong signal. They just can't get away with it."

Dufka judges harshly. Maybe her views are culturally determined. "Justice is a very Western concept," I read in *The Guardian Weekly*. A political scientist specializing in African conflicts is quoted: "Sierra Leone has a tradition of seeking consensus. Justice is obtained by dialogue within the community."

The amiable Professor Kaikai also has more nuanced views on the peace treaty. He finds it difficult to conceal his irritation over the wave of criticism expressed primarily by human rights organizations. "For years, people ignored the problems in Sierra Leone.

Intervention would have settled it all long ago. It's hypocritical to criticize us now because we have signed an agreement with the rebels. What else were we supposed to do? Should we have just allowed our people to go on suffering? Peace was so important that we decided to pay a price for it. Yes, it is a bitter pill, but no medicine is sweet."

Kaikai goes a step further and cites the discrimination against the blacks in America as an example. "When the time was ripe, the minorities there also decided to cooperate with the government. The blacks could have said they wanted nothing to do with the people who had set fire to their homes and churches, who had lynched them, shot them, and given them syphilis." Kaikai knows his history. He knows all about the bloody race riots in Watts, the Ku Klux Klan in Tennessee, and the notorious Tuskegee experiment in the 1950s where black syphilis patients were deliberately left untreated for a study of the long-term effects of the disease.

Kaikai's logic might be faulty, but the underlying message is clear: Dialogue was unavoidable. Besides, we're not the only people to engage in barbaric practices. Take a look at yourselves.

Kaikai does not mention that the government has been forced to the negotiation table because the second component of the two-track approach—the military option—was becoming a dead one. Obasanjo, the new civilian president of Nigeria, announced at the beginning of 1999 that he wanted to withdraw most of the twelve thousand Nigerian ECOMOG soldiers. After all, the peace operation, in which hundreds of soldiers had returned home in body bags and which is costing Nigeria a million dollars a day, is not so popular in his own country. The Sierra Leoneans would have to make do with a poorly trained and underpaid national army, aided by the unpredictable Kamajors. In some areas, the latter have even entered into a temporary alliance with the rebels. Recently the Nigerians have decided to stay until they are replaced by the UN's blue helmets, news that was enthusiastically received in Sierra Leone. Without the Nigerians the Kabbah government would be a dead duck.

But didn't Kaikai confidently state last April that there could be no question of power-sharing? He smiles and is once again the Spin Doctor. "The president is still the president. There are twenty-two seats in the government. Only eighteen percent of them are in the hands of the RUF. That's not power-sharing, that's simply participation in the government."

I don't know what to say to that. I just note it down literally. Next question. What does he think of Sankoh and his rebels? Can they be trusted? I'm attempting to provoke Kaikai. Come on, Professor, don't you think Sankoh is just crazy, a fruitcake, as the Americans call it? Kaikai knows how to deal with journalists, he can already see the headlines: "Sankoh Nuts, Says Kaikai!" He smiles again and folds his hands. "We are convinced that Sankoh welcomes the peace process wholeheartedly," he replies diplomatically.

What does Kaikai think of the disarmament process then? It started in July 1999, and the deadline by which the estimated forty-five thousand combatants are supposed to surrender their arms is only two weeks away. Apart from a few hundred Kamajors and a few ex-junta soldiers who are fed up with the fighting, no one, let alone any rebels, has done so.

"Indeed," Kaikai speaks delicately. "There is a certain degree of mutual mistrust, but there have been no serious violations of the peace treaty so far." That rebels have been terrorizing the main road to neighboring Guinea for the past few months, brazenly attacking and ambushing anyone passing their way, Kaikai waves away as isolated incidents of banditry. "Sooner or later the ECOMOG will take care of that."

A few days later, the ECOMOG has indeed arrested several rebels who carried out a series of attacks on the Port Loko Highway with machine guns and grenade launchers. Sankoh intervenes personally to free the rebels. No one wants to offend him. It appears that the amnesty also applies to highway robbers.

30

Cease-Beating

Meanwhile, Alfred is getting fed up. He is still waiting for the situation around Kalangba to normalize so he can open his school again. "Every day is the same here in Freetown. Waiting and doing nothing. It makes you lazy." Alfred had also anticipated the reopening of his school last September. He had sent a couple of teachers on ahead to see how the land lay. They came back a week later, alive, but beaten black-and-blue and stripped of everything they possessed. Conclusion: Kalangba remains a no-go zone. The teachers were first robbed at a checkpoint, then beaten up. "There might be a cease-fire," the rebels had jeered sadistically, "but that doesn't mean there is a cease-beating as well."

Apart from that, the teachers reported that the school has gone from bad to worse: doors, windows, and furniture have disappeared, burned as firewood. One classroom is half-collapsed after the rebels used it as a temporary barracks. The books are all gone from the library. Rebels have most likely used them for toilet paper or for rolling cigarettes and joints. Dr. Samai's clinic, where I spent a couple of nights, is still occupied by a group of rebels who have set up a control post. A local commander has even been staying in the Kanu family's house for a while, making a complete pigsty of the place.

What's more, the food shortage and lack of medical facilities is taking on increasingly distressing proportions. Relief organizations are refusing to work in the area. Not only because of the risks, but also because the rebels have set up an umbrella structure to channel all relief activities. The organizations have to hand over their relief resources to the RUF, which will then "ensure" honest and efficient distribution. The umbrella organization has been given the Orwellian name of the Organization for the Survival of Mankind.

The campaign we started in Belgium for Alfred's school, however, has taken off successfully. With a couple of students and a Flemish woman who used to work in Sierra Leone, we have held several fund-raising events, which have brought in some $6,000. That money is now in the special bank account Alfred opened.

But in Freetown there are other problems. High-ranking officials in the Ministry of Education have embezzled millions of dollars over the last year. That money was earmarked for paying the twenty thousand teachers in Sierra Leone their eight-month-overdue salaries. "Corruption is now rampant in most government ministries, and the newspapers are full of these disgraceful stories," Alfred wrote me, scandalized, in an E-mail. Alfred has at least been able to use the money from Belgium to alleviate his staff's most serious plights.

Another official at the Ministry of Education, who once

praised Alfred's unselfishness so expansively in front of the TV cameras, turned out not to be quite so innocent. He kept badgering Alfred as to whether the money from his Belgian friend had arrived yet. It was something between pure curiosity, intimidation, and blackmail. Alfred finally gave the man $50 to get rid of him. "Greed and selfishness," says Alfred sadly. "We have the richest mineral and natural resources, but greed and selfishness are destroying everything."

In addition to advancing most of his teachers' salaries, Alfred is busy purchasing materials for his school. They are being stored temporarily in the bedroom of his tiny apartment in Freetown. He shows me the boxes full of fresh exercise books he has had made with "Kalangba Agricultural Secondary School" printed on the cover in big letters. Alfred is currently combing all the secondhand-book markets in the city to gradually build up the library again. He has already bought a couple of kerosene lamps so the students can carry on studying in the evenings. He has also bought essentials such as rice, cooking utensils, and cutlery, so the students can at least be provided with school lunches.

The school also desperately needs a dispensary: Alfred has stocked up on large quantities of medicines for the most common ailments—malaria and stomach and intestinal complaints. Some children stay away from school because they have nothing decent to wear, so Alfred is having some cheap school uniforms made up. "The parents are penniless," says Alfred. "In fact, nobody has anything. With all the extras like food, clothes, and medicine, we hope we can soon entice the children back to school."

Alfred's dedication is moving. "You have to be committed to run a country school," he says modestly. The Kalangba School used to be one of the top ten in the country. "We have enthusiastic teachers, and what's more, there aren't as many distractions in the country as there are in the city." Here is the strict principal speaking again. "No bars or cinema. Our students study more hours a day than their peers in the city." Their English is also better. "In the interior there is no interference from the Krio they speak primarily in the coastal regions."

Alfred remains optimistic. Disarmament may be progressing painfully slowly, but he sees hopeful signs everywhere. Such as the return of Biguzzi and his Xaverians. Alfred can't help laughing a little at Biguzzi. "That bishop. He always maintains he is such good friends with the rebels and they have never harmed a hair of his head. But he never mentions how often he has been robbed and threatened." Another hopeful development is the decline of the paramount chief of Kalangba, who has always been an obstacle for any kind of progress.

Traditionally, the chiefs have a lot of power. Since the war started, this has increased due to the absence of any central authority. Some paramount chiefs rule like enlightened despots; the one in Kalangba, however, behaved like a greedy and selfish ruler.

Alfred explains that it is customary for the people to pay 5 percent of their cassava as tax and to donate several days' labor at harvesttime. The chief of Kalangba, however, imposed a 50 percent rule and treated his subjects as slaves. Alfred has studied in Freetown, which is where he got a more cosmopolitan perspective. Unlike his fellow villagers, who shiver in the presence of the chief, he has little respect for the traditional hierarchy. "If money came from Freetown for the school, the chief demanded half of it," says Alfred. "Of course I refused. 'That money is for my students,'" I would say. "The chief accused me of being a revolutionary and a communist."

Paramount chiefs are chosen from a group of candidates nominated by the village. A conclave of village elders ultimately chooses the new chief. "Our chief had his own ideas about campaigning," says Alfred. "He was also a member of the police force. So he had all the village elders brought to his estate. They stayed there for a week as so-called guests, while he plied them with drink and food and 'persuaded' them to vote for him. They couldn't leave. In truth they were hostages."

Now, the chief is getting old and suffering from paralysis. "I feel sorry for him," says Alfred. "He's become a pathetic old man, no longer taken seriously by anybody. He swims with the political tide. During the junta he was a major collaborator. Now, they don't even invite him to the consultations with all the national chiefs in Freetown anymore." Alfred doesn't know who will succeed him. A power struggle may erupt between his children. He must have close on a hundred by now, Alfred guesses. The exact number is not known. Families offer their daughters as brides to gain blood ties with the chief, says Alfred, explaining the hordes of children. In 1990, the chief had some fifty-seven. Alfred is sure of that, because the chief received a couple of thousand dollars from Caritas around that time for setting up an agricultural project. Villagers went to him for their share of the support. "I swear by my fifty-seven children that I will keep it all in the family," the chief answered. When word of this got back to Caritas, all funds were cut off.

The chief's children are a pain in the neck, too. A couple of them are involved in shady dealings such as arms and diamond smuggling, and Alfred only now reveals that one of them was responsible for the plundering of the Kanu family's house. The soldiers had heard rumors of a car somewhere in the area. They thought the chief would have one, but he had safely hidden his long before. Then they worked on one of his sons until he eventually told them that there should be an ambulance at Alfred's house. Later, the son came to the Kanu family to apologize and bring gifts to make up in some small way for the damage. Alfred accepted his apology.

January 2000 it is, then. That's when Alfred will reopen the Kalangba Agricultural Secondary School. Another group of teachers is going to investigate the situation next week. If they give him the thumbs-up, then Alfred will follow with the school materials he has bought.

31

Tjuz Piz!

Tjuz Piz!—"Choose Peace!"—cries the poster with a laughing child hanging in the office of UNICEF press attaché Nance Webber. I'm determined not to miss out on the child soldiers this time and have an impressive string of recommendation letters with me. Nance is extremely helpful when I inform her of my intentions. She disappears to make a couple of phone calls. When she comes back, she has printed out a busy program for me. I even get a UNICEF car with chauffeur and air-conditioning. The working day can begin.

Child soldiers are a delicate subject. And UNICEF doesn't call them that, either: they are CEDCs, or children in extremely difficult circumstances. CCs, child combatants, is a subcategory of CEDCs. This is not only intended as a euphemism. It is also to show the complexity of the problem. Most children in Sierra Leone have been involved in the war in many more ways than just carrying a weapon. They have experienced kidnapping, murder, pillaging, fleeing, loss of family, wounding, mutilation, rape—

whether passively as victim or witness or actively as perpetrator. Often in both roles at the same time.

Journalists want stories; UNICEF wants publicity. As far as that goes, we need each other. Dramatic stories about children increase circulation; publicity makes the funds flow faster in Brussels and New York. And of course, journalists in Sierra Leone wanting to do anything on children can't easily get around UNICEF. It has a few projects itself but functions primarily as an umbrella organization. UNICEF is the subsidy middleman for and introduction to the dozens of other relief organizations that "do something" with children. Because every organization in Sierra Leone has recently set up some kind of project relating to children and the war. Development work is trend sensitive, and the welfare business has noticed that child soldiers have become fashionable in recent years. "There's no money for a proper agricultural or educational project," an old hand in the business complained to me at the bar of the Camayenne in Conakry. "That's not sexy. But you come up with a few child soldiers— preferably with traumas—and the subsidies pour in." The organizations' preference for child-soldier projects is understandable. They can be set up quickly and easily, they require no expensive infrastructure, and they are short-term projects. "You just fly in a few white doctors and you are done," the anthropologist Paul Richards said. "It's far easier to work with a politically neutral subject like children than to touch the deeper underlying causes such as corruption and misgovernment."

It is therefore more than logical that journalists are so eager to talk to child soldiers. Journalists don't want boring stories. Stories have to be gripping, spiced with emotion and sensation.

A journalist isn't only thinking of his boss, he is also thinking of his public. A complex problem like the war in Sierra Leone has to be made appealing. No complicated statements on the United Nations, the International Monetary Fund, and the collapse of the nation-state in the postcolonial era. And where can you get your hands on anecdotes that spark public interest? In Freetown, they are out there on the streets. With the amputees and the child soldiers in particular.

The amputees have become weary of the press. At the entrance to their camp in Aberdeen a board has recently been erected, with a sign indicating "no photography." "We have information that certain journalists have been exploiting us," amputees' spokesman Muctar Jalloh even stated in *The Democrat*. "Most of the pictures taken of amputees are used for economic reasons." What Jalloh means is that journalists are earning their bread and butter from other people's misery. Of course they have to; otherwise they can't report on it. The amputees, however, are getting fed up with being featured in distasteful pictures and are hitting back at the press where it hurts: their pockets. There were varying entrance fees for a theater performance by the War Wounded and Amputee Drama Group: free for amputees, half a dollar for Sierra Leoneans, two dollars for foreign relief workers and local press, ten dollars for foreign photographers. The highest rate, fifty dollars, was for foreign TV crews.

The child soldiers can't defend themselves, at least not against pushy journalists, which is why UNICEF is standing up for them and wants to carefully monitor the number of contacts with the press. "We are trying to get the children to forget their past," Padre Chima, a relief worker at the Lakkah Beach crisis center, explained. "The press keeps raking it all up again. A lot of journalists are only interested in how many people the children have killed. Some of them have started exaggerating and boasting, just to make an impression." There is a big sign outside Lakkah Beach now, too: "Visitors by appointment only. Please respect the privacy of our kids."

Subtlety and caution are therefore to be recommended. You can't just drop into one of the shelters and ask children to describe atrocities with all the gory details, whether they have been on the giving or the receiving end. In some African cultures, it is even taboo to talk about the dead. Skepticism is also advisable. You never know when a kid is taking you for a ride. Sometimes they will invent a whole story for a moderate fee so the poor journalist doesn't have to go away empty-handed. "They are very well aware that journalists are fleecing them for stories," a UNICEF worker warned me. "These kids are as hard as nails."

"They are lazy, arrogant, undisciplined, aggressive, used to an enormous degree of freedom, and, well, maybe spoiled as well," Wilfred Taylor says lovingly about his little clients. Taylor works for ADRA, Adventist Relief Agency, and runs a home for some thirty CEDCs. "If they don't like the food, they threaten to run away. Where to, they don't know themselves. They just say, 'Back to the bush.'"

UNICEF has handed over 253 children to ADRA over the past year. Some had managed to escape from the RUF; others were separated from their parents during raids. "A lot of attacks take place at night," Taylor explains. "In the panic, everyone runs off in different directions." The vast majority have already been reunited with their family, the ultimate objective of most relief organizations. The thirty children who are still with ADRA are problem cases who can't be placed. Neither with their family—as the members are still unknown, missing, or simply slaughtered—nor with a foster family, because some of the children are completely unmanageable. Sometimes a family doesn't even want its child back.

A few children gather as I stand talking to Taylor in the courtyard of the shelter and stare inquisitively at the white guest. Most of them are leaning on crutches because they are missing a leg. Hacked off by the rebels or amputated at the hospital because gangrene set in after a bullet wound, explains Taylor. Other children sit apathetically in a corner, staring at nothing. A girl is slouching, bored, against the entrance gate.

Fourteen-year-old Alimani Korom is one of the boys on crutches. His foot was cut off by the rebels. After a serious infection, his leg has been removed to above the knee. "I was with my family in the fields," Alimani tells me, "when the rebels attacked. Everyone ran in different directions. Three rebels followed me. They caught up with me and grabbed me." Two of them were Liberians, says Alimani, because he recognized their accent. The Liberians wanted to kill him; the Sierra Leonean only wanted to cut off his foot.

"I saw their angry faces." Alimani speaks softly, falling silent now and again, casting his eyes to the ground with a pained expression. "They started to argue about what they should do with me. Then suddenly one of them hacked off my foot. I fainted." Alimani was lucky government soldiers were tracking down the rebels. The soldiers found him and took him to a field hospital where he received slapdash treatment. What would he do if he ever set eyes on his attackers again? "I would be very angry," says Alimani. "But I would only insult them. Now we're all at peace. If I took revenge, I would be in trouble with the law." Taylor gives him a satisfied look. Alimani is a good boy.

Tamba Marah, who comes from the Kono district, is also on crutches. But he still has his legs and is recovering from a major operation. "The rebels came in the night," Tamba begins his tale, which is much like Alimani's. It suddenly occurs to me, are they deliberately trying to make a fool of me? Have they unconsciously included elements of each other's story in their own or do the rebels simply always deploy the same modus operandi? I decide to believe the two boys. They come across as reliable, and Taylor, who is also listening attentively, is nodding now and again. He has probably heard the stories many times before.

"Everyone ran into the bush," continues Tamba, "but the rebels caught us. Dem big, big," says Tamba, his eyes wide. He thinks some of the rebels came from Burkina Faso, because they were so tall. Apart from which he could barely understand them. But he did catch some Liberian expressions. "They forced us to march in front of them in groups of ten." He says that he needed to go to the toilet, but as soon as he left the path, he was shot in the leg.

Again, the rebels discussed what they should do. "We should kill him," said one. "Let's leave him to suffer and die," said another. They left him behind alive. But not before inflicting a serious bayonet wound "for no reason." Tamba treated his own wounds with leaves until he was found by an old man who was also on the run. He begged the man to take him with him. The old man took Tamba on his back and together they reached the ECOMOG lines. The troops had just received supplies by helicopter, and Tamba was able to fly back to Freetown. There, it turned out that the bullet had hit the bone. But as he got treatment quickly, he has a good chance of recovery. Tamba will play soccer again. He's a goalie.

Alimani's father died a long time ago and his mother is untraceable, explains Taylor. But yesterday, Alimani came across two old friends who told him that his aunt is back in their village. Taylor wants to take him there. Tamba's parents are missing, but he has an uncle in Freetown who can probably take him in.

When two other children start fighting, Taylor has to intervene. Then the bored girl starts to throw stones at a boy. Taylor tells her to stop and sighs. Sometimes the work with the children gets on top of him. Before this, he was helping the amputees. "The first time I saw one, I started to shiver and shake. I could not look at them. It was such a dreadful sight, someone without hands or ears. When we were kids, we had never seen a dead body. Now, if someone is lying dead out on the street here, the kids run out whooping with joy." But Taylor has got used to a lot of things by now. "Nevertheless, you still hear unbelievable things. Unthinkable things . . ." He beckons to the bored girl slouched against the gate and invites her to tell her story.

Adama is her name. She sits down on a chair with a sullen expression. "Dem rebels do attack," Adama begins. All the stories start out the same—attacked, then kidnapped—and end the same—escaped or rescued during a counterattack by the ECOMOG or government troops. But there's a striking difference with Adama: it was a female commando, armed with serrated spears, who carried out the attack. Adama only lets this last detail drop later in the conversation, as if it's completely unimportant.

It's difficult to get a complete picture of everything that has happened to the children. They don't like to talk about the past: they are ashamed and it's too painful. Also, the events happened over many years and are not easy to summarize into a single, coherent story with a continuity of place and time. Some incidents have been forgotten or suppressed, others have faded and flow into each other.

Sometimes it seems as if the children are unaware of the importance of their information. Corinne Dufka of Human Rights Watch told me that years of horror are often recounted in two brief sentences. She had asked a girl without hands what had happened. "Dem beaucoup. They cut my hands" was the answer. Only after four, five interviews did Corinne get to hear the whole story. Gang rape, executions, amputations, people being burned alive. Only at the last meeting did the girl briefly mention that white mercenaries were also involved.

Adama was treated well by the female commando, she says. Whenever the rebels carried out another attack, the freshly kidnapped children were taken to an open space in the jungle, where they were guarded by the women. "They were nice to us. They didn't hit us." But there were rules, too. "If you do bad things, they kill you." Stealing from each other and running away, for example, carried the death penalty.

Now the truth is coming out. For years, Adama was servant to the feared rebel leader Maskita. A friend from her village was kidnapped at the same time. The friend was an extremely pretty girl, and Maskita asked her to marry him. As said before, nobody turns down marriage proposals from rebel leaders. Once married, Maskita's new bride asked whether her old friend could become their household help. Maskita agreed and Adama got the job. They all moved to the village of Zogoda on the Liberian border, where the rebels have their main base.

Life there was easy for Adama. She was no longer on the front line and was given only light tasks such as washing, cooking, and shopping. Maskita was not such a bad person, either. "He wasn't bossy. He was easygoing." Adama was afraid of the other commanders. "The lieutenants were bad, bad." There was a special group, the Cut Hands Squad, headed by a short, fat commander, whom Adama feared the most, particularly if Maskita was away for a few days. "The commander demanded a number of hands every week. Sometimes he drink blood. He eat hands," Adama tells me. Did she ever eat them herself? Adama casts her eyes to the ground and doesn't answer. "It's all right, tell him," Taylor urges her cautiously. "There's no reason to be ashamed." Adama speaks softly: "They kill enemies. They force you to eat the humans. To become fierce." She is unwilling to say more.

Taylor is familiar with such stories: "One boy told us the rebels often made sacrifices of prisoners just before an attack. They were fattened up specially. Sometimes they even told them they were going to be slaughtered and eaten the next day. 'The sweetest meat I ever ate,' another boy boasted." Adama doesn't hear this. She has lost interest in the conversation. She has got up without a word and gone off to lie on a low wall to glower at us from a safe distance.

"A difficult case," says Taylor. "Adama still behaves like a princess. She won't work; she steals from the others. She has learning difficulties and she can't concentrate on anything for more than ten seconds. When she gets angry, she says she will go back to the bush again. It's a recurring mechanism with many of the children: they turn the bush into a kind of utopia. God knows what they really did down there; there's a lot of lying and denying."

At Lakkah Beach, the former holiday paradise that is now a home for all kinds of children in extremely difficult circumstances, a red Mercedes-Benz stops. A slim woman with flaming red hair steps out, strips off her clothes to reveal a bathing suit, walks under the palm trees over the virginal beach, and throws herself into the surf, where dozens of naked former child soldiers are playing in the fierce waves. Dr. Rita Erica Fioravanzo, *psicoterapeuta*, her business card states. The Milanese doctor of psychology, also director of a pediatric clinic, has been hired temporarily by UNICEF as a consultant and troubleshooter. Rita, as I can call her, specializes in PTSD, post-traumatic stress disorder. In children in war zones, in particular. She has previously worked in Somalia and Bosnia. Rita is definitely at the right place.

"Every war is different and causes other kinds of trauma," Rita begins when we meet later at her office. "You can't compare Sarajevo with Mogadishu or Kigali. The problem is that hardly any in-depth research has been carried out into post-traumatic stress disorders. A state of emergency breaks out, experts are flown in, subsidies pour in. Then the worst crisis is over and the next one breaks out somewhere else. Everyone leaves again. Donors are hardly willing to invest in long-term research. Right now PTSD is the big hype. But how are these children going to develop in ten or twenty years' time? What will become of the next generation?

"We have to be careful when using the word *trauma*. It is rapidly becoming a meaningless slogan," Rita says. "Life itself is traumatic." She points out that issues that are traumatic for a European are entirely normal for Africans. In Rwanda, no comparable word for trauma or stress even exists. "A European couldn't stand living in the bush, without any guarantee of safety or security. The same goes for being separated from parents and family. Here, the concept of the family is interpreted broadly: everyone from the region you come from is actually related. Take infant mortality, too. In Europe it's a drama; in Africa it's the most normal thing in the world."

Rita praises the resilience of the Africans to the skies and picks European children to pieces. They are completely dependent on their parents, a safe environment, and routine. Milksops in comparison with their African peers, who are far more flexible and able to deal with problems. "European children have an anxious attachment style. Compulsive bonding and desertion anxiety," she says, explaining the psychological term. "If they are not wrapped up in security and protection, they have a nervous breakdown. In Africa, the children possess a kind of basic tranquility and self-assurance."

In Milan, she sees a lot of neurotic rich kids in her clinic. "They have an ambivalent upbringing. On the one hand they are overprotected. On the other they have to fulfill the expectations of their parents. They have to be cute and clever, they can't be aggressive or wild. They are tamed for molding into perfect mini-adults. All for the greater glory of their parents. There's something perverse about it," says Rita indignantly. "Maybe we can learn something here. We're not only here to protect the rights of the African children, we're also here to question the treatment of European children, so we can understand what's wrong with our kids."

Rita tells of the reunification of a mother with her young son after he had been in the rebels' hands for four years. "The mother took the child by the hand, lifted him up, took him gently in her arms, looked into his eyes, and just smiled softly. Try to imagine how it would have gone in Italy. Drama and theater. Fits of crying. Everyone shouting, "Mama, Mama!" Here, it went quietly and casually. A totally different way of dealing with life."

So much for what's wrong with little Europeans. But how are things with their Sierra Leonean peers? What symptoms of PTSD do former CCs suffer from? In addition to some psychosomatic ailments—skin complaints, stomach problems, headaches—which are the result of being generally worn down, there are the psychological problems Taylor from ADRA has already pointed out: compulsive behavior, aggression, refusal to accept discipline. One of the most characteristic things, however, is a totally distorted control of impulses. Explains Rita, "They don't acknowledge danger. It's as if their thermostat is broken. They explode at the slightest little thing, but remain stoical under the most horrific circumstances. No connection between input and output.

"The children had a very strong identity," Rita continues.

"They were soldiers; they carried a weapon, had power and authority. They were surrounded by all the symbols of manhood. In one way, their dreams had come true. We all have such innocent fantasies as children; we play soldiers, dress up as cowboys and Indians. It's very hard for the children to return to reality." According to Rita, many welfare workers make the mistake of either attempting to suppress this aggression or systematically ignoring it. Rita is now studying the way in which the local relief workers deal with the children. She will present me with the results in two weeks' time.

"Everything is aimed at gaining control over the children. Which will never work, unless we throw them in prison or execute them. That aggression has to be vented in some other way." Individual therapy for thousands of children is practically impossible. Rita therefore feels that more good will come of dramatic expression, in which the children can unburden themselves. In some places, the children are performing plays in which they act out amputations, rapes, and kidnaps. Competitive sports, such as soccer, could also be another release valve.

"We can't teach them to be sissies. You can't just go up to an ex-murderer and say, 'You have to be a good boy, now. Learn a trade and become one of the millions of unemployed young people in Africa.' "

32 | The New Water

Word is that the main road to Bo is safe, but to avoid all risks, I take a plane from Hastings, the national airport in Freetown. The rebels have shot the roof off the little terminal and the building is completely blackened and burned out, but the airport personnel have installed some new furniture and voilà! Everything is functioning fine. Flights leave for the interior three times a day for a reasonable price.

Bo is in the eastern part of the country, alongside the diamond regions. After Freetown, it is the largest town in Sierra Leone and strategically important, as it is the home ground and the operating base of the Kamajors. They have had the area firmly under control for years now, and Bo therefore radiates a certain affluence and tranquility. The main street is packed with the stores of Lebanese diamond merchants, selling everything one could possibly want. In the evenings the cinemas are full; during the day children cycle to school on mini–mountain bikes, sharply dressed in impeccable school uniforms. A couple of hours' walk from Bo, the tranquillity disappears into thin air: there starts the RUF territory where commander Maskita rules the roost. The disarmament is not making any headway: all parties are standing firm under the motto "first the others, then us." Nevertheless, there is a degree of détente. There has been no fighting at the front line for months now, and buses are running to the RUF territory once again. Sometimes the rebels even come into Bo to take a look around, visit family, and shop. As long as the rebels pay for their groceries, no one minds.

I've come to Bo to see how they are treating the child soldiers in the interior and have been given the name of the local organization CAW, Children Associated with War. Its director, the Reverend Theophilius Momoh, is reputed to be rather bullish. And sure enough, I have hardly set foot in his office when Momoh comes straight to the point: "UNICEF hasn't got a clue," he snorts. "They throw child soldiers in with refugees. Then they dump the children with a foster family and take off again. UNICEF is always talking about orphans. But orphans don't exist in Africa. A child belongs to the community all its life." Momoh also has his own views on the term *child*. "A child is someone who has not yet completed the initiation rites. If a child of eleven kills a lion, then he is an adult." Momoh fails to mention that lions have been extinct in the country for over a century. But his point is clear. UNICEF is an incompetent bunch of morons where ethnocentricity reigns supreme.

Momoh's criticism is not entirely new. The Western world occasionally admits its own failings. In 1996, the influential English organization Save the Children organized a major conference that resulted in the anthology *Rethinking the Trauma of War*.

In several poignant essays, the authors denounced the usual psychiatric views that are clearly rooted in a Western individualistic and secular culture. Often, traditional knowledge and assimilation mechanisms are all but ignored. As one author said, the West considers people primarily as passive victims instead of the active survivors that they actually are.

It is a nasty case of clashing civilizations: psychiatry and its concepts are the product of the highly developed Western world, while the bloodiest conflicts and mass slaughtering take place in an underdeveloped Africa. "Western psychiatry pretends that its laws are scientific and therefore hold universal truth. It ignores not only local concepts of suffering, misfortune and illness, but even undermines the underlying cosmology of these concepts," concludes the editor of the anthology, psychiatrist Patrick Bracken.

Perhaps Momoh's fierce attitude also has something to do with UNICEF's having put a stop to subsidies for Momoh and his consorts a year ago. "They're corrupt as hell," Helen Moore comments later at the UNICEF office in Bo. "CAW is quite simply run by and for the Kamajors." I note this down politely and don't enter further into the discussion. Momoh probably holds an African view on the expenditure of subsidies and, as likely as not, has distributed the money at his own discretion, honestly and fairly, among his friends, relatives, and tribe members. Corrupt or not, however, Momoh faultlessly deploys the Western relief workers' jargon: "Our strategic components are psychosocial counseling, empowerment, family tracing, sensibilization, reunification, and reintegration." The words trip, sparkling, off his tongue. I can't hear them anymore.

Luckily, the Reverend Theophilius Momoh soon turns to the specific approach of CAW and the traditions of the Mende, the dominant tribe here in the east. "There is something terribly wrong when well-brought-up children just start killing at random," he says, summarizing his argument. "The Mende value life very highly. Some of us find it even disturbing to take the life of a chicken. God gives life; God takes it away. We don't have a word for abortion in our language. No one has the right to decide over the life of another. Now you see children murdering village elders. The bush was been desecrated. The spirits of the forefathers have been offended. That cries out for healing and purification."

In the Mende culture, people communicate with the "living dead" at sacred places in the bush. "Physically our forefathers may be dead, but they live on in our memory," explains Momoh. "We have respect for our dead. In Africa you are expected to attend the funeral. If you are not there, then the spirit of the deceased is hurt. It's not like in Europe, where you just deposit someone in the hospital, then have them cremated and have the bill sent home without ever having been present."

After this minor reprimand, Momoh goes on to tell me more about the bush. There are also certain designated places where the initiation rituals of the secret Poro and Bondo Societies take place. The societies are secret because the men know nothing of the rituals of the women's society and vice versa. Anthropologists are not admitted. On the other hand, the societies are open:

every member of the tribe is expected to join upon reaching adulthood. One should not see the societies as too mysterious; as Momoh states, "The rituals are transfer points of knowledge and values."

Admission to the places of initiation is surrounded by all kinds of taboo. You cannot wear shoes, but entering entirely naked is also out of the question: special clothing is required. Women cannot enter the men's bushes, neither can men enter the women's. It goes without saying that the rebels have been stomping around like an elephant in a china shop. Places of prayer have been trampled underfoot and soiled with excrement; murders and rapes have been carried out in the sacred bush.

"One of the first signs of something being wrong is when the harvests fail," explains Momoh. "Don't think that we are primitive. What do you do when you have mad cow disease? Exactly," says Momoh without waiting for my reply. "You appoint a specialist, a veterinarian who will investigate the affair. We, too, call in a specialist, a traditional healer or a high priest. He tries to find out what is wrong. He may conclude that certain activities—sex, murder, defilement—have taken place in the bush that have angered the spirits of the ancestors. Prayers and offerings then take place to carry out repentance and reestablish communication."

The acceptance rituals for former child soldiers are similar. The entire village comes together, and the parents present their child to the high priest, who has been fasting for ten days to please the spirits. The child is dressed in old, torn clothes and smeared with clay to symbolize his impurity. The high priest disappears with the parents and child into a hut where a basin of sacred water is standing, which they refer to as new water. This water, soaked with medicinal leaves and herbs, must come from a flowing river, which symbolizes purification. It cannot be water from a stinking pool or even out of a bottle from the fridge, Momoh points out. In the hut, the high priest prays to the spirits of the ancestors, asking them for forgiveness. The child is then washed with the new water and dressed in clean clothes. Then they all come out of the hut again to present the new child to the village. The community almost always accepts the child, and a great feast commences with palm wine, big meals, and wild drum music.

Before the final rituals take place, the community has already extensively discussed all the crimes the child has committed, all the murders he has on his conscience. Most important, the child has to demonstrate remorse to the community. The parents, too, must offer their apologies; after all, it is their child who has caused the damage.

The other organizations in Bo have also started to realize that reunification without thorough preparation does not work. Brother Alex Bangura of the UNICEF-backed organization Christian Brothers tells of previous errors: "We went and delivered a whole bunch of children at one time, without warning the village beforehand. One of the children had done the most terrible things in his own village as a rebel. The reception was ice-cold. The parents ignored the child; the entire village revolted. The family refused to accept the child for fear of reprisals. We finally had to take him back with us to Bo." The child in question disappeared during an attack by rebels on Bo. Kidnapped or run away of his own accord, Brother Alex doesn't know.

Momoh once more emphasizes the importance of repentance

during the reunification ceremony: "The children have been used by the warring parties; they have done things because they were under the influence of drugs, because they were forced to. Understandable, but nevertheless, remorse is essential. Only once that has been demonstrated sincerely can the victims and the community grant forgiveness." Cases of amputees being offered money by the perpetrator are also familiar to Momoh. "That doesn't work. Accepting money means selling your hands."

CAW claims to have demobilized some six hundred children who had fought with the Kamajors and the government troops. Momoh takes me to visit several projects to show the results of his work. First, we visit a garage where children are being trained as car mechanics. There's not much to work with: under a lean-to stand a couple of wrecks without wheels, doors, or steering wheel. But the aspiring mechanics can still practice their skills on the engine blocks, explains Momoh.

One of CAW's showpieces is Sesay Braima, a hefty nineteen-year-old who joined the national army when he was only eleven. He joined up voluntarily to avenge his uncle's death during a rebel attack. Once he felt he had spilled enough blood—Braima estimates he killed fifteen rebels—he left the army. "I took revenge, then I withdrew," Braima declares energetically. No, he doesn't regret having killed: "I enjoyed killing." He was not afraid either because the young recruits were injected with stimulants or had to swallow pills just before they went into action. Amphetamines, heroine, cocaine, Braima doesn't know exactly what it was. "You feel off your head, you are not yourself." Just as with the rebels, the government troops also showed little respect for prisoners of war. Prisoners were killed immediately during fighting; those who survived were questioned. "We interrogated them, and if we were not satisfied, we killed them," explains Braima matter-of-factly.

Is he glad to be out of the army? Braima beams. His parents were proud of him for having avenged an uncle's death, but even happier to welcome him back alive into their arms. He's had enough of the army now, though. No future, no money. At that time a soldier's pay was five dollars a month. He hopes to earn ten times that as a mechanic. "I like my work," says Braima, sauntering back over the oil-drenched floor to his wreck.

At the Sani Abacha Vocational School—another ode to the Nigerian dictator—youthful ex-Kamajors are learning the trade of carpenter or tailor. The lack of materials is pitiful, but with a few blunt chisels, worn-out planes, and thirdhand nails, the boys still somehow manage to produce handsome chairs and tables. Six apprentice tailors share one rickety old sewing machine. Most of them left the Kamajors voluntarily after the peace treaty and hope to return to their villages after their apprenticeship. If the rebels should attack again, however, they would not hesitate for a moment to take up arms again to defend their villages, explains Momoh.

"We are invulnerable," says Bockary More, one of the apprentices. "In fact, that's what makes us Kamajors." He is now fifteen and fought with them for eighteen months. Don't Kamajors ever get killed, then? Hardly ever, maintains Bockary. Sometimes accidents happen when they get hit by stray bullets from their own side. They are not protected against those. RPGs—rocket-propelled grenades—also sometimes pose problems. In addition to being bulletproof, the Kamajors also possess other magical powers. "Have you seen that rusty airplane on the landing strip at Bo?" asks Samuel Hakawah, another sixteen-year-old Kamajor. "The junta was using it to transport weapons. We put it out of action with our secret powers. No engineer has ever managed to find out what was wrong with it. We can even stop your camera from working," he says self-assuredly.

I don't know whether they are bluffing, but I dare not challenge them. If they don't succeed, then I will have made fools of them; if they do, then I can forget about taking any more pictures. Plenty of people in Freetown have warned me never to mock the Kamajors, assuring me that they do indeed have supernatural powers. One had personally seen a Kamajor fire a gun at another from a distance of three meters during a test. The bullet glanced off. Different laws apply in Africa.

Hakawah was once taken prisoner by the rebels. He was tied to a tree so he couldn't pull any tricks. But he managed to escape. "I performed a miracle and disappeared," he explains. He is unwilling to give away any more, but it had something to do with wriggling his hands free and then making himself temporarily invisible.

The Kamajors' magical power is achieved through all kinds of elaborate rituals. Sloppiness in their performance reduces their invulnerability. They also adorn themselves with colorful amulets and talismans. And certain issues are taboo. Drugs, for example, which render the amulets powerless. Furthermore, a Kamajor should abstain from sex for several days before battle. With all the specific rules and exceptions, the Kamajors have a foolproof system: any irregularities are caused by contravention of particular laws and only confirm the invulnerability of the Kamajors.

The amulets may be necklaces of shells, but they can also be all kinds of mysterious substances sewn into little bags. Which rituals and which substances, the Kamajor refuse to say. That's secret. If I want to know that, then I will have to become a Kamajor myself, says Hakawah. It's not that hard, he says; initiation rituals don't take long and are open to whites. A couple of weeks in the bush learning secret spells and taking medicinal drinks and powders. You are not allowed to wash during that period. Then some tattoos and little notches on your chest with razor blades. The supreme test comes last. A hunting rifle is shot at the candidate Kamajor. Accidents sometimes happen, meaning the novice has clearly transgressed several rules. The Kamajors respect my decision to decline the invitation.

Back in Freetown, Rita Fioravanzo presents me with the conclusions of her study of the relief workers. She had them make a list of those rights of the child they considered the most important. This produced some striking revelations. The right to play Ping-Pong was mentioned once. The right to be protected from sexual exploitation only twice. The right to protection and care scored just as badly. On the other hand, the kind of rights that children have little to do with, such as the right to freedom of speech and the right to organize and associate, had high priority in the view of the relief workers.

In Rita's opinion, the relief workers are projecting their own desires and frustrations here. Most of them come from traditional

families with authoritarian family relationships. A liberal upbringing and studying in the big city were out of the question
for them. More than that, Rita suspects the relief workers of
secretly harboring a kind of envy of the former child soldiers,
who have achieved a high degree of autonomy in the bush.
"Many of the children have a more highly developed personality
than the relief workers," Rita says. Once they are back behind a
school desk, some children even achieve surprising results, thanks
to their inventiveness and flexibility.

Rita also thinks that some relief workers are suffering from an
inferiority complex, which causes that fixation on control. "What
they actually want is to subject the children to their own pattern
of values and norms" is her harsh judgment. Like Theophilius
Momoh, Rita is critical of organizations that rush into reunifi-
cations: "Those can be more traumatic than the original sepa-
ration. For years, the child has been building up an armory of
psychological self-preservation mechanism in the bush. Mistrust,
detachment, hardness. Then the child is suddenly expected to
throw it all away and be open to a new environment: Be happy.
Just trust."

Waiting for Sankoh. I try a couple more times to see him, spending hours on the sandbags in front of the gate of his heavily
guarded villa. This time I've been smart enough to bring a good
book with me, *White Man's Grave* by William Golding. A hilar-
ious novel about an American development worker missing in
the bush of Sierra Leone. I forget the time until the RUF press
officer, Mr. Collins, comes to tell me that Sankoh is not in Freetown today. "Try again tomorrow," Collins lisps.

There's no way I can come back tomorrow, I say, because then I'm taking the helicopter back to Conakry and I want to say good-bye to Alfred in the morning.

"Who is more important," asks Collins, "your friends or the chairman?"

I give a diplomatic answer and leave.

PART FIVE

ATTEMPTS AT ANALYSIS

BRUSSELS, FREETOWN, WAGENINGEN, ANTWERP, BO, DECEMBER 1999–MARCH 2000

33

Indulging the Young Ones

Are the rebels simply degenerate barbarians and bloodthirsty cannibals? Or does the *R* in RUF stand for something after all? At home in Brussels, I surf www.sierra-leone.org. I stop for a moment at the Kamajors' home page, which is still under construction, click through, and the RUF manifesto "Footpaths to Democracy" appears on the screen. The revolutionary rhetoric is evident from the very first few lines: "We can no longer leave the destiny of our country in the hands of a generation of crooked politicians and military adventurists. . . . We must be prepared to struggle until the decadent, backward, and oppressive regime is thrown into the dustbin of history. . . . We call for a national democratic revolution—involving the total mobilization of all progressive forces."

The manifesto, published in 1995, is one of the few documents that attempt to clarify what the RUF wants. It doesn't tell me much I didn't already know. With the exception of a few noncommittal recommendations—better education, health provisions, land reforms—the manifesto sticks to vague terms such as an "integrated economic system" and the "anti-neo-colonial struggle."

It does, however, go into some detail on the origins of the RUF and the artful attempts of the successive regimes in Free-town to squash the movement. This has never succeeded. On the contrary, the harder the action of Freetown, the more the flames of the revolutionary fire have been fanned. The RUF does make one small concession to conscience-searching by admitting that they initially had some help from a handful of Liberian volunteers. Due to their misconduct, however, they were soon removed. All further accusations of Liberian support are calcu-lated lies. The RUF then paints itself as the underdog, retreating into the bush, mercilessly hunted down by money-grubbers from Freetown and their foreign cronies. "We moved deeper into the comforting bosom of our mother earth—the forest." There, in the bush, a new minisociety was created, without any outside help. Children went to simple schools, and there were elemen-tary medical facilities. Prayers were said twice a day, to God and Allah successively. After all, in the view of the people, these two are one and the same God.

The RUF lauds its humane principles: prisoners were treated with the greatest respect, recruitment was never carried out under force. It wasn't necessary because the ranks of the RUF swelled naturally with deserting government soldiers, prisoners of war who suddenly saw the light, and children who spontaneously offered their services to help liberate the fatherland. The RUF does not loot or pillage, the manifesto states. That is more the style of demoralized government soldiers. No, the RUF is actually one big united family of soldiers and dirt farmers who work hard on the land and sometimes even treat the kids: "Sometimes we have the presence of mind to indulge our young ones with sweets and toys," the manifesto declares touchingly.

In December 1999, two reporters from *The Washington Post* visited Maskita's territory. They were there at the invitation of the rebels, who understood that something was wrong with their image and wanted to show the world that they were not "limb-amputating psychopaths, but revolutionaries with legitimate grievances and political goals." The reporters' reception by Maskita, a former nightclub dancer and ladies' hairdresser, was warm. Maskita declared that he had no aspirations to political leadership; his only aim was the "total revolution." Then he started a tirade aimed against the international community in general and the United Nations in particular.

Maskita did not go any further into formulating his revolutionary objectives. His press officer lashed out at "elitist" human rights activists who criticized the use of child soldiers: they refused to see that a people's war is fought by everybody, even children. To prove his point, the press officer drummed up a number of child soldiers who, under his watchful eye, informed the Americans of how happy they were to be RUF volunteers. Then, naturally, followed the obligatory denial of all atrocities. Those were committed by government militia or by ex-junta soldiers operating under the guise of the RUF, he argued.

The dividing line between the parties is, admittedly, unclear. Frustrated government soldiers—badly equipped, underpaid—

who had to fight against the RUF in the mid-1990s changed sides at nightfall and went out looting, dressed as rebels. These were popularly known as sobels—soldiers by day, rebels by night.

Contradictory stories are also circulating regarding the commando structure of the RUF. Some former child rebels talk of well-organized camps where order and discipline reigned and drugs and rape were taboo. Other children were with independently operating groups—freelancers—who acted like wild animals without any RUF authority.

Mary Rose, a girl I met at Lakkah Beach, was with the rebels for several years and told me expansively about the various units: War Unit, Small Boys Unit, Strike Force Unit, Signal Unit, Bodyguard Unit, Military Police Unit. There was a War Office, where you went to get a pass if you wanted to travel. There was also a tribunal that sentenced undisciplined rebels to death. Out of fear of punishment, some rebels—those who had clearly gone over the line—never returned to the home base. They went their own way murdering and living off their own spoils. Mary Rose knew of a boy who had shot his parents dead, screaming, "You made me suffer. You never sent me to school." That was too much, even for the rebels.

I learn more about the methodology of the combatants—both the rebels and the government troops—when I hear an incredible story from an older businessman in Freetown. He was kidnapped with his family by rebels and stayed with them for a year, from 1992 to 1993. The businessman knows a lot—too much even—and wishes to be referred to only as Chief K out of fear of reprisals. Unlike other witnesses, he has meticulously documented his experiences. Chief K has made a map of his entire trek with the rebels, with exact indications of where and for how long they stayed at each stop. He managed to surreptitiously make notes throughout the entire experience, writing on blank sheets using a straw dipped in lemon juice, so they were invisible, and telling any suspicious rebels it was his stock of toilet paper.

He escaped from the rebels during a counteroffensive and defected to the government soldiers. That was where the real agony began. Formerly a wealthy man, he was accused of being the moneyman behind Sankoh. "At that time, anyone who had been with the rebels was automatically a collaborator," says Chief K. "It was only years later that people came to understand that many had been forced by the rebels to fight on their side."

Government soldiers subjected him to the most brutal interrogations and torture. They bound him naked with ropes to a thorny tree for days on end, leaving him prey to insects and exposed to the elements. They stabbed him in the chest with a bayonet. He kept the wound clean himself with sand and herbs. "I couldn't believe how mean they were," says Chief K. There followed five days of continual flogging, without food or water, forced to drink the other prisoners' urine to stay alive. Then he was transferred to Bo. There, they threw him into a cell with a group of other people, tossing in a tear gas grenade after them. Two fellow prisoners choked to death; Chief K survived by lying flat on the ground and breathing through a damp cloth.

Chief K was lucky he had been a rich man and had powerful friends. His wife secured his freedom through the intervention of Western ambassadors and the International Red Cross, but only after he had spent four more months in various prison cells in

Freetown. "The government troops treated me worse than the RUF. As long as the rebels were not under the influence of drugs, you could get along with them," says Chief K.

He spent the majority of the his time with the RUF around the Pendembu and Kailahun rebel bases, in the east of the country. Together with other prisoners he was forced into slave labor, working on the coffee and cacao plantations and helping to extract palm oil. They had to take the products to the Liberian border, as bearers. Then they retraced their steps, this time carrying crates of weapons and ammunition. The forced laborers lived in a separate house. There was not much need for security, as no one would have dreamed of running away.

They had to find their own food and then hide it well, before the rebels had a chance to pilfer it. Sometimes they had to accompany the rebels, helping to carry back the spoils of their looting expeditions. "They called it confiscating in the name of the interim revolutionary government." The rebels drove it home that they were of the people, for the people, and at the service of the people. But it was impossible to argue. "You couldn't ask them why they stole from the people while claiming to be fighting for those same people. 'Don't be smart,' they would say, and shoot you dead." Because apart from escaping, it was also taboo to criticize the views and methods of the rebels, explains Chief K. "The rebels often joined up with the army to go plundering together. Then the army pretended they were attacking the RUF, just to fool the people. Some army units even supplied the RUF with arms and uniforms."

Colonel Isaac was also in Kailahun at that time. "He personally wiped out half a village. Sometimes, he would line up a dozen prisoners and execute them. 'To show the bitterness of war, to show that war is no joke,' he would say." Chief K is also familiar with Eldred Collins, Foday Sankoh's press officer. "He was a bootlicker and a boaster," says Chief K. "When there was any fighting to be done, he was always at the rear, but when it came to executions, he was the first to volunteer.

"They loved to kill," continues Chief K. "They knew no shame or remorse. I heard of two boys who bet for a cigarette on whether a pregnant woman's baby was a girl or a boy. They slit the woman open alive. Later they were bragging about it." A commander named Ndopo was the cruelest. Chief K has difficulty telling the story and seeks civilized words. "Sometimes he would spend the night with a girl. The next morning, once he was satisfied, he would cut off her private parts, because he didn't want the other men possessing her as well. The girl would bleed to death. He got the prisoners to work the intimate parts into a dish of cassava. No one dared to protest. We just had to do it. Sometimes they murdered babies. I don't know why. You just didn't ask."

According to Chief K, Sankoh was well aware of these atrocities. "He was often away in Liberia, buying arms. When he got back, the rebels behaved with a little more restraint. But of course Sankoh must have known about everything that went on. He just pretended not to see it. He prized a certain amount of cruelty in his men. A cruel man makes a fierce fighter."

Chief K has not only made notes, he has also got his hands on photos taken by the rebels. Without comment, he shows me a couple of grisly pictures. Smiling rebels surrounding a man with his genitals cut off, while a little way off his raped wife lies bleeding to death with her belly slit open. A Land Rover with the severed head of a businessman tied to the top of the bumper. Complete with glasses and cigar. "An example to all capitalists, according to the rebels," Chief K remarks. A sequence of a man being stripped down to his shorts, dragged over a grass field, then shot in the head at point-blank range.

The rebels employed a special war photographer, Chief K explains, with a mobile laboratory. The chemicals and the film came from plundered photo shops. "I always stayed near the photographer because I was determined to get hold of his negatives as evidence, sooner or later. He had them neatly archived in envelopes, with date and place." During a counteroffensive the photographer was killed and Chief K grabbed the most significant films and give them to his wife. That same day was supposed to have been his last day on earth. A number of fellow prisoners from Guinea had been planning to escape and take Chief K with them. But they went off in the middle of the night without him. Next morning, the rebels were furious. "They accused me of being a double agent and were going to execute me because I didn't know where the Guineans were. I was told to say my last prayers. Then the offensive started with a bombing by an ECOMOG plane. A jet sent from heaven."

34

Frankenstein's Monster

In search of what in the world possesses the rebels, I travel to Wageningen, where the English cultural anthropologist Paul Richards is based at the Agricultural University. Richards doesn't attempt to excuse the rebels' behavior, but that's the impression I got after reading *Fighting for the Rain Forest*. Admittedly, Richards completed his study in early 1996; the biggest orgies of violence were yet to come and are therefore not included in his book.

In his study, which is regularly used and abused by Sierra Leonean experts of every description, Richards describes the conflict in Sierra Leone as a "crisis in modernity." He sees the rebel movement as a "sectarian intellectual response to the perceived corruption of a metropolitan patrimonial elite," their terror as the product of the "intellectual anger of an excluded educated elite." Although he does admit in one passage that the rebels' tactics are "devilishly well-calculated," sympathy for the new underclass

taking up arms in pure desperation is the dominant tone throughout.

I found Richards's book incredibly irritating. I have scribbled
"BS" (bullshit) in red pen in numerous places in the margin.
Labeling murderers as "excluded intellectuals" is simply going too
far, in my view. That could only have originated in the brain of
an unworldly armchair anthropologist. What does the man actually know about the country? What does he know about rebels?
On the way to Wageningen I resolve to show Richards no mercy.
I start to soften a little when I read an article by him stuck to
his study door. The anthropologist writes that a good deal of child
trauma projects are trendy nonsense and pleads simply for good,
quality education. Richards turns up ten minutes late. That's also
a good sign. I don't like people who are right on time. Richards
is around six feet tall, about fifty, dressed in a safari vest with a
lot of pockets. With his little goatee his reminds me of Padre
Victor. I'm starting to like him already. When he tells me that
he spent some ten years in the country from 1977, that he is
married to a Sierra Leonean and has even adopted a girl from
Bo, he has won me over entirely.

"People really criticized me," Richards admits. "Some people
treat me like a revisionist à la Irving, who is trying to deny the
Holocaust. But I was only concerned with studying the rebels'
rational motives instead of portraying them pejoratively as un-
organized rabble." Richards is referring here to Robert Kaplan,
who published his influential essay "The Coming Anarchy" in
1994. The subtitle of that article summarizes the content: "How
scarcity, crime, overpopulation, tribalism, and disease are destroy-
ing the social network of our planet." Kaplan is the leading

expert on "new barbarism," a theoretical model that sees the periphery of the civilized world dissolving in an impoverished chaos where madness reigns and people with nothing to lose are slaying each other like wild beasts. Kaplan's essay begins and ends with Sierra Leone as a prototype of the disintegrated state being terrorized by "loose molecules."

Richards thinks there is logic in the events in Sierra Leone. "The RUF is like Frankenstein's monster, who has grown big due to the attitude of Freetown." In his opinion, it makes little difference whether it was the one-party systems of Siaka Stevens and Momoh in the 1970s and 1980s, the military regimes of Strasser and Bio in the early nineties, or more recently, the democratically elected Kabbah government. They were all metropolitan, aristocratic elites who viewed the rebels from the jungle as a trivial problem of some revolting slaves. It is the classic urban-rural dichotomy. "What I want to say in my book is, treat the rebels as rational beings and they will respond rationally. Treat them like vermin and they will become vermin."

Richards knew many of the original RUF leaders personally. "In the beginning there was something of a coherent program and legitimate demands. The rebels were trying to set up a new society, however small and modest. There was some sort of close-knit organization, Spartan discipline, and an egalitarian command structure." Richards talked to a secretary who had to type out the combatants' battle reports. According to her, raping and pillaging fighters were punished. The greatest terrorist acts, says Richards, were therefore committed by rebels who, fearing sanctions, split off into splinter groups to operate independently.

"The rebels were betrayed. In 1996, elections were suddenly

announced without giving the RUF time to organize a political party. Elections without peace never work." Richards has his doubts about the fairness of the elections: in some districts the turnout was 120 percent; the excess was simply transferred to other electoral districts. "Later, peace negotiations were started, but without any credibility, because at the same time the counteroffensive had reached its peak." Richards is referring to the unscrupulous attitude of the mercenary outfit Executive Outcomes, who destroyed various rebel camps with heavy fighter helicopters. EO took no prisoners. Captured rebels were thrown out of EO helicopters.

"Executive Outcomes only did half a job. If you want to eliminate the RUF, then you have to do it properly. Whatever you do, don't leave a handful alive. They will become extremely ugly and nasty." At the time, Richards spoke to the supreme commander of the Kamajors, Chief Hinga Norman. "Norman stated quite bluntly that they were not interested in negotiation; they simply wanted to wipe out the RUF boys. Then I said, 'What will you do if there are a few of them left? They will go completely berserk.' 'Then the international community will come to our aid,' replied Chief Norman.

"What you get is a siege situation, a hostage taker surrounded by snipers. It's like Waco. They know they're going down, so what can they do but take a few people with them? Don't judge them by their end."

The political scientist Johan Peleman—head of the Antwerp think tank International Peace Information Service (IPIS)—fails to see bloody conflicts as unavoidable natural phenomena: wars are the work of men. The work of evil men. "What we are seeing in Sierra Leone is the total collapse of the nation-state. Criminal networks rush in to fill the power vacuum, which is an oasis of lawlessness and institutionalized corruption. Those networks have every reason to make sure the state of chaos continues. And vice versa. The local warlord economy can only exist thanks to its alliances with shady international networks."

The Heart of the Matter is not only the title of Graham Greene's novel, but also the title of a report by the organization Partnership Africa Canada (PAC). The report exposes the relationships between the diamond trade and the war in Sierra Leone. After all, diamonds are the cause and the fuel of the war. Peleman was asked by the Canadians to write the Belgian section, as he is a big expert on the shady world of arms and diamond trading. And the international trade in diamonds is concentrated in Antwerp.

The statistics in the PAC report say it all: the import of raw diamonds from Sierra Leone registered in recent years in Antwerp amounts to ninety times as much as what is registered as exports by the Sierra Leonean government; the import from Liberia amounts to fifty times as much as the actual production of the country itself. Everyone knows these are rebel diamonds, used for buying arms. It's the same in other African countries. The Angolan rebel movement UNITA is only able to survive by smuggling diamonds. An embargo has only increased profits.

Only recently has the public become aware of the darker side of diamonds: organizations such as PAC are attempting to organize a consumer boycott. After all, most diamonds are used for jewelry. Just as fur coats are taboo in politically correct circles,

PAC wants to link the wearing of diamonds with blood and violence. *The Heart of the Matter* includes recommendations for awareness campaigns: slogans such as "Diamonds are not always a girl's best friend" and "Sometimes diamonds are forever," illustrated with big photos of girl amputees from Sierra Leone. Whether this is in good taste is debatable, but the world's biggest diamond merchant, De Beers, has already seen this coming and, in February 2000, proudly announced they would be marketing only "rebel-free" diamonds. How this will be monitored is anyone's guess. Discretion and confidentiality are unwritten laws in the diamond world, and there is no "Made in . . ." stamp on diamonds. There may be certificates of origin, but these are easily falsified.

"The situation is incredibly complicated," says Peleman. "To get around the monopolies, Russian diamonds are smuggled to the Ivory Coast and Liberia in order to be imported officially from there." He talks about the trilateral relationship of money laundering, diamond trading, and arms smuggling and about the players. The Russian Mafia, Eastern European arms traders, British and Israeli secret services, South African mercenaries, Lebanese militias—they all have their fingers in the pie. Some transactions are entirely legal and authorized by Western governments; other business takes place in a twilight zone, skillfully veiled by a bevy of fake firms that are extremely difficult to track down.

In one typical case, the British government in 1998 circumvented the arms embargo against Sierra Leone with large-scale arms supplies to the exiled Kabbah government. The British ambassador in Freetown, Sir Peter Penfold, arranged it all. As a former commando in the Special Air Forces, Ambassador Penfold had numerous contacts in the military world and was therefore able to settle the business via all kinds of semilegal companies. The whole dirty affair is described in detail in the IPIS publication *Sierra Leone and the Diamond Mercenaries*, a shocking study of how, gradually, "shady networks have established a universal grip on the country and how state security and sovereignty have been allowed to fall into the hands of Mafia-like organizations."

Peleman's tiny office is full to bursting with filing cabinets, sorted according to subject. Piled on top of the cupboard are several volumes of *Soldier of Fortune* and it's French equivalent, *Raids*. On the floor is the more recent research material. Yair Klein, Serge Müller, and Executive Outcomes have two or three boxes each. Klein is a former officer in the Israeli army. He trained death squads for the drug barons in Colombia. After that gig, he popped up in Sierra Leone. He is currently incarcerated in Freetown, accused of supplying arms to the rebels. Serge Müller is the biggest diamond merchant in Antwerp and director of Rex Mining. For many years, he was the big man behind the scenes of various regimes in Freetown. Müller recently caused a furor by supplying the Kabbah government with $3.5 million in parts for fighter helicopters. That a diamond merchant supplies arms is surprising in itself, but it only became a real problem when the goods supplied turned out to be of inferior quality. Peleman would not claim that Müller is a gangster, but he confirms that he is rumored to be one.

Executive Outcomes is another story. It claims to be a private security firm, but in practice it is a mercenary organization serving the business community, with roots in the secret service of the South African apartheid regime. They have done jobs for British petroleum companies in Angola, recapturing some major oil centers from the UNITA. In 1995 they were hired by Freetown to take back the diamond mines from the rebels. In addition to their hefty fee—$35 million—the diamond concessions went to Diamondworks Ltd, which is a sister company of Executive Outcomes.

Sierra Leoneans and foreign relief organizations initially rejoiced at the arrival of the mercenaries, who wiped out the rebels who had reached the outskirts of Freetown at that time. But bringing in the mercenaries had far-reaching consequences: EO had barely turned their backs—at the beginning of 1997—when Sierra Leone sank even deeper into the quagmire. The Kabbah government was up to its ears in debt to Executive Outcomes. Kabbah thought he could economize on the army. In May 1997, disgruntled army officers staged a coup.

Peleman is currently investigating whether Executive Outcomes at an earlier stage supplied arms to the RUF. Isn't Peleman at risk with this kind of exposé? He gives a self-assured smile. "My telephone is sure to be tapped, but I haven't been threatened. It's characteristic of the kind of people I'm investigating that they try to maintain a veneer of legality. They're not going to send a hit man after me." Serge Müller is, however, trying to sue Peleman, considering him responsible for the losses of millions Müller says he has suffered since Peleman's revelations. But Peleman covers himself well: every publication is checked by a team of legal experts to prevent any claims.

Peleman has a grim attitude toward developments in Sierra

Leone. The UN peacekeepers will make little difference, he thinks. "The United Nations isn't used to fighting organized crime." Even more depressing, he feels that the reciprocal contract between the state and civilians has disappeared. "In any normal country, the government provides protection and care in return for loyalty and taxes. In Sierra Leone, the social disintegration has filtered through to the level of the family. Transactions no longer take place on the basis of trust but are now based solely on intimidation."

35

Weird Folks

The Antwerp diamond merchant Chris Bruyninckx is not so keen on intellectuals. "What a load of claptrap," he declares in a thick Antwerp accent. Nevertheless, his analysis bears traces of those of Richards and Peleman. "It doesn't take a superbrain to realize that if those people had enough to eat, there wouldn't be any war. The West simply wants Africa to remain in chaos. They give them just enough to prevent them from starving, but not enough to lead a normal life." He still gets angry about all the money that was raised in Belgium for Kosovo. "They gave those damned Albanians fifteen million dollars. Sierra Leone could have survived for twenty years on that."

Bruyninckx is short and stocky, with close-cropped hair. My first encounter with him was when he called me enthusiastically after having read an article in the Belgian newspaper *De Morgen* on the support campaign for Alfred Kanu's school. The diamond trader identified a great deal with my story and offered me all his knowledge and help. He donated a considerable sum for the school and introduced me to the Sierra Leonean ambassador in Brussels. Bruyninckx also wrote a brief but charming letter of recommendation for me—"This man is a very, very good man and a big friend of your country"—to give to his friend Professor Kaikai.

Bruyninckx considers himself to be half–Sierra Leonean. His E-mail address is Sahr.chris.sierra @ . . . and his business card reads, "Sahr Chris Bruyninckx, Freetown-Antwerp." *Sahr* is a distinguished term of address in Sierra Leone. Usually he answers the phone with "How de body?" Everyone in Sierra Leone calls him the consul. "I like the sound of that," he says proudly. Bruyninckx may not yet be consul for Sierra Leone in Antwerp, but if the Sierra Leonean ambassador in Brussels has anything to do with it, he soon will be. The ultimate decision has to be made in Freetown, and Bruyninckx is aware that his opponent Serge Müller is also in the running and busy scheming away behind the scenes.

Bruyninckx, a former paracommando, had ambitions of a career in professional soccer. He failed to make it to the top, but the director of the soccer club was a diamond dealer and awoke other interests in him. He has already been to Sierra Leone six times with $100,000 in cash to buy diamonds. All completely legit. He is a small, independent trader who seeks outside investors. He also has an export license and a business associate— Sahr James Kokero—who makes the contacts on the spot.

I've met his partner Kokero several times in Freetown, having carried out a few odd jobs for the two. Bruyninckx gives me money for Kokero and his family, who are permanently on the bread line. Kokero, in turn, hands me fat envelopes to take back to Bruyninckx, filled with maps of diamond-rich areas on which he has concessions. James Kokero is an older man with lively eyes and a snakeskin baseball cap covering his bald pate. Every time I have seen him he has been bursting with enthusiasm. "It's perfectly safe here. Tell Sahr Chris to get some investors over here immediately." The problem is that foreign investors still think they will be hacked to pieces once they set foot in Freetown.

Kokero is as colorful a figure as Bruyninckx. The two are also sworn buddies. Kokero saved Bruyninckx's life when ECOMOG soldiers wanted to lynch him. That was when the two were in Bo together to buy diamonds and a Nigerian asylum seeker was killed back in Belgium during her deportation. Lebanese diamond dealers, who tolerate no competition, had stirred the Nigerians up against Bruyninckx. Kokero calmed down a platoon of furious ECOMOG soldiers, but had to hire a bunch of Kamajors as bodyguards, who were even posted outside the door of their hotel rooms at night.

Kokero has saved the life of several whites. In 1996, he set up a mining company with a British adventurer. For a paltry $50,000, they had bought digging machines and other equipment with foreign capital. Everything was going fine until the rebels confiscated their land and possessions. Kokero and the Brit were put to work. But they sabotaged the machines and kept up the story for months on end that they couldn't work due to lack of parts. The rebels fell for it, but then their patience ran out. Kokero and his friend were put up against a wall to be executed. Kokero began to fall about laughing. "What is there to laugh about?" asked the rebels. "We're all brothers," Kokero spluttered.

"If you shoot us, what use are we to you, then?" The rebels were unable to cope with such a disregard for death. They fired in the air a couple of times and let the two of them go. After wandering through the bush for a month, they reached safety.

Kokero's last stunt was when he took a group of seventy members of one family under his wing and got them to safety in Freetown after a perilous trek through rebel territory. Kokero hasn't been awarded any medal. He doesn't consider it necessary, either. After all, anyone would have done the same, right?

Plenty of wild adventures, but Kokero and Bruyninckx have failed to become rich up until now. Gigantic sums of money may be involved in diamond trading, but the profit margin is small and the risks are great. "The market has been ruined by gangsters who pay ten to twenty percent too much for the stones," Bruyninckx complains. They always use the word *stones* in the trade. He suspects money laundering. "I don't know where the money comes from—drugs, arms, or prostitution. . . . I only know it's not clean money." Millions of dollars might have passed through Bruyninckx's hands, but he can count himself lucky if he has covered the costs of his trips to Sierra Leone.

Bruyninckx is friendly with the Sierra Leonean ambassador and often has dinner with him in Brussels to discuss plans for saving the country. Bruyninckx is not short of unconventional ideas. He was furious when Belgium threatened to deport a dozen Sierra Leonean refugees. "We earn millions from them. Surely we can afford to let those few people stay." He wanted to call a press conference with the ambassador to publicize the plight of the Sierra Leoneans, but it came to nothing. So he took in a refugee himself and let him stay in his attic room until he had found the young man a job and an apartment.

Another plan involved training the Sierra Leonean army. With his connections in the world of paracommandos, Bruyninckx would have been more than capable of putting together a group of instructors for such a job. He also has some friends in the military industry and offered to mediate arms sales between Freetown and Brussels. "Absolutely legal," says Bruyninckx. "Simply a transaction between two legal governments." The plans were scrapped. He is still hopping mad about it. "The fools. They'd rather buy rubbish from Serge Müller."

Bruyninckx's reckless plans may seem shady at first sight, but they are child's play compared with what British ambassador Peter Penfold—like Bruyninckx, an ex-paracommando—has actually carried off. Now, Bruyninckx has advised his friend Professor Kaikai to hand over the arrested Yair Klein to his family for a big ransom. Bruyninckx would be pleased to carry out the negotiations. "What's the point of keeping that man in prison? Let his family pay half a million dollars for him and use that to set up a mining project in the interior. Or a beer factory, for all I care. As soon as the people have work, things will calm down." Kaikai is still considering the plan.

Bruyninckx finds it all disheartening. A while ago, he suggested to the Sierra Leonean ambassador that they start a fundraising campaign amongst Antwerp diamond merchants for subsidizing disarmament. One of the reasons it is progressing so slowly is the lack of liquid assets. Kokero is doing the same thing in Freetown under the watchful eye of the government. Months later, Bruyninckx is still waiting for a response from the ambassador. "Sometimes I just give up," he sighs.

But Bruyninckx doesn't give up; he's crazy about the country and the people. "The most honest and friendly people in all of Africa," he says. "You can leave a hundred thousand dollars lying around in your hotel room and they only peel off the top hundred-dollar bill. Optimists from cradle to grave. Look at James Kokero. Been bankrupt four times. His ramshackle house collapsed in heavy rains recently. But never a cross word; he just picks up the pieces and starts over again with a smile. No, they're weird folks, those Sierra Leoneans. You've only known them five minutes and they're already your best friend. Risk their life for you."

36

Lois and Mambu

"Your daddy saved my life," says the big white stranger to the two small children who sit quietly, their eyes cast to the ground. T-Boy was right: Lois and Mambu, Eddie's kids, are cuties. Lois has colored ribbons in her hair; Mambu has close-cut curls and big, dark eyes. They have no idea how important their father was for me. They fidget nervously on the big couch, probably hoping the visitor will soon leave.

I'm in Bo, looking up Eddie's children, who have now been taken in by their aunt Mary. Aunt Mary is feeling a bit taken off-guard, too. She is an elderly, fat woman, with a few whiskers on her chin. They are doing well at school, she tells me in an attempt to get the conversation going. The money from the Journalists' Association means she is able to pay for books and school fees and put Lois and Mambu into green-and-white-checkered uniforms. I go with her to take the children to school. When we arrive, they run straight off to join their schoolmates. All the children line up neatly, class by class, to go in to lessons. When the teacher gives the signal, they disappear, singing, into the school building.

I walk back with Mary. She was at Eddie's memorial service, somber affair, here in Bo. An uncle gave a brief address, after which everyone observed a few minutes' silence. Eddie's mortal remains have now been recovered, says Mary. They were unrecognizable. Together with the bodies of the ECOMOG soldiers who died in the same ambush, he now lies somewhere in an anonymous mass grave in Freetown.

Afterword

Since *How de Body?* was first published in Amsterdam in June 2000, the situation in Sierra Leone has again deteriorated. The twenty-five thousand UN peacekeepers that were stationed in the country by February 2000 proved to be largely ineffective. Civil war flared up, cease-fires and treaties were broken, and most recently, the fighting has spilled over the border to Guinea and Liberia.

Sierra Leone made headlines again in May 2000 when the RUF rebels took hundreds of peacekeepers hostage. A peaceful march to the house of RUF leader Foday Sankoh ended in a massacre when rebels opened fire on the crowd. Later, angry protesters stormed and looted Sankoh's house. For a few weeks, fighting raged near the capital, and the threat of a new rebel invasion became imminent.

Eventually, Sankoh was arrested again and accused of plotting a coup. I was in Sierra Leone at that time. Writer Sebastian Junger and I were on assignment for *Vanity Fair*. Somehow, the trip became a "How de Body Revisited." Just before boarding the Sabena flight from Brussels to Conakry, I had finished my Dutch manuscript, making the people in the book vivid in my mind again. I even saw some of them again. In Antwerp, Johan Peleman and Chris Bruyninckx briefed us on the diamond business. From Brussels, I made a call to Sankoh spokesman Eldred Collins to try to set up a meeting with the chairman. We also called Bruyninckx's partner James Kokero, who was to be our guide. In Conakry, we met with Zainab, and finally back in Freetown, I saw many old friends again: Alfred, T-Boy, Chief K, and the journalist brothers Joe and Lesley Mboka. We met Major Johnny Paul Koroma, who had now become a "man of God" and had turned into a staunch opponent of the rebels. At a Sankoh press conference, *Star* editor Foday Fofanah was once again praising the wisdom of the chairman. We even bumped into Colonel Croma, who was now fighting the rebels.

And of course, when the whole international press corps descended on Freetown, Miguel Gil was one of the first to arrive. We became quite good buddies with Miguel. The three of us took some trips together, and at the end of the day we'd all meet for a swim at the beach, after which we'd dine on barracuda steaks while discussing the latest developments.

Meeting some of the main characters in my book was the good part of the "How de Body Revisited" experience. The bad part was the fear and that same old feeling of being trapped. When Sebastian and I arrived in Freetown at the end of April 2000, things were as quiet and peaceful as they could be. After spending a few days in the capital, we took off for Bo. Within a matter of days, the country plunged into total chaos.

As a general rule, things in Sierra Leone get worse before they get any better. First peacekeepers taken hostage, then the massacre at Sankoh's house. It was rumored that the rebels had overrun Freetown and were on their way to take the city of Bo. With all flights suspended, we were stuck. I had visions of us being cut up into pieces by rebels and seriously questioned my judgment in coming back to the country. This time, we hadn't come to Sierra Leone to report on the war; the war had crept up on us. But I should have known: You never know in this country.

Luckily, the crisis lasted only a few days. Advancing rebels were eventually beaten back by government troops and Kamajors. We could hitch a ride back to Freetown with a UK army helicopter that had come to Bo to evacuate foreign nationals.

We stayed another week in Freetown and visited the front line a few times. Scary trips indeed. Packed in the back of a pickup truck with Kamajors and government soldiers, all armed to the teeth, drunk and high. Driving over roads where rebels might be lurking in the bush, ready for an ambush. The ride back to Freetown was worse. The soldiers who had escorted us were accused of deserting by those who remained on the front line. Screaming, yelling, that familiar sound of guns being cocked, a tense standoff until miraculously the situation would cool down.

After two excursions, I had seen enough and decided to take a day off. Sebastian went to the front again. He returned alive, but pale and shaken. This time friendly troops had again become very unfriendly with each other. Sebastian's driver was nearly shot with an RPG, at point-blank range. We decided to leave the armed part of the conflict for what it was and focused on the diamond trade, our original assignment after all.

A week after I arrived safely back in Brussels, the phone rang. It was Sebastian. "Have you heard about Miguel?" he asked. He didn't need to say any more.

Miguel Gil de Moreno died the same way Eddie had. Traveling through dangerous territory, ambushed by rebels. Miguel's companion, Reuters correspondent Kurt Schork, also got killed. I felt sick all over again.

Sometimes, in dark moments, I think that journalists make no difference at all. A huge international press corps covered the indiscriminate shelling and sniping of civilians in Sarajevo for years. One of the most tangible results was that the locals grew weary of reporters and asked them to leave so they could die in dignity. And the killing continued for a few more years. On the other hand, the images of the 1994 massacre at Sarajevo's main market shocked the public and eventually triggered an international intervention. Much too late, but still . . .

For most of the 1990s, the world was unaware of the war that was raging in Sierra Leone. True, the international press had its hands busy with the other crises in ex-Yugoslavia, Rwanda, and Haiti. Also, major news organizations didn't want to invest money in another obscure war in another obscure African country. It was thanks to a few brave individual journalists who reported the 1999 invasion that eventually Sierra Leone came into the spotlight and finally onto the UN agenda. Of course, whether the UN intervention made a difference for the population of Sierra Leone is a question only the future will tell.

Triggering political action is not the main aim of journalism. It is only a desirable side effect of the media's most important task: bearing witness and showing the world what is happening.

Some of the people I met in Sierra Leone showed gratitude that at least their fate wouldn't remain undocumented. I could not promise them their fate would change. But at least we gave some people hope.

And, yes, some things have changed. For a long time, the relation between diamonds and African wars was known only to a small group of experts. Thanks to the media's exposure, the issue has now become mainstream. Journalists contributed their findings to a UN commission that produced a devastating report about the diamond industry. Liberia was hit with a diamond boycott. Legislation is on its way to regulate the business. Needless to say, this is a complicated task, since shady traders will always find loopholes.

In May 2000, journalists found incriminating documents in Sankoh's compound. The documents proved the RUF was preparing a coup by digging diamonds and stockpiling weapons, all in flagrant violation of the Lomé peace treaty. Chief K's gruesome photos were smuggled out of the country by other journalists. These images are the only ones known up until now that show visual proof of the rebels' atrocities. Not only were these documents and images widely publicized, they were handed over to the authorities that are currently collecting evidence for a tribunal to convict those guilty of war crimes. In Sierra Leone, I'd like to think that my colleagues and friends didn't die a senseless death.

Often, I am asked if I don't get desperate from all the misery I expose myself to. The answer is a definite no. It is utterly amazing to see the strength and courage some people show in the most dire circumstances possible. The deeper the darkness, the brighter these traces of humanity light up. People such as Alfred and Eddie keep me going. Of course, the fund-raising campaign for Alfred Kanu's school is continuing. (For information, go to www.teunvoeten.com.) The school has reopened, but has had to close down a few times. At least we have been able to alleviate the plight of most of the pupils and teachers, some of whom have temporarily sought shelter in Freetown. Sooner or later, the school will function again.

Despite the difficulties, I believe there is hope for Sierra Leone. Eventually, peace will come. To quote Alfred: "We just have to be patient."

New York, August 2001

Notes

1. AT THE BORDER

5   *"Vive la francophonie!"*: Chauvinistic motives—the promotion of fran-
cophony—still play a role in French foreign policy. The 1994 genocide
in Rwanda is a typical example. The Hutu death squads were trained
by France and continued to receive military support even while the
killings were in full swing. France was worried that a victory by the
anglophone Rwandan Patriotic Front, supported by Uganda, would
mean the end of a francophone bastion in East Africa (Gourevitch, pp.
154–160).

5   "Countries neighboring on war zones": A strange case is that of the
countries of Rwanda and Burundi, which border each other and have
both been plagued, in turn, by conflicts. My colleague Van Langendonck, who has covered the conflicts in both countries, always using
the other, temporarily safe country as an operating base, has had similar
experiences of the phenomenon of "neighboring countries."

2. IN SEARCH OF CHILD SOLDIERS

15   "UNICEF published a major report": The report, *Impact of Armed Conflict
on Children*, was compiled by Graça Machel, the present wife of Nelson

Mandela. It was one of the first in-depth studies of the use of child soldiers worldwide.

15   "a UN resolution": Countries such as the United States, Great Britain, and the Netherlands are obstructive. They want to keep the minimum age of enlistment down to seventeen.

19   "ECOMOG": ECOMOG is an acronym for ECOWAS Monitoring Group. ECOWAS in turn means Economic Community of West African States, with Nigeria, Sierra Leone, Guinea, Liberia, Ghana, Senegal, and Togo among its fifteen members.

3. WELCOME TO MAKENI

24   "Abiola": Moshood Abiola was a Nigerian opposition leader who won the presidential elections in 1993. General Sani Abacha prevented him from taking office by staging a coup. In 1996, Kurdiat Abiola, the wife of Moshood Abiola, was murdered. Mohammed Abacha, the son of Sani Abacha, is currently awaiting trial for the crime. I have not come across any indication of Kabbah's involvement in any literature I have consulted.

25   "Sani Abacha": General Sani Abacha ruled Nigeria from 1993 until his death by natural causes (a heart attack after excessive use of Viagra, it is rumored) in 1998. Under his regime, corruption and violation of human rights reached unprecedented heights.

25   "But Belgium . . . that's giving them a bit too much credit": The Netherlands has always pretended to be the moral guiding light in the world. Since a new socialist/liberal government came to power in Belgium recently, this country seems eager to take over the torch. In 1999, Belgium was the first country to ostracize Austrian right-wing leader Jörg Haider. The same year, Belgium tried to have General Augusto Pinochet extradited from England to prosecute him in Brussels. A new law in Belgium makes it possible to prosecute persons suspected of having committed war crimes even if they took place outside Belgian territory.

25 "Dutroux, the Flemish National Front, the Nijvel Gang, and King Leopold II": Dutroux is the famous child molester, accused of having killed
at least four girls (two of them were starved to death in a secret cellar)
and suspected of being the ringleader of an extensive pedophile network
in Belgium. Arrested in 1996, he has yet to stand trial. The Nijvel
Gang (aka Les Tueurs de Brabant) was a criminal group operating near
Brussels who were responsible for a spate of cold-blooded killings in the
mid-1980s. The indiscriminate slayings have never been solved. Some
say it was a right-wing plot to provoke a military coup. The extreme
nationalist and anti-immigrant Flemish National Front (Vlaamse Blok)
won 30 percent of the seats in the 2000 Antwerp city council elections.
King Leopold II was the mastermind behind the criminal exploitation
of the Congo, in which an estimated 10 million natives died. "A forgotten black holocaust," according to Adam Hochschild's classic study,
*King Leopold's Ghost: A Story of Greed, Terror, and Heroism in Colonial
Africa*. Leopold II is still celebrated as a national hero in Belgium.

32 "golden wheelchair insurance": This term was coined by the Dutch reporter Harold Doornbos, who covered the war in the former Yugoslavia.

32 "They're still fighting out old school quarrels": "The birth of all wars is
personal humiliation:" this quote is not from some heavy philosophical
work, but from the novel *Die Luftgängerin* by Robert Schneider, 1999.

32 "Escuela de las Americas": The school closed its doors in 1984. It is
currently called the U.S. Army School of the Americas and has moved
to Fort Benning, Georgia. Torture is no longer part of the curriculum;
these days such subjects as human rights are taught. The My Lai blood-
bath is even used as a case study. Visit their Web site at www.benning.
army.mil.

5. TROUBLE HAS STARTED

49 "Now, they dominate the lucrative diamond sector": Profits from diamond trading were not invested in Sierra Leone, but diverted to Beirut
to support the various factions in the Lebanese civil war in the 1980s.

7. BANDANNA AND COCONUT

63   "They think that the vests are bulletproof": The Mai-Mai in the eastern Congo are convinced that their magical powers turn enemy bullets into drops of water. Bearing this in mind, a life vest is entirely logical.

63   "a photogenically villainous face": The Spanish photographer Gervasio Sánchez made a series of wonderful portraits of combatants in full regalia in Liberia (*El País Semanal*, May 1995).

8. WHAT WENT THROUGH MY HEAD

65   "A bullet fired": Detailed information can be found in the paper "Understanding the Mechanisms of Bullet Wounds" written by the surgeon Pierre Gielis for Doctors Without Borders–Brussels.

67   "You fucking foreigners started this war": Antiwhite attitudes are quite common amongst warring parties in Africa. During the fall of Kinshasa, August 1998, all white journalists—the only foreigners still around—were declared outlaws. Correspondent Alfonso Rojo from *El Mundo* was almost murdered by local militia shouting slogans such as "You whites are the cause of everything bad that happens in Africa, we're going to kill you like dogs" (*El Mundo*, 29 August 1998).

21. BY LAND, SEA, OR AIR?

136   "the gates of Freetown": Some support a conspiracy theory. Nigeria wanted to withdraw its troops from Sierra Leone. It therefore allowed the ECOMOG to be "caught unawares" and overrun to show that the military option was not working and thus encouraging the Kabbah government to negotiate a peace treaty with the rebels.

136   "Thousands of civilians": The figures quoted originate from the Human Rights Watch report *Getting Away with Murder*.

137   "American cameraman was shot dead": AP television producer Myles Tierny was driving through no-man's-land with two colleagues with an armed escort of ECOMOG soldiers. A few rebels walked up to their car and suddenly opened fire for no apparent reason. Tierny was killed, the

two colleagues wounded. The accompanying ECOMOG soldiers shot the rebels dead.

22. WELCOME TO THE NUTHOUSE

154   "drug cartels are trading cocaine for diamonds": According to the PAC (Partnership Africa Canada) report *The Heart of the Matter* (p. 46), "Western intelligence agencies" are investigating the possibility that a criminal network of cocaine cartels and diamond merchants is supporting President Charles Taylor of Liberia. The latter is suspected of wanting to get his hands on Sierra Leone's diamond resources through an RUF puppet regime.

23. DEM BATS BEAUCOUP

166   "Tupac": After hundreds of rebels dressed in Tupac T-shirts attacked the village of Kukuna in September 1998, some speculated whether the aggressive rapper was the rebels' patron. The mayor of Kukuna banned the public display of Tupac images. All over Freetown, however, you see people—from children to pregnant women—walking round in Tupac caps and T-shirts.

24. CO CUTHANDS

167   "by Belgian colonizers": The Belgians even had a special administrator, the "hand keeper," who not only administered the bullets used and the hacking off of hands, but even smoked and dried those hands above a fire so they would not perish in the tropical climate. See *King Leopold's Ghost* by Adam Hochschild.

169   "the anthropologist doesn't mention": Richards told me that the RUF also had another reason for sabotaging the rice harvests: large quantities of rice are needed for the initiation rituals of the Kamajors, the archenemies of the rebels.

26. PRESS TRIPS

184   "misconduct of the ECOMOG": During the January 1999 invasion, it was suicide to work alongside the rebels. Most journalists therefore worked alongside the ECOMOG. The controversial film *Cry, Freetown*

by filmmaker Sorious Samara, in particular, showed the hard-as-nails approach of the peacekeeping force. Sorious Samara was initially on the rebels' side of the front, was captured and almost executed, but escaped in the nick of time to continue his work under ECOMOG supervision.

27. TESTIMONY OF HOPE

196 "into Freetown to buy drugs": Nigeria is a major transit point in international drug smuggling. PAC's *Heart of the Matter* states that rebels in the district of Kailahun, near the border with Liberia, which is controlled by the rebels, grow opium poppies and coca, which are processed in Liberia.

197 "gunpowder:" The use of gunpowder as a stimulant features in many statements. Girls even take it as a form of contraception. The exact effect is unknown. It is said that gunpowder makes the combatant fearless; some refer to the placebo effect. In New York I heard about a man who mixed gunpowder with his pit bull terrier's food to make him more ferocious.

28. LET WE FORGIVE

208 "involved in an unsuccessful coup": *The Washington Post Magazine* gives the following version of the facts: photographer Sankoh was sent to take pictures of the coup, but became so enthusiastic that he ended up joining it.

208 "source of inspiration was the film hero Rambo": In *Fighting for the Rain Forest*, Paul Richards quotes an anecdote about a woman who fled into the bush after a rebel attack. She said she drew strength and inspiration from the hounded Rambo in *First Blood*.

209 "to bring him to his knees in Liberia": The ECOMOG's looting in Liberia earned it the nickname Every Commodity Movable Gone. In Liberia, the warlord Charles Taylor was the archenemy of the ECOMOG. It is ironic that the same ECOMOG had to keep the peace during the elections in 1997 in which none other than Charles Taylor came to power.

29. GETTING AWAY WITH MURDER

217   "The Liberian president Charles Taylor is reputed": The African specialist Stephen Ellis accuses Taylor of cannibalistic practices in his book *The Mask of Anarchy* (1999). Taylor has sued Ellis for defamation of character.

218   "war is fought with cheap weapons": This quote is from Paul Richards: "It makes no sense to call one kind of war 'barbaric' when all that is meant is that it is cheap" (*Fighting for the Rain Forest*, p. xx).

219   "the same fate awaits Chairman Sankoh as General Pinochet": Pinochet has now returned, immune, to Chile, but his case has set an important precedent. In February 2000, ex-dictator Hissene Habre of Chad, who had fled to Senegal, was placed under house arrest. After local human rights activists brought him to trial, the activists said that the Pinochet case had inspired them. Sierra Leonean member of parliament Liz Lavalie announced in March 2000 that Sankoh would have to be handed over to the international community sooner or later.

221   "the Nigerians have decided to stay until": In fact, Nigeria has several times announced its intention to withdraw, only to later decide to stay after all. Withdrawal of the Nigerian ECOMOG troops was one of the election promises of the new civilian president Obasanjo.

31. TJUZ PIZ!

230   "welfare business": With a turnover estimated at tens of billions of dollars, the development and welfare sector may well be referred to as a business. See the revealing book *The Lords of Poverty* by Graham Hancock.

231   "A journalist isn't only thinking of his boss": For an explanation of market mechanisms, journalists' choices, and public demand, see the book *Who Stole the News?* by Mort Rosenblum. Instead of blaming the sensationalization and simplification of news on a few multinational media conglomerates, Rosenblum also points at the responsibility of the public that gets what it asks for.

231   "Muctar Jalloh even stated in *The Democrat*": "The majority of journalists visiting the camp should be properly screened," stated Muctar Jalloh. "Pictures of amputees from Sierra Leone are seen all over the globe, but not much has been done to alleviate their plight" (*The Democrat*, 19 November 1999).

232   "In some African cultures": In her book *Spelen met vuur* (Playing with Fire), Tangelder mentions Western relief workers who interviewed former child rebels in Mozambique: "You don't talk about the dead in that country. And definitely not about someone you have murdered, because the spirit of the dead person who is looking for you will have found you as soon as you speak out his name" (p. 11).

232   "invent a whole story:" In a chapter on Liberia, Tangelder tells about the strained relations between journalists and child soldiers. She herself is followed by children who pretend to be former combatants and are eager to tell the grisliest stories for a few dollars. An Irish priest complains that the journalists have "spoiled" the children and tells an embarrassing anecdote about a French journalist who takes down a story she knows to be entirely fictitious (p. 25).

239   "long-term research": Rita told me that Israel has a rich tradition of psychological research into the long-term effects of war traumas. Not only because of the Holocaust, but also because it is one of the few highly developed countries that has been in a virtually permanent state of war for decades.

240   "No connection between input and output": For years, a friend from Sarajevo appeared to be completely untouched by all the people he had seen killed by snipers' bullets and grenades. After the Dayton peace treaty, he was watching a Tom and Jerry cartoon. For the first time in years, he broke out in tears when Jerry hit Tom on the head with a hammer.

241   "power and authority": Victoria Brittain describes in *The Guardian Weekly* a twelve-year-old boy who reported at a disarmament camp claiming to be a lieutenant colonel. He was accompanied by a forty-

year-old man who was carrying his bags, calling him sir, and saluting
him in a military fashion.

241   "Competitive sports, such as soccer": Caritas currently has several projects running in Liberia in which former child soldiers are encouraged
to play soccer. The initial results are promising.

32. THE NEW WATER

243   "commander Maskita rules the roost": Sam Bockarie, aka Maskita, disappeared from the scene in December 1999. Around that time, he pro-
tested the disarmament and the stationing of Nigerian UN troops by
kidnapping two people from Doctors Without Borders. The embarrassed
Sankoh ordered the release of the two Western hostages. The two were
indeed released, upon which Sankoh sent an RUF commando to arrest
the recalcitrant Maskita. After a scuffle, in which several people were
killed, Maskita escaped to Liberia.

243   "orphans don't exist in Africa": In some cultures, even the concept of
biological fatherhood does not exist, as no connection is made between
sex and reproduction.

244   "psychiatry and its concepts": The whole concept of PTSD was thought
up by American psychiatrists who had to give a name to a host of
complaints suffered by Vietnam veterans. For the history of how PTSD
came about, see Allan Young's book, published in 1995, *The Harmony
of Illusions: Inventing Post-Traumatic Stress Disorder*.

244   "psychiatrist Patrick Bracken": *Rethinking the Trauma of War*, p. 57.
Bracken was affiliated with the Medical Foundation for the Care of
Victims of Torture, a London research institute.

245   "Poro and Bondo Societies": The Poro Societies are for the men, the
Bondo for the women. The initiation period for the Bondo Society used
to be as long as three years, in which the women learned everything
the community expected of them (farming, housekeeping, child care,
traditional medicine). Formal education took over many of these tasks.

Nowadays, the initiation rites have been cut down to a few weeks. In the past, clitoridectomy was an important element (Bangura, p. 2).

247 "final rituals": There are variations on the rituals. Sometimes, cola nuts are exchanged between perpetrator and victim. In incest cases, similar cleansing rituals take place. Those involved are sprinkled with sacred water in a flowing river in the presence of the community.

249 "RPGs . . . also sometimes pose problems": Thomas Davies-Langba, director of operations for the Kamajors in Freetown, claimed that he himself was resistant to RPG fire. Another Kamajor once shot twenty-nine grenades at him; all these projectiles ducked between his legs or swerved around his body in a curve.

250 "the Kamajors have a foolproof system": The Mai-Mai warriors in the eastern Congo, who claim to be able to turn enemy bullets into water, also always have a sound explanation—sex, bad thoughts, unclean food—when something goes wrong. In *Witchcraft, Oracles and Magic Among the Azande* (originally published in 1937), the anthropologist Evans-Pritchard describes the beliefs and philosophy of the African Azande tribe as an internally coherent and entirely logical system.

33. INDULGING THE YOUNG ONES

260 "soldiers by day, rebels by night": This phenomenon also appears in other wars: in the Congo, they are called *démi-kabilas*, a play on words on the name of ex–rebel leader Laurent Kabila, who became president.

260 "freelancers": Paul Richards uses this term to describe loose groups of bandits who go around robbing under the guise of being rebels. The word *freelancer* is derived from the medieval term for a mercenary, who would at that time have been armed with a spear or lance.

263 "the intimate parts": Corinne Dufka links some atrocities to bloody rituals. Bangura states that, during the female circumcision rituals in the traditional women's Bondo Society, the removed parts are dried in the sun and then ground to a powder and mixed with rice. The con-

sumption of this rice—and the secrecy of the ingredients—is the most important part of the graduation ceremony (Bangura, p. 33).

34. FRANKENSTEIN'S MONSTER

265 "used and abused": Richards complained that RUF legal representative Sam Golley quoted parts of his study to lend credence to the political integrity of the RUF.

266 "his influential essay 'The Coming Anarchy' ": The article—the basis for Kaplan's bestseller *The Ends of the Earth*—was faxed to all American embassies in the world as if it were a blueprint for the future.

267 "treat them like vermin": In the RUF manifesto, too, the rebels state explicitly that they are treated as "despicable aliens from another planet."

268 "supreme commander of the Kamajors, Chief Hinga Norman": Hinga Norman is currently the minister of defense under President Kabbah. The Kamajors have become a considerable military force, which calls itself the Civil Defense Forces.

269 "registered as exports": According to *The Heart of the Matter* by Smilie et al., in 1998 the Sierra Leonean government registered exports of 8,500 carats (a carat is 0.2 gram); the Diamond High Council, in Antwerp—the diamond merchants' central body—registered imports of 770,000 carats. The annual Liberian production is estimated at between 100,000 and 150,000 carats; between 1994 and 1998, an average of 6 million carats were exported annually.

271 "officer in the Israeli army": For further background on Yair Klein, see *The Arms Fixers* by Wood and Peleman, pp. 83–85.

35. WEIRD FOLKS

275 "*Sahr* is a distinguished term of address in Sierra Leone": *Sahr* is the Mende word for "firstborn." The eldest son of a family may use this title. Chris was given the title by his Sierra Leonean associate James

Kokero because he considers Chris a brother, who is therefore the first-born white in the family.

276　"a Nigerian asylum seeker": Sémira Adamu violently resisted her deportation by plane in 1998. Two Belgian state policemen attempted to silence her screams by pressing a pillow over her face. She died of suffocation.

AFTERWORD

283　"on assignment": See "The Terror of Sierra Leone," *Vanity Fair*, August 2000 (also published in *Fire* [New York: W. W. Norton, 2001]). The photos of Chief K were published in the October 2000 issue of *Vanity Fair* and were later shown on CNN TV.

287　"UN commission": See the "UN Panel of Experts Report on Diamonds and Arms" (New York, 2000). Johan Peleman of the IPIS and Ian Smilie of the PAC are some of the experts.

287　"a tribunal": In August 2000 the UN Security Council requested that the secretary-general negotiate an agreement with the Sierra Leone government to establish a "special court" to prosecute war crimes committed during the ongoing war. The hybrid court will be jointly administered by the United Nations and the Sierra Leone government. Currently it is still awaiting final approval from the Security Council. See www.crimesofwar.org.

Important Dates in the History of Sierra Leone

1462	The Portuguese explorer Pedro da Sinta "discovers" Sierra Leone.
1600	The English establish a trading post and transshipment base for the slave trade.
1774	An English charitable organization buys land from a chief in Freetown where freed slaves can settle.
1807	England abolishes slavery. Some fifty thousand freed slaves are taken to Sierra Leone over the next fifty years.
1808	Sierra Leone officially becomes an English colony. The English inculcate a high degree of self-management over the next century.
1961	Sierra Leone becomes independent. Successive Milton Margai, Siaka Stevens, and Joseph Momoh governments.
1989	The rebel movement the Revolutionary United Front (RUF) is set up.

IMPORTANT DATES IN THE HISTORY OF SIERRA LEONE

1991   The RUF invades the country from Liberia.

1992   Coup by the twenty-seven-year-old army officer Valentine
                Strasser. He becomes the youngest head of state in the
                world.

1994   RUF has large parts of the diamond region under control.

April 1995   Strasser hires the mercenary outfit Executive Outcomes to
                combat the rebels.

June 1995   Executive Outcomes recaptures the diamond region from
                the rebels.

January 1996   Valentine Strasser is removed by the army chief of staff,
                Julius Bio.

March 1996   Democratic elections. The RUF does not participate. Tejan
                Kabbah becomes president.

June 1996   Peace negotiations between President Kabbah and RUF
                leader Foday Sankoh begin in Abidjan (Ivory Coast).

October 1996   Executive Outcomes destroys the RUF's most strategic ba-
                ses.

November 1996   Kabbah and Sankoh sign the Abidjan peace treaty.

January 1997   Executive Outcomes leaves.

March 1997   RUF leader Foday Sankoh arrested in Nigeria.

May 25, 1997   Coup by the army officer Major Johnny Paul Koroma. The
                junta names itself the AFRC, Armed Forces Revolutionary
                Council, and enters into an alliance with the RUF rebels.
                President Kabbah flees to Conakry.

IMPORTANT DATES IN THE HISTORY OF SIERRA LEONE

June 1997   The Economic Community of West African States (ECO-
                   WAS) instigates a boycott against the AFRC/RUF junta.

December 1997   AFRC/RUF junta signs a peace treaty in Conakry, promising
                   to step down in March 1998 and hand back power to the
                   exiled president, Kabbah.

February 1998   The West African peacekeeping force ECOMOG starts at-
                   tacking the junta headquarters in Freetown. On February
                   13 the AFRC/RUF junta falls.

March 1998   President Kabbah returns to Freetown, where he is rein-
                   stated.

October 1998   Foday Sankoh is condemned to death. Twenty-four junta
                   loyalists are executed.

December 1998   RUF starts a big counteroffensive with an attack on Mak-
                   eni.

January 1999   RUF invasion of Freetown.

February 1999   ECOMOG repels RUF from Freetown. Peace negotiations
                   begin in the Togolese capital, Lomé.

July 1999   President Kabbah and Foday Sankoh sign the Lomé peace
                   treaty. Foday Sankoh is released. Amnesty for AFRC/RUF
                   junta leaders and collaborators.

October 1999   Foday Sankoh returns to Freetown and becomes vice pres-
                   ident. The United Nations decides to send peacekeepers.

November 1999   First contingent of peacekeepers arrives. Six thousand have
                   arrived by the end of the year.

IMPORTANT DATES IN THE HISTORY OF SIERRA LEONE

January 2000

United Nations decides to expand the number of blue helmets. By the end of February, 25,000 are in the country, making the peacekeeping operation in Sierra Leone the biggest in the world.

May 2000

RUF rebels take hundreds of peacekeepers hostage. A peaceful demonstration to Sankoh's compound ends in a massacre when rebels open fire at the crowd. Sankoh flees his compound but is arrested a few weeks later.

January 2002

After a slow start the disarmament process reaches a final stage. Rebel leaders and hundreds of their followers, including many child soldiers, burn their weapons in a symbolic bonfire. A month later, both the government and the rebels declare the civil war to be over.

March 2002

Foday Sankoh undergoes a preliminary hearing at the National Court in Freetown, where he will be charged with high treason and murder. Preparations for the Sierra Leone War Tribunal are in full swing. The Kalangba Agricultural High School reopens after being closed for two years.

Sources

Bangura, Peter. "An Inquiry into the Health Hazards of Female Genital Mutilation in Gbendembu Ngowahun Chiefdom." Makeni: Unpublished final thesis for Makeni Teachers College, 1999.

Bongiovanni, P. Vittorio. *Testimoni di speranza in Sierra Leone: Un popolo in agonia dimenticato da tutti.* Rome/Makeni: Xaverian Mission Center, 1999.

Bourke, Joanna. *An Intimate History of Killing: Face-to-Face Killing in Twentieth-Century Warfare.* London: Granta, 1999.

Bracken, Patrick, and Celia Petty, eds. *Rethinking the Trauma of War.* London/New York: Free Association Books, 1998.

Brittain, Victoria. "Return of Sierra Leone's Lost Generation: Aid Workers Strive to Rehabilitate Child Soldiers Brutalized and Brainwashed by Years of Civil War." *Guardian Weekly,* 9–15 March 2000.

Coll, Steve. "In Mosquito Country." *Washington Post Magazine,* 9 January 2000.

Dooling, Richard. *White Man's Grave.* New York: Picador, 1995.

Dufka, Corinne, ed. *Getting Away with Murder, Mutilation, Rape: New Testimony from Sierra Leone.* New York/Brussels: Human Rights Watch, June 1999.

Fofana, Lansana. "Rap Star Inspired Sierra Rebel Brutality." *Johannesburg Mail & Guardian,* 7 October 1998.

Gourevitch, Philip. *We Wish to Inform You That Tomorrow We Will Be Killed with Our Families: Stories from Rwanda.* New York: Picador, 1999.

Greene, Graham. *The Heart of the Matter*. London: Penguin Books, 1994 (orig. publ. 1948).

Hancock, Graham. *The Lords of Poverty: The Freewheeling Lifestyles, Power, Prestige, and Corruption of the Multibillion-Dollar Aid Business*. London: Macmillan, 1989.

Hochschild, Adam. *King Leopold's Ghost: A Story of Greed, Terror, and Heroism in Colonial Africa*. Boston: Houghton Mifflin, 1998.

Huntington, Samuel. *The Clash of Civilizations and the Remaking of the World Order*. London: Simon & Schuster, 1997.

Kaplan, Robert. "The Coming Anarchy." *Atlantic Monthly*, February 1994.

———. *The Ends of the Earth: A Journey to the Frontiers of Anarchy*. New York: Random House, 1996.

Misser, François, and Olivier Vallée. *Les gemmocraties: L'économie politique du diamant africain*. Paris: Desclée de Brouwer, 1997.

Ourdan, Rémy. "Uneasy Peace Follows a Brutal Past." *Guardian Weekly*, 16–22 December 1999.

Peleman, Johan. *Sierra Leone en de diamanthuurlingen*. IPIS Brochure 114. Antwerp: International Peace Information Service, 1998.

Peters, Krijn, and Paul Richards. "Fighting with Open Eyes: Youth Combatants Talking about War in Sierra Leone." In Bracken and Petty, eds., *Rethinking the Trauma of War*.

Richards, Paul. *Fighting for the Rain Forest*. Oxford/Portsmouth, N.H.: Currey/Heineman, 1996.

Rosenblum, Mort. *Who Stole the News? Why We Can't Keep Up with What Happens in the World and What We Can Do about It*. New York: John Wiley & Sons, 1993.

Smilie, Ian, Lansana Gberie, and Ralph Hazleton. *The Heart of the Matter: Sierra Leone, Diamonds, and Human Security*. Ontario: Partnership Africa Canada, 2000.

Tangelder, Simone. *Spelen met vuur: Kindsoldaten en hun strijdtoneel*. Amsterdam/Gent: Mets/Globe, 1999.

Wood, Brian, and Johan Peleman. *The Arms Fixers: Controlling the Brokers and Shipping Agents*. Oslo: International Peace Research Institute, 1999.

A Word of Thanks

I am eternally grateful to many, many people. First and foremost, Eddie Smith, Zainab Fofana, Samuel Baker, and above all, the Kanu family. They showed me just how wonderful and brave people can be. Without them, I would almost certainly not be alive. A special word of thanks to Right Makkah and Colonel Momodu. I am extremely thankful to Bishop Biguzzi and Padre Victor from the Catholic mission in Makeni, and Gabriel Mani and Nancy Dankey from Caritas Makeni, for all the help and support they gave me during my first trip. I would like to thank a certain O. for a note she left in my passport.

It is virtually impossible to mention everybody who went to such efforts while I was missing, but let me make an attempt. My friends and colleagues Charlotte Zwemmer, Linda Polman, Gert Van Langendonck, Robert Dulmers, Kadir van Lohuizen, Sebastian Junger, Corinne Dufka, Peter Tetteroo, and Wim Van Capellen. And of course, my father, Ad; my sister, Margje; my brothers, Pieter and Jaap; and my aunt Blanche.

Also, Hans Verploeg and Nina Eberlijn from the Dutch Journalists' Association; Louis Zaal from the Hollandse Hoogte photo agency; Anouk Delafortrie, William Bourgeois, Bettina Saerens, Pierre-Pascal Vandini, Pascal Vignier, Wouter Kok, and Freek Landmeter from Doctors Without Borders in Brussels, Paris, and Amsterdam; Henriëtte van Gulick and Henk van Gent from the Dutch Ministry of Foreign Affairs; Commodore Berlijn from the Dutch Ministry of Defense; Gijs Westerouen van Meeteren, HM ambassador to the Vatican.

A WORD OF THANKS

The boundless enthusiasm and efforts of Brigitte Jaspard, Sabine Hirsch, Camille Noël, and Hilde Demoor, who made the campaign for Alfred Kanu's school possible (for further information on the campaign: www.teunvoeten. com). Without the critical remarks of Tilly Hermans, Linda Polman, Riekje von Drigalski, and Gert Van Langendonck, this book would never have seen the light of day. And I would like to thank all the child soldiers and Joe Mboka, Septimus Kaikai, Nance Webber, Theophilius Momoh, Rita Fioravanzo, Paul Richards, Johan Peleman, James Kokero, and Chris Bruyninckx for all the time and information they were willing to share with me.

Brussels, April 2000